The European Union and Global Financial Regulation

The European Union and Global Financial Regulation

Lucia Quaglia

OXFORD
UNIVERSITY PRESS

OXFORD
UNIVERSITY PRESS

Great Clarendon Street, Oxford, OX2 6DP,
United Kingdom

Oxford University Press is a department of the University of Oxford. It furthers the University's objective of excellence in research, scholarship, and education by publishing worldwide. Oxford is a registered trade mark of Oxford University Press in the UK and in certain other countries

First Edition published in 2014

Impression: 2

Published in the United States of America by Oxford University Press
198 Madison Avenue, New York, NY 10016, United States of America

British Library Cataloguing in Publication Data
Data available

Library of Congress Control Number: 2014933808

ISBN 978–0–19–968824–1

Printed and bound by
Clays Ltd, St Ives plc

In memory of my parents

Preface

In 2008, I was awarded a Start-up Grant by the European Research Council (Grant 204398 FINGOVEU) for a research project on financial services governance in the European Union (EU). The first part of that project analysed the 'internal' (i.e. intra-EU) dimension of EU financial services regulation. The main findings of that part of the research were reported in my book *Governing Financial Services in the EU* (Routledge, 2010). The second part of my ERC project examined the 'external' dimension of EU financial services regulation, whereby the main focus was on the effects of EU legislation for third countries.

In the meantime, the global financial crisis was followed by new waves of regulation in the EU and worldwide. The EU and some EU countries took a prominent stage in the global post-crisis regulatory debate. Hence, I realized that it was increasingly important to consider the interaction of the EU and its member states in international regulatory fora. In 2012, I was awarded a small British Academy–Leverhulme Trust grant for a research project on the EU and global financial regulation (SG 120191). At the same time, I was awarded a one-year research fellowship at the Hanse-Wissenschaftskolleg. This book reports the main findings of the second part of the project and builds on the research I had previously conducted at the Max Planck Institute in Cologne and the European University Institute in Florence. I am also grateful to the University of York research priming fund.

The book examines the influence of the EU in global financial regulation, arguing that such influence varies over time and across financial services. By and large, it has increased (albeit unevenly) over the last decade. In the past, the EU mostly 'downloaded' financial regulation from international financial fora or 'passively' 'cross-loaded' it from the US. From the 2000s onwards, the EU has been able to 'upload' its regulatory templates internationally or has 'actively' cross-loaded them to third countries. Across financial services, EU influence has been stronger whenever the EU has developed a robust 'regulatory capacity'. Regulatory capacity has mostly been the result of intra-EU developments, first and foremost the role of the Commission as policy entrepreneur and the agreement amongst the main member states, whose preferences were informed primarily by domestic political economy.

While writing this book, I had to make some consequential decisions. First, after the global financial crisis, financial regulation was continuously revised and became a moving target. Thus, the content of this book had to be updated over time. In the end, I decided to cover the period up to June 2013, even though some important issues, such as the proposal for Banking Union in the EU, have yet to be settled. Second, it was not easy to discern the EU position, as such, on certain issues; or to distinguish the EU position from that of its member states. Unlike trade policy, for example, which is an EU competence, financial regulation is a shared competence between the EU and its member states. The member states are represented in international regulatory fora and often have their own distinctive preferences. Hence, the EU sometimes fails to speak with one voice externally. In the empirical chapters, I have tried to point out whenever this was the case, even though for the sake of simplicity, in the introduction and conclusion of each chapter and in the introductory and concluding chapters of the book I speak of the 'EU'.

Third, there was a trade-off between the array of financial services examined and the deepness of the analysis. I opted for a broad coverage by looking at all the main financial services, i.e. banking, securities markets (including rating agencies, hedge funds, and derivatives), insurance, accounting, and auditing (which are often considered part of securities market regulation). In each empirical chapter I had to be selective about the material included. Since this book is about the EU and global financial regulation, the sections on financial regulation in the EU and international financial regulation are far more developed than the sections on financial regulation in the US. The US is included, however, because it is the main counterpart of the EU and is an important player in international regulatory fora. I have adopted the same structure for all the empirical chapters so as to make them more easily comparable, but they could also be read as self-standing chapters.

Some of the assessments of this book are deemed to be provisional because financial regulation in the EU remains a work in progress. That said, this research takes a historical perspective by considering the evolution of financial regulation over recent decades. Hence, the main findings of the book highlight and explain consolidated trends rather than ad hoc events.

Acknowledgements

This research was funded by the European Research Council (Grant 204398 FINGOVEU), the British Academy and Leverhulme Trust (SG 120191), and the Research Priming Fund at the University of York—this financial support is gratefully acknowledged. This book was researched and written while I was visiting fellow at the Max Planck Institute for the Studies of Societies (Cologne), the European University Institute (Florence), and Hanse-Wissenschaftskolleg. I am grateful to these institutions for providing a stimulating intellectual environment, as well as several opportunities to discuss my research. I wish to thank the University of Sussex first and the University of York later for granting me research leave. I am also in debt to my fellow colleagues in all these academic institutions for providing an inspiring and supportive environment in which to carry out my research, as well as a sense of real community.

The primary research for this book could not have been completed without the help of many practitioners and experts in several financial institutions, interest organizations, and private companies based in Brussels, in several European countries, in the US, and in international bodies. I was able to benefit from forthcoming and helpful interlocutors, who generously gave me their time, despite their very busy diaries, and who were willing to share some of their insights with me. I am very grateful to all of them. It was agreed with all the interviewees that, although I could use the information they gave me, they would not be individually attributed. I am sure they would not agree with all the evaluations expressed in this book. All errors, omissions, and interpretations in this book are mine.

Since I started my research, several academics have generously given me their advice, and some have commented on parts of the book, conference papers, and other academic publications in which some of the findings of this research were presented. In particular, I would like to thank Michele Chang, Chad Damro, Shawn Donnelly, Kenneth Dyson, Enrik Enderlein, Dermot Hodson, Peter Holmes, David Howarth, Till Kaesbach, Patrick Leblond, Huw Macartney, Ivo Maes, Renate Mayntz, Mick Moran, Manuela Moschella, Daniel Mügge, George Pagoulatos, Eliot Posner, Uwe Pütter, Claudio Radaelli, Eleni Tsingou, Alasdair Young, Amy Verdun, and Nicolas Veron. I also wish to thank the anonymous reviewers of my book proposal and manuscript.

I am especially grateful to David Howarth, with whom I have had a very productive, ongoing collaboration and several intellectual exchanges over the years. Some of the material on Basel III in Chapter 3, hedge funds in Chapter 4, and Banking Union in Chapter 7 is based on collaborative research with David. I am grateful that he gave me permission to draw from our joint work for this book. Tables 2.1 and Table 7.1 are revised and extended versions of two tables that appeared in my article in *New Political Economy* (Quaglia 2013). Nina Arbabzadeh provided extremely valuable research assistance for the collection of the data reported in the tables. Peg Murray-Evans and Dan Keith very efficiently copy-edited and formatted the manuscript. Jane Robson provided very professional copy-editing for OUP, and Fiona Barry carefully proofread the typeset text. Apologies if I have forgotten anyone who kindly commented on or helped me in my research. At a personal level, Carla, Massimo, and Soeren offered unfaltering support and encouragement for my project. Paola, Francesca, Stella, Debora, Anna, Giovanna, and Alessandra reminded me that, while financial regulation is important, time with friends is also important and sometimes special.

I also wish to thank the participants to various conferences of the University Association for Contemporary European Studies (UACES), the European Union Studies Association (EUSA), the British Political Studies Association (PSA), the British International Studies Association (BISA), and the European Consortium for Political Research (ECPR) for their perceptive comments. Parts of this book were presented at research seminars and workshops at the Sussex European Institute, the Max Planck Institute for the Study of Societies, the European University Institute, the Hanse-Wissenschaftskolleg, the University of Edinburgh, the College of Europe, the University of Amsterdam, the University of Cardiff, the University of Glasgow, the University of York, and the Austrian Academy of Social Science.

Last but surely not least, I wish to thank my editor, Dominic Byatt, for his interest in and commitment to my project.

Professor Lucia Quaglia,
York, November 2013

Contents

List of Tables

List of Abbreviations

BCBS	Basel Committee on Banking Supervision
BIS	Bank for International Settlements
CCP	Central Counterparty
CDS	Credit Default Swap
CEA	Comité Européen des Assurances
CRD	Capital Requirements Directive
DG	Directorate General
EBA	European Banking Authority
ECB	European Central Bank
ECOFIN	Council of Economic and Finance Ministers
EFSF	European Financial Stability Facility
EMU	Economic and Monetary Union
EP	European Parliament
ESM	European Stability Mechanism
ESMA	European Securities and Markets Authority
FASB	Financial Accounting Standards Board
FDIC	Federal Deposit Insurance Corporation
FSA	Financial Services Authority
FSAP	Financial Services Action Plan
FSB	Financial Stability Board
FSF	Financial Stability Forum
G4	Group of Four
G7	Group of Seven
G10	Group of Ten
G20	Group of Twenty
G30	Group of Thirty
GAAP	Generally Accepted Accounting Principles
IAASB	International Auditing and Assurance Standards Board

IAIS	International Association of Insurance Supervisors
IAS	International Accounting Standards
IASB	International Accounting Standards Board
IASC	International Accounting Standards Committee
IFAC	International Federation of Accountants
IFRS	International Financial Reporting Standards
IMF	International Monetary Fund
IOSCO	International Organization of Securities Commissions
ISA	International Standards on Auditing
ISDA	International Swaps and Derivatives Association
OECD	Organization for Economic Co-operation and Development
MEP	Member of the European Parliament
MOU	Memorandum of Understanding
NAIC	National Association of Insurance Commissioners
PCAOB	Public Company Accounting Oversight Board
QIS	Quantitative Impact Study
SEC	Securities and Exchange Commission
SME	small and medium-sized enterprise
SRM	Single Resolution Mechanism
SSM	Single Supervisory Mechanism
WTO	World Trade Organization

1

Introduction

The global financial crisis that began in the US in 2007 and subsequently spread worldwide brought into the spotlight the political salience of financial governance. The crisis underscored the need for 'fit-for-purpose' financial regulation and supervision.[1] It also highlighted how financial instability can spread quickly across national borders due to the internationalization or globalization of finance (Cerny 1993, 1995; Cohen 1996; Helleiner 1994; Porter 1993). The sovereign debt crisis in the euro area, which began in 2010, drew further attention to the link between financial services regulation and fiscal policy. In other words, there is a (potentially very large) 'price tag' on getting financial governance wrong. These two interconnected crises cannot be understood without a proper explanation of the regulatory 'patchwork' that is a core feature of global finance. Similarly, it is impossible to draw the right policy conclusions without addressing the challenge of the multi-level governance in finance.[2]

The regulation of financial services has become increasingly complex due to the large number of cross-border financial institutions that exploit regulatory gaps to engage in risky activities. Moreover, there is a variety of (often poorly coordinated) international, regional, transnational, and national bodies involved in rule-making and monitoring (Porter 2003, 2005). The multi-level governance of financial services (Baker et al. 2005) is characterized by two main interrelated regulatory phenomena: the interaction between rule-making processes in multiple arenas; and the 'accommodation' or 'coexistence' of their rule-making outputs (Goldstein et al. 2000).

[1] The academic literature on the global financial crisis is vast. In economics, see the comprehensive work of Reinhart and Rogoff (2009). In political economy, several special issues were published in the aftermath of the crisis, see e.g. *Review of International Political Economy*, 19/4 (2012); *New Political Economy*, 15/1 (2010); *Journal of Common Market Studies*, 47/5 (2009). There were also several edited volumes, such as Helleiner et al. (2010), Maynz (2012), Hardie and Howarth (2013), and Moschella and Tsingou (2013).

[2] I wish to thank a reviewer for this point.

The multi-level governance of financial services is complicated further in regional jurisdictions, such as the European Union (EU), where an extra (supranational) level of regulation exists, alongside that taking place in national, international, and transnational arenas. Amongst regional regulatory regimes, the EU is by far the most advanced because its legislation is legally binding in the member states and to a large extent it provides the framework for national financial services regulation. Moreover, the European Commission is in charge of monitoring the implementation of EU rules in the member states, and the European Court of Justice has jurisdiction over compliance with those rules.

Nowadays, the EU is one of the largest financial jurisdictions worldwide. Drezner (2007) considers it as one of the 'great powers', together with the US, and Damro (2012) characterizes the EU as a 'market power'. Over the 2000s, the EU devoted considerable efforts to the completion of the single financial market in Europe (for some comprehensive accounts, see Donnelly 2010; Macartney 2010; Mügge 2010; Posner 2005; Quaglia 2010a), promoting regulatory harmonization within its borders and strengthening the institutional framework for financial regulation and supervision. Moreover, the EU is increasingly active in international financial fora and is one of the main interlocutors of the US in the policy debate on this subject (Posner 2009a, 2010). For all these reasons, the EU is an important player to consider in global financial governance.

Yet, we know relatively little about the EU and global financial regulation. How influential is the EU in regulating global finance? What accounts for its influence (or the lack of it)? Are there variations over time and/or across financial services? This research evaluates the influence of the EU in regulating global finance by promoting formal international regulatory convergence, which is defined as the deliberate approximation of legislation across jurisdictions (see Drezner 2007; Posner 2009a; Simmons 2001; Singer 2004, 2007). The focus on international regulatory convergence, defined as the approximation of regulation across jurisdictions, is important because financial services are inherently borderless. Therefore, their effective regulation requires, to some extent, harmonized rules across jurisdictions to prevent regulatory gaps and arbitrage (Bach 2010). Yet, international regulatory convergence has transaction costs when it is negotiated and it has implementation costs when domestic rules are changed to comply with either international rules or rules from third countries (Simmons 1998).

The Empirical and Theoretical Puzzles

The research starts with an empirical puzzle: in some (very few) cases, the EU 'uploads' its financial services rules internationally; in other (very many) cases, the EU 'downloads' international financial rules domestically; in other cases, the EU actively 'cross-loads' its rules to other jurisdictions, or passively 'cross-loads' rules from other jurisdictions (mainly the US); finally, in some instances, no international rules are created and in the absence of domestic rules, private-sector governance prevails (these terms will be defined later).

For example, just by looking at capital requirements, there is considerable variation across banking, securities, and insurance. Capital requirements in the banking sector have been agreed internationally by the so-called Basel accords and have subsequently been incorporated with some modifications into EU directives. By contrast, capital (solvency) requirements in the insurance sector have been set by an EU directive, the Solvency II Directive, which has partly been incorporated in embryonic international regulation. Capital requirements for investment firms have not been agreed internationally. However, the EU has decided to apply the content of the Basel accords to investment firms.

Capital requirements, which had considerable prominence over the past two decades or so (Alexander et al. 2005; Barth et al. 2006; Scott 2005; Tarullo 2008), are only one type of the rules that govern global finance. After the global financial crisis, the perimeter of international financial regulation has expanded to financial institutions and activities previously unregulated, such as hedge funds, rating agencies, and over-the-counter derivatives. Accounting and auditing standards are other important topics in international financial regulation.

Why does the EU upload international financial regulation in some (few) cases, download it in (many) other cases, and cross-load either actively or passively in other instances? Has this changed over time, especially after the completion of Economic and Monetary Union (EMU) and the single financial market, or after the global financial crisis? Under what conditions is the EU more or less likely to upload, download, or cross-load rules? Through which mechanisms does this take place?

This research focuses on the uploading, downloading, and cross-loading of financial regulation by the EU as a way to promote international regulatory convergence. It is important to understand when, how, and why the EU uploads, downloads, and actively or passively cross-loads financial regulation because uploading and active cross-loading are forms of EU 'power' in regulating global finance: it means that international or third-country rules are set according to EU terms. In these instances, the EU is a 'rule-maker' and other jurisdictions are 'rule-takers'. In the case of downloading and passive cross-loading, the EU mainly 'adjusts' to rules set by third jurisdictions or international bodies, hence it is a rule-taker. This raises an interesting theoretical puzzle: which theoretical approaches better account for the EU's ability (or otherwise?) to upload and actively cross-load its rules?

The terminology of 'uploading', 'downloading', and 'cross-loading' has been borrowed from the literature on Europeanization (Börzel 2002; Bulmer and Radaelli 2005; Howell 2004), with some adaptations. 'Downloading' is defined in this research as the incorporation of international financial regulation (or parts of it) into EU rules. 'Uploading' is defined as the incorporation of EU rules (or parts of them) into international financial regulation. 'Cross-loading' is the incorporation of rules agreed in one jurisdiction into another jurisdiction, without the adoption of these rules by international regulatory fora. In this research, cross-loading occurs either from the EU to third countries, first and foremost the US (this is referred to as 'active' cross-loading for the EU), for example through equivalence clauses in EU legislation; or from the US to the EU, especially through the extra-territorial effects of US legislation (this is referred to as 'passive' cross-loading for the EU).

International regulatory convergence can take place through the creation of international standards (in which case it is 'international regulatory harmonization'), or through bilateral regulatory changes, whereby rules originated in one jurisdiction are adopted in full or in part in another jurisdiction. An example of bilateral regulatory convergence was the change of US regulation of financial conglomerates in order for it to be judged as equivalent to EU rules (Posner 2009a; Dür 2011). The focus in this research is on *formal* regulatory convergence that is accompanied by the change of rules across jurisdictions, not on de facto or market-driven convergence (Knill 2005). As Drezner notes, some of the most salient issues in world politics concern the making of international financial regulation and regulatory disputes (Drezner 2007: 6; Farrell and Newman 2010).

The Overall Argument

Through a theoretically informed empirical investigation, this research argues that EU influence in regulating global finance has varied across financial services and over time. The EU has mostly downloaded or passively cross-loaded rules. Less frequently, it has uploaded or actively cross-loaded financial regulation. The key explanatory variable used in this research is 'regulatory capacity', as elaborated by Bach and Newman (2010). This concept is applied in a dynamic (temporal) way with reference to the EU and the other main 'great (financial) power' (paraphrasing Drezner 2007), namely the US. A distinction is made between 'strong' and 'weak' regulatory capacity. A two-by-two explanatory matrix is created, with weak/strong EU regulatory capacity on one side and weak/strong US regulatory capacity on the other side. International regulatory convergence and the influence of the EU therein depend on the various combinations of EU and US regulatory capacities.

When EU regulatory capacity is weak and US capacity is strong, the US will mainly upload its national rules to international regulatory fora and the EU will mainly download them. The US will also actively and bilaterally cross-load its rules to the EU, which will passively cross-load them. When the EU regulatory capacity is strong and US regulatory capacity is weak, the EU is able to upload its rules internationally or to actively cross-load them to the US (and other third countries). When EU and US regulatory capacities are weak, international and national rules are mostly absent, hence there is neither uploading/downloading internationally, nor cross-loading bilaterally. Private-sector governance prevails. When both the EU and the US regulatory capacities are strong, both jurisdictions seek to upload some of their rules internationally, and to actively cross-load their rules to other jurisdictions.

The temporal dimension is also important in two ways (for a similar argument see Posner 2010; Mügge 2011a). First, there is the sequencing between the development of domestic regulatory capacities in the EU and the US. There are 'first-mover advantages' to be gained by the EU and the US in international standard-setting if they are the first to set in place robust domestic regulatory templates that can be uploaded internationally or cross-loaded bilaterally. Second, there is the sequencing between the setting in place of robust domestic regulatory templates and the development of international standards, creating a process of path-dependence. If the EU has strengthened its regulatory capacity in a given sector by establishing its own regulatory template prior to international capacity building, then it is better positioned to influence the making of international standards by uploading its regulatory templates. Vice versa, if international regulatory capacity is already developed in a given sector, the EU will continue to download international standards.

This research design considers EU and US regulatory capacities as independent variables: their different combinations give rise to different values of the dependent variable, namely the influence of the EU in international regulatory convergence. However, what explains different regulatory capacities? The literature on US regulatory capacity is well developed, hence it does not need to be rehearsed here. In the case of the EU, drawing from the literature on EU financial regulation, the building up of regulatory capacity in the EU is explained by the role of policy entrepreneurs and the convergent (or at least compatible) interests of the main jurisdictions and their financial industries.

Caveats

There are three main caveats to this research. First, it focuses on the EU and its influence (or in certain cases, the lack of it) in the making of rules for global finance. Although the US regulatory capacity and preferences on key issues are discussed in the book, this is done concisely because of space constraints. Yet, there is an extensive literature on financial regulation in the US and the existing international political economy literature has mainly focused on the US, whereas this research innovatively looks at the EU.

The second caveat is that an in-depth investigation of the uploading, the downloading, and the cross-loading processes would require three somewhat different research designs, namely 'bottom-up', 'top-down', and 'horizontal'. Nonetheless, the three aspects, in particular downloading and uploading, should be jointly examined because they mutually affect each other. Hence, this research deals with all of them at the same time.

Third, this book mainly deals with the uploading, downloading, and cross-loading of rules (or at least, regulatory templates), not so much of ideas or interests. The advantage is that rules are more easily observable than ideas or interests. Moreover, the focus on rules is the most suitable in order to investigate the influence of the EU in international regulatory convergence. The shortcoming is that the EU can also attempt to upload, download, and cross-load interests and ideas. These are interesting venues for further research.

The Content of the Book

This research contributes to three main bodies of scholarly work: the international political economy literature on the politics of international harmonization, regulatory coordination, and transatlantic economic relations; the EU literature on the external economic relations of the EU and the role of the EU in the international financial system; and the literature on the politics and political economy of EU financial services regulation. The book is structured as follows.

Chapter 2 reviews three main bodies of scholarly works in political science and political economy. First, there is the international political economy literature on the politics of financial regulation and standard-setting. Second, there is the EU literature on the role and influence of the EU in international economic arenas, primarily in trade and competition policy. Third, there is the literature on the politics and political economy of financial services regulation in the EU. The second part of the chapter discusses the research design, the dependent and the explanatory variables, the analytical framework, the choice of the case studies, the methodology, and sources. It also delimitates the scope of the research, outlining the timeframe and the empirical coverage.

Chapter 3 discusses the EU and global banking regulation by focusing on the Basel I, II, and III accords, which were issued by the Basel Committee on

Banking Supervision (BCBS) and were downloaded by the EU into the Capital Requirements Directive, subsequently revised over time.

Chapter 4 examines the EU and global securities markets regulation. It discusses the rules issued by the International Organization of Securities Commissions (IOSCO) on securities trading. The chapter also examines the regulation of previously unregulated financial institutions or activities: credit-rating agencies, hedge funds, and over-the-counter derivatives in the EU, the US, and internationally, discussing the potential cross-loading of EU rules to third countries.

Chapter 5 examines the EU and global insurance regulation. It discusses the setting of embryonic international capital requirements for insurers and the principles for group supervision by the International Association of Insurance Supervisors (IAIS) in 2008–9. The content of these provisions was partly uploaded by the EU from the (then newly issued) Solvency II Directive, which also contains provisions concerning third countries.

Chapter 6 examines the EU and global accounting and auditing standards. It explains why the EU decided to download the international financial reporting standards of the International Accounting Standards Board (IASB) into EU legislation. It also discusses the convergence between the international standard and US standards. As far as auditing is concerned, prior to the crisis international standards were mainly set by a private-sector body. After the crisis, the EU has proposed new far-reaching legislation on auditing, as well as the downloading of international auditing standards.

Chapter 7 engages in a cross-sectoral assessment, teasing out the mechanisms for the uploading, downloading, and cross-loading of financial rules by the EU and evaluating the main scope conditions. It summarizes the main theoretical and empirical findings, putting forward proposals for further research. It also discusses the ongoing proposal on Banking Union.

2

State of the Art and Research Design

This chapter begins by reviewing several bodies of scholarly works that are relevant to this research. It then outlines the research design, the analytical framework, and the selection of case studies, the methodology, and the sources. Finally, it clarifies the empirical coverage, the timeframe, and the scope of the research.

State of the Art

This review first deals with the international political economy literature on standard-setting and regulatory convergence in finance, which primarily explains what affects the outcomes of international negotiations and whose preferences (including existing regulatory templates) are adopted as international standards. In the terminology of this research, this includes the uploading or active cross-loading by different parties. Second, it reviews the literature on the external economic relations of the EU, especially in trade policy, which is also essentially about uploading and active cross-loading, but focuses on how and how well the EU does it. Finally, the literature on financial services regulation in the EU is reviewed in order to explain the building up of regulatory capacity in the EU, which determines whether there is anything that the EU can upload or actively cross-load. Thus, these literatures deal with (in reverse order): preference formation, representation, and negotiated outcomes.

The Politics of International Regulatory Convergence in Finance

The early academic literature on international financial regulatory convergence stresses the importance of the preferences and the power of the 'hegemonic' country, the US, for or against international harmonization[1] (Simmons

[1] The expression 'regulatory harmonization' is used because this body of scholarly work mainly focuses on standard-setting in international fora, which is one form of regulatory convergence.

2001). The assumption is that international regulatory cooperation benefits some countries more than others, and therefore has redistributive implications (Oatley and Nabors 1998).[2] Consequently, international cooperation and regulatory harmonization will take place only when they are in line with the preferences of the dominant country, as determined by incentives to emulate its rules and by policy-specific externalities. This approach highlights the importance of the preferences of the US and its bargaining power, mainly on the basis of its market power. Hence, international regulatory convergence takes place towards US rules.

Reflecting the changed global context in the twenty-first century, some works question the hegemony of the US in regulating global finance by considering other jurisdictions that have large financial markets (Drezner 2007; Singer 2004, 2007).[3] Like Simmons, these works mainly focus on market size in order to explain international bargaining power. Singer (2004, 2007) investigates the domestic politics of preference formation for or against international financial harmonization in the US, the UK, and Japan, arguing that international cooperation is a way for domestic regulators to restore the domestic balance between competition and stability in response to an external shock. Drezner (2007: 5) examines the role of the 'great powers', defined as 'governments that oversee large internal markets', namely the US and the EU, in a variety of regulatory regimes, including finance. These works point out that the preferences of regulators in large markets, other than the US, should be considered. Hence, international regulatory convergence tends to reflect the existing rules of the great powers.[4]

Recent historical institutionalist works on international market regulation (see the special issue of *Review of International Political Economy* (2010), 17/4; Bach and Newman 2007; Büthe and Mattli 2011; Mattli and Büthe 2003; Posner 2009a, 2010) challenge the market power explanation and argue that 'domestic regulatory institutions are the sources of both power *and* preferences on the global stage' (Drezner 2010: 794). A key concept used by this literature is 'regulatory capacity', defined as 'a jurisdiction's ability to formulate, monitor, and enforce a set of market rules' (Bach and Newman 2007: 831). It links market size to power in international market regulation (Bach and

[2] This approach contradicts early 'functionalist' explanations of international financial harmonization, such as Kapstein's (1992) account of the making of the Basel I accord. His argument is that regulators promote international regulatory harmonization as a way to solve common problems or realize joint gains. To some extent, he considers central bankers and financial regulators engaged in the negotiations of Basel I as an 'epistemic community' (Haas 1989).

[3] For a similar argument about the role played by European countries, in particular France, with reference to capital liberalization, see Abdelal (2007).

[4] Drezner's model also explains what happens when the great powers have incompatible regulatory preferences.

Newman 2007) because neither market size alone nor regulatory capacity alone are sufficient to regulate a certain market.

In his investigation of EU–US regulatory relations, Posner (2009a) focuses on 'regulatory centralization' in the EU, arguing that this institutional change has increased EU leverage *vis-à-vis* the US. More recently, he has examined the sequencing in the development of financial standards across jurisdictions, pointing out first-mover advantages for (large) jurisdictions that first set rules in a certain sector (Posner 2010). This approach highlights the importance of regulatory capacity in the EU and the US in order to settle the terms of transatlantic regulatory disputes in finance. However, it has not been applied with reference to international regulatory fora, and because of space constraints it has not paid enough attention to explaining the building up of regulatory capacity in the EU.

With reference to private standard-setting, including international accounting standards, Büthe and Mattli (2011) argue that, even though rule-making has shifted to the international level in several sectors, domestic regulatory institutions remain paramount. They stress the 'institutional complementarity' between the domestic and the international levels. Influence on international private standard-setting is not a function of market size, but of the ability of domestic (mainly private) standard-setters to provide timely information and speak with a single voice in international fora (Büthe and Mattli 2011: 13).

A less state-centric perspective is taken by scholars who emphasize the role of private-sector governance in financial services (Underhill and Zhang 2008; Underhill et al. 2010). The argument is that international regulatory convergence reflects the interests of industry, i.e. the rules that the financial industry finds more advantageous (or less burdensome). For example, some authors argue that the lowering of capital requirements in banking were a clear example of a race to the bottom and industry's capture of regulators (Lall 2012; Tsingou 2008; Underhill and Zhang 2008).

It is undoubtedly true that the financial industry is a powerful lobbyist, with plenty of financial, human, and technical resources at its disposal (Baker 2010; Underhill et al. 2010). Nonetheless, this explanation is somewhat problematic if one considers the diversified interests of industry on several regulatory issues across financial services and over time (Helleiner and Pagliari 2011; Young 2012). For example, on important issues raised by the Basel II accord, such as operational risk capital charge, the financial industry had different (opposing) preferences (see Chapter 3). In some cases, the rules eventually agreed were more stringent than those initially proposed, as a result of lobbying from certain parts of the industry (Young 2012). In accounting, prior to the crisis, some financial companies, such as investment banks, preferred fair value accounting, whereas others, such as continental European banks with a traditional business model, resisted mark-to-market accounting (Donnelly 2007, 2010; Véron 2007).

Another non-state-centric approach has focused on the institutional features and working dynamics of a number of financial regulatory bodies, arguing that financial governance arrangements no longer belong to the realm of intergovernmental negotiations, but fall within the responsibility of a 'transnational policy community of expert actors' (Tsingou 2010: 21). These actors have common professional and educational backgrounds (Chwieroth 2010) and share similar epistemological views (e.g. Kapstein 1992 defined the Basel Committee on Banking Supervision (BCBS) as an embryonic 'epistemic community'). The broadly social constructivist argument is that small groupings of experts facilitate information exchange and processes of deliberation (Baker 2010) which, in turn, lead to the socialization of the experts involved and to the formation of common beliefs (Baker 2006: 54). International regulatory convergence takes place towards 'groupthink' (Gieve and Provost 2012).

On the one hand, it is true that the members of international regulatory bodies are regulators and not politicians, unlike, for example, the Group of Twenty (G20). The shared professional dimension and the sharing of similar mindsets are important in international financial negotiations. However, as one regulator put it, 'the devil is in the details' (interview, Washington, 5 August 2011), because international rules have compliance costs and economic effects which are different across countries, and regulators are mindful of that. Moreover, in the aftermath of the global financial crisis, financial regulators gathering in the BCBS were less insulated than in the past from politics and politicians (Helleiner and Pagliari 2011). Post-crisis, financial regulation became politically salient—it was no longer 'quiet politics', paraphrasing the title of Culpepper's book (2011).

Most of the literature just reviewed was published prior to the global financial crisis. The literature on the international regulatory response to the financial crisis is burgeoning (see the special issues of *Review of International Political Economy* (2012), 19/4; *New Political Economy* (2010), 15/1; *Journal of Common Market Studies* (2009), 47/5; see also Hardie and Howarth 2013; Helleiner and Pagliari 2010; Helleiner et al. 2010; Mayntz 2012; Moschella and Tsingou 2013). By and large, it highlights three common trends, across jurisdictions as well as internationally, which are relevant to the overall argument of this book.

The first trend is the extension of the perimeter of regulation to previously unregulated activities or institutions, reducing the scope for private-sector governance and introducing prescriptive regulation. The second trend is the slow pace and the incremental nature of the regulatory reforms implemented either internationally or nationally, rather than any path-breaking change. The third trend is the (open or hidden) resistance of industry to major reforms, as well as the persistent disagreement amongst jurisdictions, that to some extent account for the piecemeal character of the reforms implemented. Moreover, partly because the crisis originated in the US, this jurisdiction has become less influential than in the past in international regulatory fora.

The Politics of EU Trade Policy and the External Representation of the Euro Area

The second body of literature reviewed deals with EU trade policy, focusing on the formation of EU negotiating positions in international fora and the effectiveness of the EU's external representation. These two aspects are mostly overlooked by the international political economy literature just reviewed. Indeed, the vast majority of works dealing with international regulatory convergence in finance does not consider the EU as an international financial player. There are notable exceptions, such as Drezner (2007) and Posner (2009a, 2010) which, however, do not pay enough attention to different positions amongst the member states in international regulatory fora or with reference to transatlantic relations. As explained in the following section, different national preferences are often rooted in different regulatory frameworks and configurations of national financial systems.

By contrast, in trade policy and competition policy there is a consolidated body of literature that identifies the increasing bargaining power of the EU as such (see the special issues of *Journal of Common Market Studies* (2007), 45/4; *Journal of European Public Policy* (2006), 13/6). Most of these works also pay attention to the different preferences of the member states and how these shape the EU negotiating position internationally (see also Collinson 1999; Moyer 1993; Patterson 1997). A significant body of the literature on EU trade policy adopts a 'principal-agent' approach, which emphasizes the relationship of delegation and control between the member states and the Commission as the key to understanding the EU's trade policy output (da Conceição 2010, 2011; Delreux and Kerremans 2010; Elgström and Frenhoff Larsén 2010; Elsig 2002, 2007, 2010; Kerremans 2004; Meunier 2007; Pollack 1997; Woolcock 2005; Woolcock and Hodges 1996). A further set of literature seeks to 'bring economic interests back in' (Dür 2008) to the study of EU trade policy by emphasizing the effects of lobbying by interest groups at both the member-state and EU levels (De Bièvre and Dür 2005; Dür 2007, 2008, 2010; Heron and Siles-Brügge 2012; Shaffer 2006; Woll 2006, 2008). Young (2007) notes that the literature on EU trade policy, somewhat mirroring the literature on international regulatory convergence, asks two interrelated questions: what shapes the EU's trade policy preferences and what affects the EU's ability to achieve them?

As for the first question, i.e. how the EU determines its regulatory objectives, EU preferences in finance are explored by the literature on the politics of EU financial integration, which I review shortly. As for the question of what affects the EU ability (or otherwise) to achieve its preferences in international or bilateral trade settings, some authors highlight specific features of EU market power, such as the need to secure access to EU markets for non-EU producers and service providers (Dür 2010, 2011). Other authors maintain that institutional factors determine how potential market power materializes into actual power, pointing to the importance of robust institutional arrangements for the conduct of EU trade policy internally and externally (Damro 2006; Meunier 2000, 2005; Young 2007).

While some of these explanations could be extended to the EU role in international regulatory convergence in finance, there are several important differences between trade policy and financial services regulation. The most important differences concern the legal competence and the institutional arrangements for external representation of the EU. After the Lisbon treaty, trade policy is a true supranational policy, it is an exclusive competence of the EU, and the Commission represents and negotiates on behalf of the EU in trade policy fora, following the mandate given by the member states gathered in the Council, which also monitors the activity of the Commission through the so-called 'article 133 committee' (Young 2007).

By contrast, in finance the member states (or at least some of them) are active participants in international regulatory fora in their own right, whereas the Commission and in some cases the European Central Bank (ECB) might (or might not) be present, and if they are present, they have observer status, as detailed in the chapters. With reference to international financial regulation, Mügge (2011a) has argued that the 'European voice' is reduced when both the EU as such and the member states are represented in a given forum. Other authors (e.g. Hodson 2011) have argued that the mechanisms for the external representation of the EU do not make much of a difference in finance.

Some issues at stake in international financial negotiations are similar to those concerning the external representation of the euro-zone (not the EU) in international fora (Bini Smaghi 2006; Cohen 2008; Frieden 2004; Hodson 2011; McNamara and Meunier 2002). After the establishment of the Economic and Monetary Union (EMU), the member states were reluctant to sacrifice their representation in international organizations and other regulatory bodies for the sake of the euro area (Bini Smaghi 2006). The same is true with reference to financial regulation. Moreover, non-EU countries were eager to avoid any over-representation of the EU/euro area in certain fora, such as the Group of Seven (G7) (Padoa-Schioppa 2004a). This resulted in ad hoc (and somewhat unsatisfactory) arrangements for the external representation of the euro area. Some of the literature explicitly laments the fact that the euro area is unable to speak with one voice and argues in favour of unified representation (Cohen 2008; McNamara and Meunier 2002).

The Politics of EU Financial Regulation

The third body of literature reviewed deals with the politics of financial services regulation in the EU. It is useful in order to explain the building up of regulatory capacity in the EU, as well as the preferences of the EU and its member states in international financial regulation.

The early political economy literature on financial services regulation in the EU stressed the intergovernmental character of the negotiations on financial market regulation in the EU in the 1970s, 1980s, and early 1990s (Story and Walter 1997). As the title of their book suggests, their work regarded financial market integration as the 'battle of the systems', whereby the member states were keen to set EU rules that were in line with their domestic regulatory approach and did not create comparative disadvantages or adjustment costs to national industry and the public authorities. Underhill (1997), like Story and Walter, highlighted the way the 'triangle' of the three main financial systems in the EU—the British, the French, and the German—shaped EU financial regulation in the 1980s and early 1990s.

More recently, Buckley et al. (2012) and Howarth and Quaglia (2013a, 2013b) have examined how the configuration of national banking systems shapes member states' preferences on international and EU capital requirements. To some extent, this approach builds on the literature on varieties of capitalism, rooted in comparative political economy. The vast literature on varieties of capitalism (for some comprehensive analyses, see Amable 2003; Hancké et al. 2007; Hall and Soskice 2001; Schmidt 2002; for a review, see Jackson and Deeg 2008) has paid limited attention to the financial system. To the extent that it has, it has mainly investigated the sources of corporate finance and the effects of this on corporate governance (see Zysman 1983; see also Deeg 2010). Only a handful of works have examined varieties of national financial systems (Allen and Gale 2000; Deeg 2010; Hardie and Howarth 2013). Given their focus on the member states, these accounts of the politics of financial regulation in the EU tend to be intergovernmental, overlooking the role of other important actors, such as the European Commission and financial industry.

A second body of scholarly works has viewed the Commission as the core supranational actor driving financial market integration (Posner 2005; Jabko 2006). Posner (2005: 20) stressed the 'intended and unintended bureaucratic actions' of the Commission in the creation of new stock markets in Europe in the 1990s. By contrast, Jabko (2006) showed that the Commission was able to 'construct' the single market by emphasizing different meanings of the word 'market' to different audiences, forming a coalition that pushed through financial market reform in the late 1990s and early 2000s. These accounts somewhat overemphasize the role of the Commission in the making of financial regulation. This policy area is still jealously guarded by the member states. Moreover, the Commission has seen its influence reduced in the EU policy process since the time of the charismatic presidency of Jacques Delors. Yet, in certain cases, the Commission has been proactive in promoting financial market harmonization in the EU, often with the support of the main member states, as in insurance.

A third stream of literature has focused on the role of the private sector in promoting European financial market integration (Bieling 2003; Mügge 2006, 2010; Macartney 2009, 2010; Van Apeldoorn 2002). These works emphasize either the structural power of transnational capital or the lobbying activities of financial institutions which 'captured' the public authorities in various ways. Amongst the most prominent were 'economic' or 'material' capture, given the size and importance of the financial sector in certain countries and the economic resources available to industry for lobbying, and 'intellectual' capture, based on the high level of expertise and technical knowledge at the disposal of the private sector and often tapped into by the regulators themselves (Baker 2010). Like its counterpart in international political economy, this literature tends to overlook the fact that the financial industry, even the main transnational players, often have competing interests, and that public officials are able (though not always willing) to withstand industry pressure.

Other scholars have focused on networks of supervisors in the EU (Coen and Thatcher 2008; De Visscher et al. 2008; Quaglia 2008), an approach which bears some similarities to the transgovernmental networks approach in international political economy. This approach has limited explanatory power in the making of level one EU legislation (or framework legislation), because the 'technical' authorities (i.e. financial supervisors) are only consulted during the legislative process, whereby legislation is proposed by the Commission and co-decided by the Council of Ministers and the European Parliament. The network-based approach is more successful when applied to level two legislation, in which the so-called 'committees of supervisors', recently transformed into EU authorities, are the main players.

Other studies have applied a constructivist analysis to the subject, pointing out that in the 1980s and 1990s a dominant paradigm for financial services regulation emerged internationally and in the main jurisdictions, including Europe. They have referred to it as the 'neoliberal' paradigm (Best 2003; Gamble 2009) or as a 'governance light' approach, which favoured 'market-based governance', based on a benign view of financial markets and grounded in efficient market theories (Underhill et al. 2010: 10). This regulatory paradigm was sponsored by the US and the UK which prior to the crisis, exercised considerable influence in international regulatory fora (Baker 2010; Helleiner and Pagliari 2010).

In the EU, regulatory liberalism came to dominate EU financial regulation from the mid-1990s onwards until the outbreak of the global financial crisis (Mügge 2011b). Over time, according to Donnelly (2010), there was a gradual convergence, which he refers to as 'collusion', amongst member states' norms of financial market regulation, paving the way to an agreement to delegate functions to the supranational level in the early 2000s. In a similar vein, but with more emphasis on persistent differences between regulatory approaches, Quaglia (2010a, 2010b; see also Grossman 2004) pointed out two main competing coalitions of interests and ideas struggling to shape financial regulation in the EU in the 2000s: the 'market-making' coalition, led by the UK, also including Ireland and the Nordic countries; and the 'market-shaping' coalition, led by France, also including Italy, other Mediterranean countries, and, in several instances, Germany (see also Zimmerman 2010). This literature draws attention to the persistent ideational differences on financial regulation amongst the member states.

The literature on the EU response to the crisis very much mirrors the main themes pointed out in the post-crisis international political economy literature, namely the extension of the perimeter of regulation, the incremental nature of change, and the reduced influence of the UK in the making of EU rules. Indeed, from the late 1990s until the unfolding of the global financial crisis, EU financial regulation to a large extent reflected Anglo-Saxon preferences (Mügge 2011b; Posner and Véron 2010). After the global financial crisis, the legislative measures adopted by the EU were principally market-shaping (Quaglia 2012), reflecting a shifting balance of power in favour of continental Europe. By contrast, British policy-makers (Moschella 2011) and the industry (Pagliari 2011) were on the back foot, at least in the short and medium term.

To sum up, the literature on the politics of financial regulation in the EU argues that the size of the EU financial market and its regulatory capacity have increased from the late 1990s onwards, as a consequence of the completion of EMU, the Financial Services Action Plan (FSAP), and the so-called Lamfalussy reform. These initiatives were mostly pushed through by a proactive Commission and a supportive ECB, which were keen to show the financial benefits ensuing from EMU and from the completion of the single market. They were also supported by a powerful transnational financial industry that had much to gain from further market integration and regulatory harmonization in the EU.

Distilling Lessons from a Composite Literature

Several important insights can be distilled from the three main bodies of scholarly works reviewed in order to develop the research design. The international political economy literature suggests that one should pay attention to the preferences of the US on key regulatory issues: although this country is no longer the 'hegemon' in finance, it carries considerable weight in international regulatory fora, and its market rivals that of the EU. With reference to national or regional jurisdictions, two aspects are important: market size and regulatory capacity. One should also pay attention to the preferences of the financial industry, in particular the big transnational players.

The literature on EU trade policy confirms the importance of EU capacity to regulate access to its market as a source of bargaining power in finance as well. It also highlights the way the different preferences of the member states and their domestic industries contribute to shaping the EU positions in international fora and *vis-à-vis* third countries. The literature on the external relations of the euro area draws attention to the modalities for the external representation of the EU in international fora and *vis-à-vis* the US.

Finally, the literature on the politics of financial regulation in the EU teases out three important features in the development of EU regulatory capacity in finance. The first feature is the policy entrepreneurial role of the Commission and the UK, which, at least prior to the crisis, were instrumental in the building of regulatory capacity in the EU by promoting financial market integration and financial harmonization in the EU. After the crisis, the Franco-German coalition has been (at least temporarily) in the ascendancy. Second, this literature alerts us to the different preferences of the member states, mostly rooted in national varieties of financial systems, concerning EU and international financial regulation. Third, it draws attention to the preference of national financial industries and specific features of different financial services that can slow down or enhance the development of regulatory capacity in the EU.

The Research Design

Building on the literature on international standard-setting in finance just reviewed, I acknowledge that the US and the EU have been the main players in the development of international standards by standard-setting bodies over the past decades. In finance, the international power configuration has moved from US 'hegemony', to US–EU 'bipolarity' (Posner 2010: 641; see also Leblond 2011). The literature on the trade policy and external relations of the euro area alerts us to the perils of considering the EU as a fully unitary actor and the need to consider the modalities of the external representation of the EU in international financial regulatory fora.

The *dependent variable* of this research is international regulatory convergence, both as a 'process' and an 'outcome'. Uploading, downloading, and cross-loading, as well as the absence of any of them, are the values that the dependent variable process can take. In the case of uploading and cross-loading from the EU to third countries, the outcome will be international convergence towards EU rules. In the case of downloading and cross-loading from third countries, the outcome will be convergence towards the rules of other jurisdictions. Finally, there are cases in which the outcome is the lack of regulatory convergence or the presence of private-sector rules.

The key *explanatory variable* is 'regulatory capacity', defined as 'a jurisdiction's ability to formulate, monitor, and enforce a set of market rules' (Bach and Newman 2007: 831). This concept can be applied not only to national jurisdictions but also, *ceteris paribus*, to regional polities, such as the EU (see Bach and Newman 2007; Posner 2010). Regulatory capacity involves the degree of regulatory centralization and the presence (or absence) of 'regulatory templates'—that is, coherent sets of rules concerning certain financial activities in a given jurisdiction. There are several causal mechanisms that account for the importance of domestic regulatory capacity in global financial regulation.

First, a jurisdiction with regulatory centralization can preclude access to its markets to third-country firms that do not comply with its domestic rules, including those that follow international standards instead. Hence, a jurisdiction with high regulatory capacity is more influential than other jurisdictions in international regulatory fora and bilaterally can put pressure on third countries to conform to its domestic rules. Second, a jurisdiction that develops regulatory templates in a certain sector is better positioned to shape international rules. Not only does it have the expertise to interact effectively in international financial regulatory fora, it also has domestic regulatory templates that can provide solutions to the regulatory issues that international standards seek to address. In some cases, the regulatory templates adopted by a given jurisdiction might prove attractive for third countries, especially if third countries need to develop their own rules on certain financial services or if they need to reform their domestic rules because of regulatory failure.

Third, the existence of EU regulatory templates (especially if they are based on maximum harmonization) means that the (at times very different) preferences of EU member states and their national industries have already been reconciled during intra-EU negotiations. Hence, the EU is less likely to present a disjointed position in international fora and in bilateral relations *vis-à-vis* the US. This explanation could also be turned the other way round in that different (often incompatible) preferences amongst the member states and their financial industries can prevent or slow down the development of EU regulatory capacity, as in the case of rating agencies and hedge funds prior to the crisis, as elaborated in Chapter 4.

Given the bipolarity in global financial regulation, the regulatory capacity of the EU should not be examined in isolation, but rather in relation to the regulatory capacity of its main counterpart, namely the US. The different combinations of 'strong' and 'weak' EU and US regulatory capacity account for the ability (or otherwise) of these jurisdictions to shape international standards. A two-by-two explanatory matrix can be created, with weak/strong EU regulatory capacity on one side and weak/strong US regulatory capacity on the other side. The convergence of international financial regulation and the influence of the EU therein depend on the combination of EU and US regulatory capacities.

When EU regulatory capacity is weak and US regulatory capacity is strong, the EU will mainly download international rules uploaded by the US, or passively cross-load US rules, with the convergence taking place towards the rule of the main international player (namely, the US). When the EU regulatory capacity is strong and US regulatory capacity is weak, the EU is able to upload its rules internationally, or actively cross-load them to the US, with convergence taking place towards EU rules. When both EU and US regulatory capacities are strong, there will be an exchange of rule elements, i.e. both uploading and downloading by the EU and the US and well as bilateral cross-loading (Table 2.1). Alternatively, there might be 'rival standards' (Drezner 2007), instead of convergence. When EU and US regulatory capacities are weak, these jurisdictions have limited ability to shape international standards produced by regulatory fora. This activity is likely to be delegated to industry self-regulation.

There are different degrees of uploading, downloading, and cross-loading. For example, the downloading of the International Financial Reporting Standards (IFRS) produced by the International Accounting Standards Board (IASB) into the EU legislation through the so-called endorsement process tends to be detailed. By contrast, the EU's uploading of key elements of the Solvency II Directive to the International Association of Insurance Supervisors (IAIS) principles on solvency requirements for insurers is limited to some key concepts.

Table 2.1. The analytical framework

		US regulatory capacity	
		Strong	Weak
EU regulatory capacity	Strong	EU and US upload some of their rules internationally and mutually cross-load them; or rival standards, instead of convergence	EU uploads its rules as international standards and actively cross-loads them
	Weak	US uploads its rules as international standards and actively cross-loads them EU downloads international standards and passively cross-loads them	No international standards issued by regulatory fora, industry self-regulation

International standards are soft law, which means that they are not legally binding in the jurisdictions that sign up to them. They become legally binding only when they are incorporated into national or EU legislation. In the downloading stage, the EU as well as third countries have some room for manœuvre in adapting international rules to their domestic context. The (different) implementation of the Basel accords worldwide was a clear example of this.[5] In the EU, the vast majority of legislation on financial services takes the form of directives, rather than regulations. Whereas the latter are immediately applicable and enforceable in the member states, the former need to be incorporated (technically transposed) into national law. So another downloading of rules takes place from the EU to the national level. When member states transpose EU directives into national law, they can sometimes exercise 'national discretion', basically modifying EU rules with a view to adjusting them to the domestic context.[6]

This research design considers EU and US regulatory capacities as independent variables: their different combinations give rise to different values of the dependent variable, namely the influence of the EU in international regulatory convergence. However, what explains the existence of different regulatory capacities? This question considers regulatory capacity as the dependent variable to be explained. Drawing on the literature on the politics of EU financial regulation, this research explains the building up of regulatory capacity in Chapter 7 by pointing out the role of policy entrepreneurs and the convergent (or at least compatible) interests of the main jurisdictions and their financial industries.

In the EU, the role of policy entrepreneur is often fulfilled by the Commission. In financial services, the UK has often acted as a policy entrepreneur, given the large size of the financial sector in this country and the international role of the City of London. After the crisis, France and Germany often acted as policy entrepreneurs. However, for Commission and UK initiatives to be successful, the support of all the main member states is required. This support largely depends on the domestic political economy effects of the proposed EU rules and institutions—in other words, their implications for national financial industries—but also the national variety of financial capitalism.

[5] When the global financial crisis began, the US had not yet implemented domestically the Basel II accord signed in 2005 (on the domestic difficulties encountered by the US in implementing Basel, see Herring 2007). In an attempt to promote the consistent implantation of the Basel II accord across jurisdictions, the BSBS has set up the Standards Implementation group.

[6] In the case of the CRD, there were more than 100 national discretions exercised, after being reduced from a larger number. Incidentally, this has made the creation of a common EU rulebook on financial services difficult, as noted, e.g., by Padoa-Schioppa (2007).

Case Selection, Methodology, and Sources

The empirical research is based on a variety of case studies of significant international regulatory developments across financial services, whereby the new sets of rules (such as the Basel accords, etc.) are the unit of analysis. The case selection ensures variation between the explanatory variables—namely EU regulatory capacity (strong/weak) and US regulatory capacity (strong/weak)—and the dependent variable—namely international regulatory convergence—both as a process and an outcome.

Methodologically, the book uses the congruence procedure and process tracing across case studies and within case studies over time (George and Bennett 2005). According to the congruence procedure, the hypotheses or empirical expectations derived from Table 2.1 are assessed against the empirical record of the case studies, to confirm (or not) at first cut the explanatory power of the framework. This is a 'plausibility probe' rather than systematic testing. Second, through process tracing, the research explains how the various factors played out and influenced the regulatory process and outcome, mapping the causal mechanisms at play.

A methodological problem is that the EU as such is not represented in some international regulatory fora, where the member states are represented. In some cases, the Commission and sometimes the ECB may be present with observer status, as in the BCBS. Moreover, the member states are not represented by their national executive (for example, the treasury or finance ministry). They are instead represented by national central banks and/or regulatory agencies, as in the case of the BCBS, the International Organization of Securities Commissions (IOSCO), and the IAIS. In the case of the BCBS, not all the central banks and banking authorities of the EU member states are present; only seven of them sit on the Committee. The Commission sits on the IAIS without voting power. In accounting and auditing, the main standard-setting bodies are private, and the member states are not represented either by national executives or by regulatory agencies, even though there are some provisions in place to ensure public accountability.

This book uses the shorthand expression of the 'EU' 'uploads', 'downloads', or 'cross-loads' in the introductory and concluding chapters and the introductory and concluding sections of the following chapters. However, in the analytical account of each empirical chapter, the EU is 'disaggregated', distinguishing the position of the Commission and the member states, whenever they were very different. Disagreement between member states had consequences in two ways: it slowed down the development of EU regulatory capacity on certain financial services, and made it difficult for the EU to speak with one voice in international fora or with the US.

As for the sources used, a wealth of information is available from primary documents issued by international standard-setting bodies, such as the BCBS, IOSCO, IAIS, and IASB; as well as by EU bodies, such as the European Commission, and to a lesser extent, by the EP; the Council of Economic and Finance Ministers (ECOFIN Council); the ECB; the national authorities; international, European, and national financial sector associations; large financial firms; NGOs and think-tanks (e.g. Centre for European Policy Studies); academic and non-academic experts.

This material has been complemented by more than fifty semi-structured elite interviews comprising a cross-section of policy-makers and market participants. The vast majority of interviews took place at the EU level, including: the Commission; the European Parliament (EP); the ECB; all the so-called Lamfalussy committees; other (mainly advisory) committees linked to the Directorate General (DG) Internal Market; and all the main financial sector peak associations, such as the European Banking Federation, European Saving Banks Group, etc. Interviews were also conducted at several permanent representations in Brussels. At the national level, interviews were carried out in seven member states (the UK, Germany, France, Italy, Belgium, Spain, and Portugal) at the treasury (or equivalent ministry), financial services authorities, central banks, national financial associations, and individual companies.

Interviews were also conducted at the secretariats of the main international standard-setting bodies, as well as with national representatives sitting in those bodies. Finally several rounds of interviews were carried out with policy-makers and representatives of financial industry associations in the US. The main purpose of the interviews was to gather a better understanding of the preferences of policy-makers and stakeholders, the policy-making process, the formal and informal rules governing it, the interactions between various types of policy-makers and stakeholders, the resources at their disposal, their influence, etc. All the interviews were confidential, triangulated, and checked against primary documents and press coverage.

In the following chapters, systematic reference has been made to the interviews conducted when presenting the empirical material, indicating the place and date of interviews, but no names or institutional affiliations, as all the interviews were conducted on a non-attributable basis. Whenever a point was made by several interviewees, not all of them are cited. Whenever data gathered through interviews confirmed information provided in policy documents and newspaper articles, sources publicly available are quoted. There are several instances of this in the manuscript because the interviews were conducted with the policy-makers who were involved in drafting key policy documents and industry representatives who took part in consultations for the preparation of those documents. Of course, the unofficial views given during interviews did not always coincide with the official ones expressed in public documents.

Empirical Coverage and the Scope of the Research

This is the first study ever to examine in a systematic and comparative way all the main financial services, namely: banking, securities, insurance, accounting, and auditing. Corporate governance and company law can be seen as related to but distinct from financial services, and for this reason they are not analysed in the research. Similarly, macroeconomic policies are related to but distinct from financial regulation, hence they are not discussed.

As far as the time frame is concerned, the research analyses the regulatory activities that have taken place from 1999 onwards. This starting point is chosen because previous research has mainly examined international financial standard-setting until the late 1990s, whereas the developments that occurred over the past decade are under-researched (there are exceptions, as discussed earlier in this chapter). In the EU, following the FSAP and the completion of EMU, financial market integration has substantially increased and financial regulation has been overhauled over the past decade. It is therefore crucial to examine how the increased regulatory capacity of the EU influenced (or not) the making of rules for global finance. Subsequently, the global financial crisis has given momentum to a new wave of regulation—it is therefore important to examine EU influence in this hectic period. A reference is also made to regulatory activities that unfolded in the 1980s and early 1990s whenever this is necessary either to explain developments in the subsequent decades, such as in the case of securities markets, or to allow a comparison of similar rule-making processes over time, notably in the case of the Basel II accord that superseded the Basel I accord.

The potential breadth of the research means that it is important to clarify at the outset what is covered in this book and what remains outside its scope. The research focuses on the intersection between the international level and the EU level, not so much the interaction between the EU and the member states. Nevertheless, a discussion of the member states' positions is sometimes necessary in order to explain the origins and configuration of EU rules, or how the EU was able to exert regulatory influence at the international level, in particular in fora where the EU as such is not represented (e.g. the IOSCO) or where the European Commission is present only as an observer without voting power (as is the case in the BCBS and the IAIS).

The main focus of the research is on the activities of standard-setting bodies across the main segments of the financial sectors, namely: the BCBS in banking; the IOSCO in securities markets; IAIS in insurance; the IASB (and its predecessor) in accounting; and the International Federation of Accountants Committee (IFAC) in auditing. Whereas the first three bodies are fora of national regulators, the last two bodies are private-sector bodies, though subject to some oversight by the public authorities.

Other international bodies or gatherings dealing with financial and macroeconomic issues are not discussed in this book. The Financial Stability Board (FSB) (and its predecessor, the Financial Stability Forum, FSF) is not a standard-setting body, though it could be seen as the standard-setter of the standard-setters because in the wake of the crisis, it has set the agenda for standard-setting bodies, such as the BCBS, in certain respects. The G20, which came into the spotlight during the global financial crisis and is the broader political forum in which the agenda for international rules on financial services are discussed by national executives, is not a regulatory forum. Similarly, the International Monetary Fund (IMF) and the World Bank are not standard-setting bodies, even though the IMF produces periodical reports concerning the regulatory and supervisory framework of the countries subject to the IMF's assessment. These two bodies tend to focus on issues related to macroeconomic governance, which encompasses monetary and fiscal policy. The Organization for Economic Co-operation and Development (OECD) issues (non-binding) rules on taxation and corporate governance, which are not dealt with in this research.

Conclusion

This chapter has taken stock from three main bodies of literature, outlining the research design of the book. The following chapters deal with the main financial services, namely banking, securities markets, insurance, accounting, and auditing. Each chapter outlines the regulatory capacity in the US and explains the development of the regulatory capacity of the EU over time. In that section, EU regulatory capacity is the dependent variable, and policy entrepreneurs and the interests of the main member states are the independent variables. Each chapter then focuses on significant international regulatory initiatives pre- and post-crisis. These sections explain how EU and US regulatory capacities—the independent variables—played out in the uploading, downloading, and cross-loading of financial rules—the dependent variables. These chapters also consider an alternative or, as it turns out to be, a complementary explanation based on the power of the financial industry.

3

The EU and Global Banking Regulation

Banking was the first financial service to be subject to regulatory harmonization in the EU. Initially, EU rules were primarily designed to foster integration in the banking sector, rather than dealing with prudential issues. Lacking its own regulatory template for capital adequacy, the EU decided to download international standards over time (the Basel accords), albeit taking into account European 'specificities'.

In the US, banking regulation is a dual (i.e. a state and federal) competence, with several federal regulatory agencies involved. The US, together with the UK, was one of the first movers in setting in place risk-sensitive capital requirements in the 1980s. These domestic rules were then uploaded onto the international Basel I accord. Subsequently, the US agreed to download the Basel II and III accords into domestic legislation, although the domestic implementation process was fraught with difficulties.

Unlike for other financial services, global banking regulation is quite well established because the Basel Committee on Banking Supervision (BCBS) dates back to 1974. The main prudential rules on capital requirements were agreed internationally for the first time in 1989—the Basel I accord. This international agreement was superseded by the Basel II accord (2004–5) and by the Basel III accord (2010). In the negotiations for the Basel accords, the EU did not present a united front because its member states had different priorities, rooted in different structures of national banking systems and their links to the real economy.

Banks, especially big transnational players, have been powerful lobbyists in the making of the Basel accords. Their influence was greatest in Basel II because most of the innovations introduced in the accord were uploaded by the big transnational players, rather than by the US or European authorities. In the downloading of the Basel accords, small local banks have obtained concessions that have taken into account their specificities both in the EU and the US.

The Regulatory Capacity of the EU in Banking

The EU regulatory capacity in banking developed relatively early (see Table 3.1), as compared to other financial services, such as securities markets and insurance (Story and Walter 1997). Several bodies dealing with banking regulation and supervision were set up in the EU over time, but their powers and remit remained very limited because the member states were reluctant to relinquish their prerogatives in this field. EU rules were mainly designed to promote market integration. With reference to prudential regulation, especially capital adequacy, the EU has mainly downloaded international standards. The proposals for banking union are discussed in Chapter 7.

The Institutional Framework for Banking Regulation in the EU

Prior to the introduction of the so-called 'Lamfalussy architecture' in the early 2000s, the Banking Advisory Committee created in 1977 was the main forum in which banking legislation was discussed in the EU. It brought together national senior officials of finance ministries, central banks, and supervisory authorities and was chaired by the European Commission. It met regularly, serving as a discussion forum for the member states and advising

Table 3.1. The building up of EU regulatory capacity in banking in the 2000s

Policy entrepreneur	Preferences of the large member states	Industry preferences	Regulatory template—content
Commission Germany pivotal	Different preferences on core issues (e.g. definition and amount of capital, liquidity), due to different banking systems and varieties of capitalism (continental vs UK)	Different preferences on core issues, due to different banking systems (e.g. savings banks in Germany, *bancassurance* in France, international banks in the UK) and varieties of capitalism (funding to real economy)	*Capital requirements legislation: CRD III (2006) and CRD IV(2013)* – downloading Basel II and III rules – European 'specificities' – 'national discretions' (CRD III)
ECB Commission France and Germany	Franco-German agreement on core elements, but different preferences about fiscal implications	–	*Proposals for Banking Union (2012)* – single rulebook – Directive on Recovery and Resolution – Deposit Guarantee Scheme Directive – Single Supervisory Mechanism – Single Resolution Mechanism – common fiscal backstop

the European Commission on issues related to banking legislation (see, for example, Goodhart 2011). In 2001, the EU endorsed the Lamfalussy reform, named after Baron Alexander Lamfalussy, the chair of the Committee of Wise Men (2001) that proposed it to speed up the regulatory process in financial services (Mügge 2006; Quaglia 2007; see also Chapter 7).

The Lamfalussy architecture was articulated across multiple institutional levels. At level 1, the EP and the Council co-decided framework legislation (mainly directives) proposed by the Commission. At level 2, the implementing measures (generally directives, less frequently regulations) of the level 1 framework legislation were adopted by the Commission through the comitology process, which involved the so-called level 2 committees of member state representatives in banking, securities markets, and insurance. At level 3, the committees of national regulators (the level 3 committees) advised the Commission on the adoption of level 1 and level 2 measures and adopted level 3 measures, such as non-legally binding standards and guidelines.

The Lamfalussy reform transformed the Banking Advisory Committee into a so-called 'level 2 committee'—the European Banking Committee—in 2005. It has 'comitology' functions because it assists the Commission in adopting implementing measures for level 1 framework directives or regulations, co-decided by the European Parliament and the Council of Ministers. As part of the Lamfalussy reforms, the Committee of European Banking Supervisors was set up in London in 2004. It was a so-called level 3 committee, made up of senior representatives from national banking supervisory authorities as well as the ECB. It advised the Commission concerning the preparation of draft-implementing measures in the field of banking activities (level 2 measures), as well as in the preparation of level 1 legislation. It contributed to the consistent implementation of EU legislation by issuing 'standards' and 'guidelines' (level 3 measures) and to the convergence of member states' supervisory practices throughout the EU. Finally, it promoted supervisory cooperation, also through the exchange of information. The Committee aimed to work by consensus of its members. If no consensus could be reached, decisions could be taken by qualified majority, whereby each member state had the same number of voting rights as in the Council of Ministers (Quaglia 2008).

After the global financial crisis and building on the de Larosière report (2009), the EU reformed its micro- and macro-prudential framework for financial supervision. It established the European Systemic Risk Board in charge of monitoring macro-prudential risk; it transformed the level 3 Lamfalussy committees into independent authorities with legal personality, an increased budget, and enhanced powers. In 2010, the Committee of European Banking Supervisors became the European Banking Authority, with the same membership and voting rules as its forerunner, but with a full-time chair.

The European Banking Authority, like the other two authorities in securities markets and insurance (see Chapters 4 and 5), is charged with the tasks of coordinating the application of supervisory standards and promoting cooperation between national supervisors. It develops technical standards, which are binding unless the Commission opposes them. It produces interpretative guidelines to assist the national authorities in taking individual decisions. It can address decisions directly to national authorities and can also take decisions directly applicable to financial institutions whenever the European Banking Authority has addressed a decision to the national supervisor but the national supervisor has not complied with it.[1]

Regulatory Templates in Banking in the EU

The First Banking Directive (1977) removed obstacles to the provision of services and establishment of branches across the borders of EU member states and harmonized rules for bank licensing, subject to host country control. In the 1980s, the principle of 'home country control' and 'mutual recognition' were introduced into EU legislation, meaning that financial firms could operate across the EU on the basis of rules set by the country where firm headquarters were located (Story and Walter 1997). The Second Banking Directive (1989) established a single banking licence—known as 'single passport'—that allowed banks to operate throughout the EU, providing a variety of financial services, following the 'universal bank' model (Dermine 2006).

The Second Banking Directive contained a list of banking services that could be provided in all member states on the basis of a licence. The directive also stipulated that there should no longer be capital requirements at the branch level, but only at the bank level, to facilitate branching (Mügge 2010). At that time, the member states had in place different national rules on capital adequacy and these rules mostly reflected the distinctive features of national banking systems, hence it was difficult for them to agree on a common set of prudential standards. The Basel I accord provided a solution to this conundrum. The Own Funds directive (1989) and the Solvency Directive (1989) set capital requirements in the EU, building on Basel I. In order to ensure a level playing field and prevent regulatory arbitrage, the Capital Adequacy Directive (1993) basically extended capital requirements for banks to investment firms (Underhill 1997). The directive required banks

[1] <http://europa.eu/rapid/pressReleasesAction.do?reference=MEMO/10/434&format=HTML&aged=0&language=EN&guiLanguage=en> (accessed Mar. 2013).

to separate their 'trading book'[2] from their 'banking book', and to apply the building block to the former.[3]

In the development of EU regulatory capacity in banking, unlike for example in insurance and to some extent securities markets and accounting, the UK did not act as a policy entrepreneur. In several circumstances, the British authorities were on the back foot when negotiating EU banking legislation. Indeed, some observers regarded the British support for the Basel I accord as an attempt to prevent the establishment of distinctive EU rules with a strong continental imprint (Story and Walter 1997). By contrast, Germany, which has the largest banking sector in the EU and also has a distinctive three-pillared banking system, was a pace-setter in EU banking legislation from the outset.[4] The Second Banking Directive de facto promoted across the EU the 'universal bank' model, which was common in Germany, where banks could provide a variety of services, including securities trading. This was not the case in other countries, such as the UK, which had several non-bank investment firms, and Italy, where different types of banks existed (e.g. banks providing long-term credit).

The Commission acted as policy entrepreneur, but its efforts were very much directed towards promoting banking integration, rather than setting prudential regulation. Indeed, the EU legislative activity in the 1970s and 1980s mainly concerned the development of policy templates for the conduct of cross-border banking activities. To be fair, the Commission was well aware of the formidable obstacles to the development of capital requirements and prudential rules in the EU because of the different, often incompatible, preferences of the member states. It was difficult for the member states to agree on common prudential rules, such as capital requirements, because they had different national regulatory frameworks, which were rooted in their domestic political economies (Brown 1997; Story and Walter 1997; Underhill 1997).

Two features are particularly important in this respect: the configuration of national banking systems and their link to the real economy. Despite increasing cross-border banking integration in the EU over the past two decades, national banking systems remain different in certain key respects. They have different definitions of capital and allow different assets to be counted as regulatory capital. Many banks on the continent, such as the publicly owned

[2] A 'trading book' consists of positions in 'financial instruments...held either with trading intent or in order to hedge other elements of the trading book' (BCBS 2005: 55). It is different from the 'banking book', where securities are held until maturity and are not actively traded.

[3] The Banking Directive on the Taking up and Pursuit of Credit Institutions (2000) consolidated in one single legal text the previous directives—it was the equivalent of a 'European Banking Act'.

[4] The rapporteurs of the Capital Requirements III and IV were, respectively, German and Austrian, reflecting the importance attributed by these countries to EU banking legislation.

German LB, Cooperative and Savings Banks and most French Mutuals, do not have equity finance and rely on other sources of funding.[5] The Landesbanken in Germany have a variety of 'hybrid' instruments, such as 'silent participations'—state loans—that are calculated as part of their public capital. In France (but also Spain and Austria), the *bancassurance* model[6] is widespread, which permits the double counting of the capital of insurance subsidiaries and artificially increases the figures for the overall capital of banks. As for the link between the financial system and the real economy, in continental Europe most of the funding to the real economy is provided by banks, hence higher capital requirements are likely to result in decreased funding to industry. For these reasons it has proved difficult to agree on harmonized capital rules either at the EU level or internationally.

The Regulatory Capacity of the US in Banking

In the US, banks are subject to a dual regulatory system at the state level and federal level. Supervisory responsibilities are shared by a variety of federal agencies. Despite this convoluted internal division of competences amongst domestic regulatory authorities, the US was one of the first movers, together with the UK, in setting in place a domestic regulatory template based on risk-sensitive capital requirements in the mid-1980s. This move gave the US authorities a head start in shaping international capital standards.

The Institutional Framework for Banking Regulation and Supervision in the US

The Office of the Comptroller of the Currency, which is the oldest of the federal bank regulatory agencies, was established by the National Currency Act (1863) and the Bank Act (1864) to supervise national banks. The Comptroller is a bureau of the Treasury Department. The Federal Reserve, which was established as the central bank in 1913, supervises state-chartered banks, which have elected membership in the Fed. The Federal Reserve is also the primary supervisor of bank holding companies and financial holding companies. In addition, the Federal Reserve Board has authority to examine any US branch

[5] Indeed, this aspect proved problematic in the incorporation of the Basel III accord into EU legislation, which contains specific provisions for co-operative and mutual banks. Basel III was written with banks funded by equity finance in mind (hence the emphasis on common equities in core tier 1 capital).

[6] These are banks that combine under one roof banks and insurance activities.

or subsidiary bank controlled by a foreign bank (see Spong 2000). The Dodd Frank Act, discussed shortly, has given the Fed additional competences.

The Federal Deposit Insurance Corporation (FDIC), which was established as a response to the Great Recession in 1934, supervises insured state-chartered banks that are not members of the Federal Reserve System, as well as state-chartered savings banks (Spong 2000). Like the Federal Reserve, the FDIC is an independent federal agency. The Office of Thrift Supervision, which is to be abolished following the Dodd Frank Act, is responsible for supervising federal savings associations and federal savings banks. It is a bureau of the Treasury Department. The Office shares with state agencies supervisory authority over state-chartered savings associations belonging to the Savings Association Insurance Fund. It also regulates savings association affiliates and thrift holding companies.

The Dodd Frank Act (2010) contained several provisions concerning the reform of the institutional framework for banking regulation and supervision in the US, but it did not substantially reduce the number of agencies involved. It established a new Financial Stability Oversight Council, charged with identifying and responding to emerging risks throughout the financial system. It is composed primarily of federal financial services regulators and is chaired by the Secretary of the Treasury Department (see Woolley and Ziegler 2012). The Act created the Bureau of Consumer Financial Protection, housed within the Federal Reserve Board. It granted to the US Department of the Treasury, FDIC and the Federal Reserve new powers to close and wind down 'too big to fail' financial (including non-bank) institutions in an orderly fashion. It abolished the Office of Thrift Supervision, redistributing its responsibilities amongst the Federal Reserve, the FDIC, and the Office of the Comptroller of the Currency (for an in-depth discussion of the Dodd Frank Act and its effects, see Acharya et al. 2011).

The Federal Reserve was tasked with the supervision and regulation of all banks, thrifts, bank holding companies, and non-bank financial institutions with assets over $50 billion, as well as full authority to examine all non-bank subsidiaries of bank holding companies. The board was given the power to establish policies and procedures for emergency lending. The Federal Reserve became specifically responsible for the supervision of systemically important (i) financial institutions; and (ii) financial market infrastructure (notably payment, clearing, and settlements activities) (see Acharya et al. 2011).

The variety of regulatory agencies involved at the national and state level is also reflected by the 'composite' US representation in the BCBS. The Federal Reserve, the Office of the Comptroller of the Currency, and the FDIC sit in the BCBS. The Federal Reserve of New York also sits in the BCBS. In banking regulation and supervision in the US, inter-agency competition has been frequent (*The Banker,* 2 Aug. 2002; US Senate Committee on Banking 2008b), including during the negotiations of the Basel accords.

Regulatory Templates in Banking in the US

US banking regulation has evolved in a piecemeal fashion over time, largely in response to crises and policy failures. For example, after the Great Recession, the National Banking Act of 1933 (also called the Glass-Steagall Act, after its main proponents in Congress) separated commercial banking from investment banking. However, this separation became blurred over time. In 1987, the Fed allowed selected large banks to underwrite securities that previously they had not been permitted to (Calomiris 2000). In 1999, the Gramm-Leach-Bliley Act removed the legal restrictions between commercial banking and investment banking.

On the key issue of prudential rules, the three major US banking regulators adopted different capital requirements prior to 1985. In 1985, following a series of domestic banking failures, US regulators, under the aegis of the Federal Reserve Chairman Paul Volcker, agreed to adopt a common minimum fixed capital/asset ratio of 5.5 per cent for banks. Hence, borrowing from the risk-based capital requirements adopted by the Bank of England in 1980, US regulators adopted risk-based capital requirements in 1986 (Kapstein 1989). These rules were then uploaded at the international level in the Basel I accord.

Subsequently, the US, like the other members of the BCBS, downloaded the Basel I accord into domestic legislation, the FDIC Improvement Act (1991). This Act, passed at the height of the Savings and Loan Crisis in the US, introduced provisions on prompt corrective action by linking enforcement closely to the level of capital held by a bank. It introduced a leverage ratio, i.e. a risk-independent capital requirement that is proportional to the size of bank's assets (Spong 2000). The leverage ratio was subsequently uploaded by the US into the Basel III accord.

During the Basel II negotiations, the US authorities decided to apply the accord only to internationally active banks, which numbered approximately a dozen, with another dozen able to opt in (*The Banker,* 2 Aug. 2002). The remaining 8,000 banks were to be subject to a revised version of Basel I. In the end, however, Basel II was not implemented in the US because it was felt that the Basel II accord would disadvantage US banks outside its scope of application (e.g. community banks) (Herring 2007). Indeed, lower capital requirements were expected for the banks to which the Basel II accord would be applied, making them more competitive *vis-à-vis* the domestic banks to which the Basel II accord would not apply, as argued, for example, by the regulator of community banks, the Office for the Comptroller of the Currency (Parliamentary hearing, US Congress, 27 Feb, 2003).

This issue was brought to the fore by the results of Quantitative Impact Study (QIS) 4[7] conducted in the US. The study also highlighted the problem of excessive decline of capital requirements, which was addressed by maintaining a lower floor and capital ratio, forcefully advocated by the FDIC (Parliamentary hearing, US Congress, 19 June 2003 and 27 Feb. 2003). The Federal Reserve, which was the principal supporter of the Basel II accord in the US, recognized that 'creating international competitive balance under Basel II carried the potential that domestic competitive balance will become distorted' (*Financial Times,* 5 Jan. 2004).

In the downloading of the Basel III accord, the US will have to take into account the banking provisions of the Dodd Frank Act. The Collins Amendment, originally drafted by FDIC staff, imposes the risk-based and leverage capital standards currently applicable to US insured depository institutions on US bank holding companies, including US intermediate holding companies of foreign banking organizations, thrift holding companies, and systemically important non-bank financial companies (Paskelian and Bell 2013). As a result, the Collins Amendment creates a statutory floor and US banking regulators would be able to implement Basel III only to the extent it is consistent with the Collins Amendment floor. Hence, they might be able to impose more stringent Basel III capital rules on insured depository institutions and bank holding companies.[8] Both in the Dodd Frank Act and in the BCBS, the US authorities called for additional capital requirements for systemically important financial institutions. The governor of the Federal Reserve noted that 'the parallelism of the international and domestic processes should facilitate the goal of congruence between U.S. and international standards' (Tarullo 2011).

The Collins rule could have direct implications for EU headquartered banks operating in the US. Prior to the crisis, the US accorded foreign banks the same national treatment as domestic banks, and US regulators generally allowed foreign banks to choose the organization and legal structure they saw fit at the consolidated level (Tarullo 2012). The Dodd Frank Act forced foreign banks operating in the US to create holding companies, to which US capital requirements would apply. Indeed, the Collins Amendment removed the exemption from bank holding company capital requirements granted by the Federal Reserve in the past (Tarullo 2012). The change was intended to strengthen the capital regime applied to the US operations of foreign banks,

[7] These studies were field-testing exercises, run to assess the feasibility and impact of specific capital requirements.

[8] <http://blogs.law.harvard.edu/corpgov/2010/07/08/collins-amendment-sets-minimum-capital-requirements> (accessed May 2012).

including EU banks, which worried about this new requirement (interviews, New York, Nov. 2011, June 2013).

The Volcker Rule introduced by the Dodd Frank Act imposes limits to depository banks in proprietary trading, resembling the prohibition of combined investment and commercial banking introduced after the Great Depression by the Glass-Steagall Act. Banks are allowed to invest up to 3 per cent of their Tier 1 capital in private equity and hedge funds as well as trade for hedging purposes. The rule also requires systemically important non-bank financial companies to carry additional capital and comply with certain other quantitative limits on such activities, although it does not expressly prohibit them (Acharya et al. 2011).

The Volcker Rule could have significant implications outside the US, especially for the EU. Hence, the European Commission, supported by the member states, put pressure on the US government to revise the formulation of this rule (interviews, New York, Nov. and Aug. 2011). To begin with, some large European banks (mostly British, French, or German) also operate in the US. Central bankers and regulators in Europe (including in the UK), but also in Canada and Japan, were concerned that the rule, which would apply to the US operations of foreign banks, could be extended to firms' operations outside the country (*Bloomberg*, 24 Feb. 2012).

Furthermore, the Volcker Rule could hinder the ability of US banks to buy and sell European sovereign bonds on behalf of customers, reducing liquidity in those markets because the rule exempts US government debt but not non-US government bonds (interviews, New York, Nov. 2011, June 2013). This could create problems in finding traders and investors for the sovereign debt of European countries, worsening the sovereign debt crisis in Europe. Small European countries, especially those with a relatively large stock of debt, rely heavily on big banks that serve as primary dealers to buy their debt at auctions. However, those dealers may pull back from those markets because they often do not have buyers at the ready for such securities and could fear violating Volcker-imposed restrictions (*Wall Street Journal*, 27 Jan. 2012).

The BCBS and International Capital Standards

Unlike for other financial services, global banking regulation is quite well established because the BCBS dates back to 1974. International capital requirements were agreed by the BCBS back in 1989—the Basel I accord—which was superseded by the Basel II and Basel III accords. As argued by the historical institutionalist literature, a process of path-dependency 'kicked in': once an international regulatory forum has acquired a prominent position by issuing a robust set of international standards, it is difficult to claw back its powers.

The International Institutional Framework for Banking Regulation

The BCBS is the oldest financial international regulatory forum: it was established by the central bank governors of the Group of Ten (G10) countries in 1974. Prior to the reform introduced in 2009, the Committee's members came from Belgium, Canada, France, Germany, Italy, Japan, Luxembourg, the Netherlands, Spain, Sweden, Switzerland, the United Kingdom, and the US. After the financial crisis, the membership of the Committee was extended to all countries of the Group of Twenty (G20), given the fact that financial activity in other (non-G10) jurisdictions had become more important. Countries are represented in the Committee by their central bank and by the authority with formal responsibility for the prudential supervision of banking activities, whenever this is not the central bank. The only exception is the US, which is represented by multiple regulatory agencies. The European Commission and the European Central Bank participate in the working of the BCBS as observers.

Despite its small staff, hosted at the Bank for International Settlements (BIS), the BCBS has recognized expertise in banking regulation (Kerwer 2005; Wood 2005), largely through the work carried out by its working groups of national regulators, which discuss the technical details of regulation and meet regularly. The final versions of the accords drafted by the Committee are eventually negotiated and agreed at the level of governors and chairmen of the supervisory authorities (or their deputies). Although the BCBS does not have enforcement powers, it has implementation working groups that monitor how its capital rules are put into practice across jurisdictions.

Generally, the members of the Committee have the ability to enact international rules domestically and tend to be independent from the political authorities. Moreover, central bankers, who compose the bulk of the Committee, have an established ability to cooperate (Dyson and Marcussen 2009; Tsingou 2010). National politicians are one step removed from the Basel negotiations. However, national regulators negotiating in the BCBS are mindful that the agreement reached in Basel has to be acceptable to their respective national financial industries and political authorities back home.

When the BCBS was established, the US and the UK put their market power and regulatory capacity behind it (Simmons 2001; Wood 2005). Indeed, for the first fifteen years or so, the chairs of the BCBS mainly came from the US and the UK. These two countries had the largest banking markets worldwide, with many foreign banks operating in their territories (Wood 2005). A body facilitating international cooperation in banking was seen as serving their domestic political economy interests, dealing with cross-border externalities and promoting a level playing field in banking regulation across jurisdictions (Simmons 2001). Over time, the EU (or to be precise the European members of the BCBS) have become very supportive of this forum, where European countries have tended to be over-represented, at least prior to the inclusion of the G20 members.

International Regulatory Templates in Banking

Initially, the work of the Committee focused on promoting cooperation amongst banking supervisors, with a view to closing gaps in supervision (Wood 2005). Two basic principles informed the work of the Committee: no banks should escape supervision; and supervision should be adequate. The first document issued by the Committee shortly after its creation was the so-called 'Concordat' (1975), which contained guidelines for improving cooperation between supervisors dealing with banks' foreign establishments (for a history of the first two decades of the BCBS, see Goodhart 2011). In 1997, the BCBS issued the 'Core Principles for Effective Banking Supervision', which have been revised over time. The Financial Stability Forum (FSF) and its successor the Financial Stability Board (FSB) have included them amongst the 'Key Standards for Sound Financial Systems' for the financial sector assessments programme carried out by the IMF (see Drezner 2007).[9]

The second main area of standard-setting activity of the BCBS has concerned capital requirements for banks. The BCBS first reached an agreement on international capital requirements in 1988—the so-called Basel I accord on 'International Convergence of Capital Measurement and Capital Standards'. The Basel I accord was replaced by the Basel II accord (2006) and Basel III accord (2010). In the following discussion, more attention is devoted to Basel II and Basel III, which fall within the time frame of this book. Basel I is included because it set in place a path-dependent process and provides an interesting comparison with Basel III.

The Basel I Accord

The 'International Convergence of Capital Measurement and Capital Standards', also known as the 'Basel I accord', was agreed by the BCBS in 1988. The Basel accord set in place an international regulatory template for capital requirements. It was largely instigated by the US, which was subsequently joined by the UK (Oatley and Nabors 1998; Simmons 2001). A period of domestic banking instability and increasing competition from foreign banks stimulated US policy-makers to call for international rules on capital requirements (Singer 2004, 2007). The 1980s were characterized by a series

[9] <http://www.financialstabilityboard.org/cos/key_standards.htm> (accessed Dec. 2011).

of banking failures in the US. These failures were caused by a variety of factors, but ultimately they could be ascribed to low levels of capital held by banks. The Latin American debt crisis worsened the situation because many US banks had invested heavily in that region (Wood 2005).

US regulators reacted by imposing higher risk-based capital requirements domestically. These requirements were calculated as a percentage of assets to which different risk weights had been assigned. However, higher capital requirements represented a cost for US banks, damaging their competitiveness *vis-à-vis* foreign banks, which operated with lower capital requirements. The increasing market share of Japanese banks was of particular concern in the US (Simmons 2001). Hence, US policy-makers called for the introduction of risk-weighted capital standards internationally, with a view to creating a level playing field and protecting the competitiveness of their banking sector. The US was able to upload most of its capital rules to the international level.

British policy-makers joined the US authorities in calling for international capital requirements because they had similar domestic concerns (Simmons 2001; Singer 2004, 2007). Like the US, the UK had been plagued by a series of domestic banking failures, the most well-known of which was that of Johnson Matthey Bankers Limited in 1984 (Moran 1991). Like their American counterparts, the British authorities reacted by increasing risk-based capital requirements, which weakened the competitiveness of British banks *vis-à-vis* foreign competitors, first and foremost Japanese banks.

The Anglo-Saxon alliance won over the Japanese authorities. After an agreement was reached between these three countries, the other members of the BCBS decided to join in, and the Basel I accord was signed. The EU as a whole did not have its own set of capital requirements, which varied considerably across member states (Underhill 1997). Indeed, they could not even agree on a common definition of 'capital', a problem that surfaced in the negotiations of the Basel I accord (Wood 2005). In the end, the Basel I accord did not provide a common definition of capital, nor did Basel II succeed in doing so. European policy-makers had different priorities and different positions during the negotiations of the Basel I accord and there was no EU (at that time it was still called the European Community) attempt to coordinate on the issue (Wood 2005).

The 1988 Basel Capital Accord (Basel I) set capital adequacy standards for internationally active banks. It principally dealt with credit risk. The formula used for calculating capital requirements for credit institutions (banks) was relatively simple. Individual assets were divided into four basic credit risk categories (or 'buckets') on the basis of the counterparty of each financial transaction and were assigned weights ranging from 0 (loans to Organization for Economic Co-operation and Development (OECD) countries) to 100 per cent (corporate loans). The sum of the weighted values of the individual balance sheet assets was classified as a bank's risk-weighted assets. Banks were required to maintain capital of not less than 8 per cent of their risk-weighted assets. National authorities were free to set higher levels of minimum capital.[10] The Basel I accord was a non-legally binding gentlemen's agreement. Its rules became legally binding only when incorporated into the national legislation of the member countries. Over time, the standards set by the BCBS came to be applied in over 100 countries (BCBS 2001), well beyond the limited number of signatories.

The accord underwent a major amendment in 1996 so as to incorporate capital requirements for market risks in the trading book. The Amendment set out two alternative approaches to measure market risk: a standardized method and an internal model approach, whereby banks were allowed to use approved value-at-risk models (Wood 2005). This is a technique used to estimate the probability of portfolio losses based on the statistical analysis of historical price trends and volatilities. The idea of using the banks' internal models to calculate market risk subsequently found its way into the Basel II accord, which relied heavily on banks' internal models to calculate credit risk and operational risk (Underhill and Zhang 2008).

The Basel II Accord

Despite several amendments introduced over time, some weaknesses of the Basel I accord remained. The overarching criticism was that the rules devised to determine capital requirements were crude and potentially misleading (BCBS 1999a). The risk-insensitivity of the Basel I accord gave banks an incentive to move high-quality assets off the balance sheet through securitization and did not reward the use of advanced credit management techniques (BCBS 1999a, 2001).

The regulators, in particular in the US (Ferguson, Federal Reserve, Parliamentary hearing, US Congress, 27 Feb. 2003), became convinced that the Basel I accord was too simplistic to capture the increasingly complex operations of the largest banks (BCBS 1999a). Several large banks had complex risk management models in place and they lobbied hard to convince policy-makers that this should be taken into account in setting (lowering, in their case) capital requirements (Underhill and Zhang 2008; Tsingou 2008).

Beginning in 1998, the Chairman of the Federal Reserve, Alan Greenspan, and subsequently other high-level Fed officials, repeatedly made the case

[10] The Basel I accord defined crude risk classes, such as 100% risk weight for loans to all non-financial companies regardless of credit quality. Hence, a corporate exposure with a high rating and low risk had the same credit risk weighting as a corporate exposure with a low rating and a high risk. A similar comment applies to loans to OECD countries, which received the same risk weight.

for changing the Basel I rules. Executives from individual banks and banking industry associations, such as the American Bankers Association and the Institute of International Finance, also called for change (Tarullo 2008: 90). As Tarullo, later governor of the New York Federal Reserve, put it, Basel II 'even more than Basel I, resembled a trade negotiation, with extensive political and constituency involvement at times submerging the spirit of regulatory cooperation traditionally central to Basel Committee activities. And yet, no national regulator knew at the outset exactly what outcome it wanted' (2008: 87).

The negotiations for the Basel II accord gained momentum in June 1999, with the publication of the first consultative paper by the BCBS, followed by a second consultative paper in January 2001 and a third paper in May 2003. These documents were subject to open consultation and the responses from industry, experts, and national authorities flooded the BCBS. The BCBS conducted four quantitative impact studies in 2001 (QIS1), 2002 (QIS2), 2004 (QIS3), and 2005 (QIS5) concerning the implementation of the new rules. Such assessments were conducted in aggregate terms, i.e. they were not country- or sector-specific. However, since not all countries were satisfied by the results of the QIS3, the US, Japan, South Africa, and Germany decided to conduct national impact studies, which became the QIS4.

The Basel II accord was eventually agreed in June 2004 and was approximately eight times the length of the Basel I accord. Unlike the Basel I accord, which was largely based on the US regulatory template, the Basel II accord contained a new set of rules that were not uploaded from any national jurisdiction. Whereas it partly built on the Basel I rules, the new parts of the accord were informed by proposals and studies from the main banks and banking associations (Tarullo 2008).[11] The Basel II accord based capital requirements on three pillars (BCBS 2006). Pillar 1 was concerned with minimum capital requirements, covering three types of risk: 'credit risk', 'market risk', and, innovatively, 'operational risk'. Innovations were also introduced with reference to risk measurement. 'Credit risk' is the probability of loss from a debtor's default. Basically, it is the risk that a counterparty to a financial transaction will fail to fulfil their obligations. 'Market risk' is 'the risk of losses in on- and off-balancesheet positions arising from movements in market prices' (BCBS 2005: 1). 'Operational risk' is 'the risk of loss resulting from inadequate or failed internal processes, people and systems or from external events' (BCBS 2006: 140). Pillar 2 was based on a supervisory review process, aimed at covering external factors that were not fully taken into account when computing

[11] A compendium of all the relevant documents was published in 2006. *Basel II: International Convergence of Capital Measurement and Capital Standards: A Revised Framework—Comprehensive Version*, June 2006, <http://www.bis.org/publ/bcbs128.htm> (accessed Mar. 2014).

the minimum capital requirements. Supervisors were therefore enabled to take measures which, if necessary, could go beyond the minimum capital requirements. Finally, Pillar 3 was the discipline imposed by the market, facilitated by transparency requirements.

In July 2005, in close cooperation with the International Organization of Securities Commissions (IOSCO), the international body of securities supervisors, the BCBS published a document on the treatment of banks' 'trading books'. This text was subsequently integrated with the June 2004 text in a document released in June 2006. Capital requirements on the trading book were very important for investment banks and investment firms, whose main lines of business concern securities trading, whereas commercial banks have most or part of their business in the 'banking book'.

There were several controversial issues in the negotiations of the accord. On some of these issues European (mainly continental) countries presented a united front. On other issues, they did not. A disagreement that was settled early on in the negotiations concerned the initial US-led proposal to use external rating in order to assess the credit risk that is part of the first pillar of the Basel II accord (Wood 2005: 130). Credit rating agencies themselves expressed reservations about the proposal (*American Banker*, 4 Apr. 2000: 2). The European members of the BCBS suggested the use of internal rating, which was regarded as more reliable, and would penalize European banks that lent extensively to unrated companies less severely (interviews, London, 19 May 2006; Frankfurt, 17 Jan. 2006; Rome, 23 June 2006). This proposal was endorsed by the BCBS, and it was thus included in the Consultation Paper 2.

The second controversial issue was the use of internal ratings-based models by banks in order to determine their credit risk. Beside the 'standardized' model for smaller banks that did not have the internal resources to operate internal models, Basel II established an advanced internal ratings model for the very big banks, whereby banks were allowed to use their own internal model to estimate various aspects of credit risk. The Federal Reserve board was the main proponent of this change. Other US regulators, first and foremost the FDIC, were lukewarm towards this idea and so were some continental regulators (such as Germans). The big global banks that had most to gain from the advanced internal ratings-based model organized themselves effectively to lobby national regulators on this issue (Lall 2012), though they did not achieve all they wanted (Young 2012). The influence of the large financial institutions was strengthened by the fact that the BCBS had insufficient expertise to develop the advanced approach on its own and had to rely on the banks to provide technical input into the process (Tarullo 2008). Small banks that would not qualify for the internal ratings-based model feared they would be disadvantaged, an issue that re-emerged during the domestic implementation of the accord.

The third controversial issue was the operational risk charges as part of Pillar 1. These charges were criticized by banks: US-based banks and the Institute of International Finance were particularly vocal on this issue (Wood 2005: 129, 140). They admitted that this type of risk existed—for example, as a result of disruptions to their operations caused by staff fraud or natural disasters—but argued that it was better dealt with internally by banks (House Committee on Financial Services 2003a, 2003b). Provisions concerning operational risk were watered down in the final version of the accord, as a consequence of lobbying efforts from industry (Lall 2012; Underhill and Zhang 2008).

An important issue for continental European countries concerned the implications of the new capital rules for bank credit to small and medium-sized enterprises (SMEs). There was concern that risk weights for lending to SMEs would remain the same as those for lending to large unrated corporations, due to the fact that most SME borrowers do not have external credit ratings. This issue was prominent for the SMEs in Germany (see Bundesverband deutscher Banken 2003; European Savings Banks Group 2003; *The Economist,* 10 Nov. 2001), the *mittlestand,* which largely rely on bank loans for their funding, as is also the case in Italy (see Associazione Bancaria Italiana 2003) and France. The German authorities were so concerned about the domestic impact of Basel II that they decided to conduct a Quantitative Impact Study on their own (QIS4).

The changes that were subsequently made to the rules of Basel II regarding these issues can largely be ascribed to the activity of the representatives from the main European countries (interviews, Frankfurt, 17 Jan. 2006; Rome, 23 June 2006). It should also be noted that, because of its domestic political salience, the German Chancellor and the Economics Minister went public in October 2001, criticizing the accord for being detrimental to SMEs (Wood 2005: 141). It was one of the few instances of direct political interference in the process, even though there were several other instances of indirect political pressure, such as that exerted by Congress on US negotiators and evidenced in several Congressional hearings (see e.g. House Committee on Financial Services 2003a, 2003b).

Amongst the overarching regulatory and competition issues, there was concern that inconsistent implementation across countries would distort competition and could significantly increase regulatory burdens for those banks operating in more than one country. Finally, there were issues such as the inherent procyclicality induced by the content of the agreement, its negative effects on developing countries (Claessens et al. 2008; Griffith-Jones 2003), and its excessive complexity (500 pages).

The EU did not have a unified position in the making of the Basel II accord. On the one hand, the participating EU member states were keen to pursue their national preferences, largely rooted in their domestic political economy, namely the configuration of the banking sector and the link between the financial sector and the real economy (such as the implications of the accord for credit to SMEs in continental countries). On the other hand, when negotiations began on the Basel II accord, the member states agreed that the new international capital requirements would be incorporated, with some modifications, into EU legislation, as had been the case for the Basel I accord.

This meant that the Basel II accord was to be applied to all banks and investment firms in the EU, not only to internationally active banks, unlike in the US. Hence, European policy-makers had an incentive to make sure that what was agreed in Basel was suitable for the EU context (interviews, London, 19 June 2006; Frankfurt, 17 Jan. 2006; Paris, 17 July 2007; Rome, 23 June 2006). The European Commission, in particular, prioritized this aspect (interview, Brussels, 27 June 2007).[12] The Commission's review of capital requirements took place almost in parallel with the activities of the BCBS (*Global Risk Regulator*, Oct. 2004).

On some important issues, US regulators also had different views. For example, the FDIC was particularly supportive of the leverage ratio (Tarullo 2008). By contrast, the Federal Reserve considered that the existing leverage ratio was not fully reflective of the risk faced by institutions (Ferguson, Federal Reserve, Parliamentary hearing, US Congress, 27 Feb. 2003). There was an attempt by the FDIC to ask the BCBS to discuss the setting in place of an international leverage ratio, but the attempt was short-lived (*The Economist*, 4 Nov. 2006).

Moreover, the accord was criticized by some members of Congress (*American Banker*, 6 Oct. 2005; *The Banker*, 5 Jan. 2004, 5 Apr. 2004), as exemplified by the first hearing on this matter held on 27 February 2003 by the House Committee on Financial Services, which was entitled 'The New Basel Accord—Sound Regulation or Crushing Complexity?' The Basel II accord was also heavily criticized by parts of the banking sector, as evidenced in several Congressional hearings on the matter (see, for example, House Committee, 22 June 2004, 28 Sept. 2005). In particular, local community banks considered the application of the Basel II accord in the US only to the fifteen or so internationally active banks as reducing capital requirements for the big players, giving them a comparative advantage *vis-à-vis* community banks.

All in all, the Basel II process began without any clear proposal from any country and was a collective effort by national supervisors and large banks to create a new paradigm for capital rules (Tsingou 2008). At the same time,

[12] In March 2002, the European Council asked the Commission to prepare a report on the consequences of the Basel II accord for all sectors of the European economy, with particular attention placed upon small and medium enterprises (SMEs) in light of the fact that the accord's content was to be transposed into EU legislation (PricewaterhouseCoopers 2004). The report estimated a beneficial outcome for SMEs.

it resembled a trade negotiation, where banks, regulators, and subsequently elected officials pursued competitive advantages, with little regard for prudential consideration (Tarullo 2008: 136). In the end, after intense lobbying from industry, Basel II did not include new capital charges for derivatives in the trading book, and marginal levels of capital were required for securitized products (Lall 2012). As explained at the beginning of this section, these were some of the shortcomings of Basel I, which Basel II was expected to address. Specific national interests did not disappear from the Basel II process, but the process generated as many disagreements within the Committee countries as amongst them (Tarullo 2008). As the international negotiations dragged on, Basel II attracted domestic political attention, which heightened during the domestic implementation of the accord.

The Basel III Accord

The global financial crisis brought into sharp relief the inadequacy of existing capital requirements and therefore the need to revise the content of the Basel II accord. The BCBS agreed on the broad framework of Basel III in September 2009. It put forward concrete proposals in December 2009, which were then subject to public consultation. A general agreement was reached in July 2010 and a final agreement in September 2010. The G20 exerted considerable political pressure on the BCBS to agree on a draft that could be discussed by the G20 in the autumn of 2010. Indeed, compared to the Basel II accord, the Basel III accord was achieved in record time—less than two years—due to the political salience imparted to it by the crisis. However, the Basel III rules will be phased in gradually from January 2013 until 2019.

The Basel III accord built on the Basel II accord, rather than reinventing it altogether. Hence, regulatory path-dependency was at work, despite the watershed event of the global financial crisis. The new rules provided a rather restrictive definition of what counts as capital; increased the risk weight of several assets (e.g. the trading book) and introduced capital buffers; set up a leverage ratio; and outlined international rules on liquidity management. All in all, they almost tripled the regulatory capital required for banks.

The accord provides a common definition of capital, on which there had been no agreement in the past. According to the Basel III rules, the main form of 'Tier 1 capital' must be common shares and retained earnings. The remainder of the Tier 1 capital can include subordinated debt. 'Hybrid capital' instruments should be phased out (BCBS 2010a: 2). This might considerably reduce the capital base of continental European banks that used these and similar non-equities instruments in the past (*The Economist*, 23 Jan. 2010). For these reasons, policy-makers in continental European countries (unsuccessfully) opposed this change.[13] The total regulatory capital consists of Tier 1 capital and Tier 2 capital and it must be at least 8 per cent of risk-weighted assets. Tier 1 must be at least 6 per cent of risk-weighted assets and the 'Core Tier 1', which comprises common equities, must be at least 4.5 per cent of risk-weighted assets (BCBS 2010a: 12). The original proposals for higher capital requirement were watered down in a search for a compromise between the US, the UK, and Switzerland,[14] keen to set higher requirements, and continental European countries, resisting them and asking for longer transition periods (*Financial Times*, 22 Oct. 2010, 13 Sept. 2010).

Capital requirements are raised for the trading book; complex securitization and resecuritizations in the banking and the trading book; counterparty credit exposures arising from banks' derivatives; and repo and securities financing activities. The accord introduces a 'capital conservation buffer'[15] of 2.5 per cent comprised of common equities, above the regulatory minimum. Capital distribution constraints are to be imposed on a bank when capital levels fall within this range (BCBS 2010a: 55). Countercyclical buffers, designed to take into account the macro-financial environment in which banks operate, are introduced (BCBS 1010a: 57). National countercyclical buffer requirements, to be decided by national jurisdictions, can vary between zero and 2.5 per cent of risk-weighted assets. Bank-specific countercyclical buffers can also be imposed (BCBS 2010a: 58). Capital buffers are to be phased in between 2016 and 2019. The accord also envisaged a capital surcharge to mitigate the risk of systemic banks, to be agreed subsequently.

A 'leverage ratio', which is a non-risk-based leverage ratio calibrated to act as a supplementary measure to the risk-based capital requirements, is introduced. The Committee will test a minimum Tier 1 leverage ratio of 3 per cent during the parallel run period from 1 January 2013 to 1 January 2017 (BCBS 2010a: 61). This regulatory instrument was already in use in the US, but was resisted by European countries, which argued that the riskiness of the activities of their traditional universal banks was lower than that of (largely Anglo-Saxon) investment banks (*Financial Times*, 26 Oct. 2010) and that this feature would not be captured by a crude leverage ratio.

The Basel III accord establishes internationally harmonized minimum liquidity standards to address short-term mismatches (the 'Liquidity Coverage Ratio') and long-term liquidity mismatches (the 'Net Stable Funding Ratio').

[13] The Germans also complained about the exclusion of 'silent participations', state loans that make up a significant part of the capital of German banks, from core tier 1 capital (*Financial Times*, 10 Sept. 2010).

[14] Higher capital requirements were unilaterally imposed on industry in some jurisdictions, such as Switzerland.

[15] This buffer is intended to promote the conservation of capital and the build-up of adequate buffers above the minimum that can be drawn down in periods of stress.

These two standards comprise specific parameters that are harmonized internationally, but also contain elements of national discretion. Banks and other market participants already use similar methods to assess their liquidity requirements. Hence, many of the issues raised during the negotiations on liquidity requirements revolve around the calibration of the parameters, rather than the conceptual basis of the framework. After an observation period, the Liquidity Coverage Ratio will be implemented in 2015, and the Net Stable Funding Ratio in 2018 (BCBS 2010a: 8–9). The prolonged phase-in period is explained by concerns about the potential impacts of these measures on lending, in particular in the bank-based continental financial system, where banks are the main source of finance for firms, especially for SMEs (*Financial Times*, 26 Oct. 2010: 11). The UK was the first country to unilaterally introduce liquidity requirements after the crisis (Howarth and Quaglia 2013a).

In an overall evaluation, on the one hand, the Basel III accord sets risk-weighted capital requirements of 4.5 per cent as compared to a pre-existing (Basel II) level of 2 per cent, plus a new buffer of 2.5 per cent. So the new effective floor is 7 per cent. Moreover, a further countercyclical buffer of up to 2.5 per cent can be imposed by national regulators. On the other hand, some policy-makers, such as the Governor of the Bank of England, were critical of the new rules, arguing that the new level of required capital should have been many times higher than the levels set out in Basel III (*Financial Times*, 26 Oct. 2010). In a similar vein, the *Financial Times* commentator, Martin Wolf, dubbed the accord 'the mouse that did not roar', arguing that capital equities requirements should have been raised to 20–30 per cent, without risk weight, in order for banks to be able to withstand future financial distress (*Financial Times*, 15 Sept. 2010: 13).

On the other hand, other (mainly continental) policy-makers, such as the former Governor of the Bank of France, Jacques de Larosière, argued that the 'Basel rules risk punishing the wrong banks', i.e. the 'diversified' and 'safer' continental European universal banking model, rather than the 'risky' Anglo-Saxon originate-to-distribute model (*Financial Times*, 26 Oct. 2010: 11). Reportedly, German policy-makers, with some support from the French and Italians, were the most hostile to the higher capital requirements discussed during the negotiations and asked for an extended implementation period (*Financial Times*, 13 Sept. 2010) (Howarth and Quaglia 2013).

If one compares the content of the Basel III proposal over time, it becomes apparent that the July draft was less strict than the draft issued in December 2009. Thus, bankers greeted the final deal with some relief (*Financial Times*, 19 Aug. 2010). One explanation has certainly to do with the lobbying efforts of industry. The main body representing the financial industry painted a doomsday scenario of the detrimental effects that higher capital requirements could have on the real economy, reducing the amount of credit available for lending to business, as well as increasing costs for banks (Institute of International Finance 2010). This defensive stance was echoed by comments of the chief executives of several banks (*The Economist*, 29 May 2010). Regulators responded with their own study, showing that the economic effects of the proposed rules were much less draconian than the estimates provided by industry (BCBS 2010b, 2010c). Part of the explanation can however be ascribed to regulators' concerns about economic recovery (*Financial Times*, 19 Aug. 2010). The QIS in May and April 2010 showed the real-world impact of the rules as initially proposed: Core Tier 1 ratios of some (mainly continental) banks would fall by 50 per cent. This would have meant raising new capital in a volatile market or reducing lending to industry, which was a major concern for continental policy-makers.

In the negotiations on Basel III, the 'old' (i.e. Basel I) divide re-emerged between the US and the UK on the one side, and continental countries on the other side (*Financial Times*, 15 Feb. 2011). The US and the UK, which had been heavily hit by the financial crisis, wanted a stricter definition of capital, to be limited to ordinary shares; higher capital requirements, including capital buffers; a leverage ratio; liquidity rules; and a short transition period. The leverage ratio was uploaded by the US, which already had this rule in place domestically. The liquidity rules were uploaded by the UK, which had developed them at the national level in the wake of the crisis. Continental countries, in particular France and Germany, wanted a broader definition of capital, including hybrids and silent participations (which were part of the definition of capital included in their domestic regulatory template) and lower capital requirements. They opposed the leverage ratio, asked for a modification of certain aspects of the liquidity rules, and wanted a longer transition period (*Financial Times*, 15 Feb. 2011). Despite attempts by the Commission to forge a common position, the EU presented a disjointed stance during the Basel III negotiations (see Buckley et al. 2012).

Like in Basel I and II, the EU was unable to project a common set of preferences on Basel III. Unlike Basel I, in which the influence of the US and the UK was predominant, Basel III was a compromise between the positions of the two coalitions at play. In particular, continental Europeans were able to secure longer transition periods and lower capital requirements, as evidenced by the comparison of the initial document issued by the BCBS in December 2009 and the (less ambitious) document eventually agreed in December 2010.

The Downloading of the Basel Accords into EU Legislation

The Basel accords have been incorporated into EU legislation over time via Capital Requirements Directives (CRDs). There are, however, three main differences between international rules and EU rules. First, the Basel accords were 'gentleman's agreements' signed by the members of the BCBS, and subsequently domestically implemented by the signatories as well as by other jurisdictions (as noted, Basel II was de facto implemented in more than 100 jurisdictions). In contrast, the CRDs applied only to EU member states. Second, the Basel accords were 'soft law', i.e. they were not legally binding, whereas the CRDs were legally binding. Third, the Basel accords applied only to internationally active banks, whereas the CRDs also applied to all banks and investment firms, even if their activities were purely domestic.

Lacking its own rules, the EU decided to incorporate Basel I into legally binding EU legislation, via the Own Fund Directive (1989) and the Solvency Directive (1989). In this case, the downloading of international rules was a way for the EU to overcome its internal inability to reach an agreement, due to the different regulatory templates in place in the member states. Subsequently, it was decided to extend prudential rules for banks to investment firms through the so-called Capital Adequacy Directive (1993) (Mügge 2010). The Directive aimed to ensure a level playing field between firms competing within the same EU markets and thus it applied to all credit institutions and investment firms. It was passed in conjunction with the Investment Services Directive (1993), which allowed investment firms authorized by the competent authorities of their home member states and supervised by the same authorities to establish branches and provide services freely in other member states. The setting in place of EU capital requirements for investment firms was the quid pro quo for the passport to operate across the EU, granted to investment firms, which was a priority for the UK (Mügge 2010).

In the intra-EU negotiations on the first Capital Adequacy Directive, the most controversial issue was setting capital requirements for investment firms, because unlike most of continental Europe, the UK had many investment firms without a banking licence (for a detailed account of intra-EU negotiations, see Brown 1997; Underhill 1997). Indeed, the structure of the UK investment sector differs from that in much of continental Europe, where firms offering investment services are required to hold banking licences, and investment services' business lines are often integrated into the commercial banking activities of major banking groups. By contrast, the UK has a very high number of specialized investment firms.

As in the case of Basel I, the EU decided to download Basel II into a revised Capital Requirements Directive articulated on three pillars: requirements for an internal capital assessment by financial institutions (exposure to credit, market, and operational risks); a supervisory review process conducted by supervisors to evaluate the risk profile of each institution; and market discipline. Two 'sticky' issues emerged during the intra-EU negotiations on the CRD (for the details of the negotiations, see Christopoulos and Quaglia 2009).

The first was the role and powers of the 'consolidating supervisor' for the supervision of EU cross-border groups, namely the national supervisor in the member state where the group's parent firm is authorized. Banks with cross-border activities (mainly British-based banks and large private German banks) were largely in favour of the establishment of a 'lead supervisor' (British Bankers' Association 2003; European Banking Federation 2003), with greater decision-making power compared to that proposed for the consolidating supervisor. Cross-border banking groups pointed out the disadvantage of duplicating compliance costs, because under consolidating supervision their activities would still be subject to different national systems of supervision (British Bankers Association 2003). The concept of leading supervisor was ultimately successfully opposed by the national supervisors, eager not to see their supervisory power diluted and by purely domestic banks (interview, London, 8 Dec. 2005; Frankfurt, 17 Jan. 2006).

The second issue that required attention, as in the case of the previous CRD, was the calibration of specific parts of Basel II, namely the trading book, for investment firms (HM Treasury 2003a, 2003b). Capital requirements for securities trading were a priority for the associations of international securities dealers and investment banks[16] and the British authorities (*European Voice,* 9 June 2005). In the end, a satisfactory solution was found and the Capital Requirements Directive was formally adopted by Council and European Parliament in June 2006. It came into force at the beginning of 2007, with the most sophisticated approaches available from 2008.

The downloading of the Basel III accord into the CRD was more fiercely contested than in the case of Basel II. In July 2011, after extensive consultations conducted in parallel with the work of the BCBS, the EU Commission adopted the CRD IV legislative package designed to replace the CRD II with a directive that governs the access to deposit-taking activities (Commission of the European Communities 2011a) and a regulation that establishes prudential requirements for credit institutions (Commission of the European Communities 2011b). The proposed directive (Commission of the European Communities 2011a) contains rules concerning the take-up and pursuit of the business of banks, the conditions for the freedom of establishment and the freedom to provide services, the supervisory review process, and the definition of competent authorities. The directive also incorporates two elements of the Basel III accord, namely the introduction of two capital buffers in addition to the minimum capital requirements: the capital conservation buffer, identical for all banks in the EU; and the countercyclical capital buffer, to be determined at national level. The proposed EU regulation (Commission

[16] See the joint letter by the European Banking Federation et al. (2004) ; see also Association of Private Client Investment Managers and Stockbrokers (2003).

of the European Communities 2011b) contains prudential requirements for credit institutions and investment firms. It covers the definition of capital, increasing the amount of own funds that banks need to hold, as well as the quality of those funds; it introduces the Liquidity Coverage Ratio—the exact composition and calibration of which will be determined after an observation and review period in 2015; and the need to consider a leverage ratio, subject to supervisory review.

The Commission's CRD IV draft, which would implement Basel III into EU law, involved watering down or modifying the Basel III guidelines in ways that met EU member state demands. Indeed, the CRD IV draft was criticized by many regulators and by the IMF for significantly watering down key Basel III elements (IMF 2011). Speaking at a meeting of the economic and finance ministers held to discuss the CRD IV, the British Treasury minister complained that 'We are not implementing the Basel agreement, as anyone who will look at this text will be able to tell you' (*Financial Times,* 2 May 2012).[17]

The Commission 'softened' its definition of Core Tier 1 capital relative to the Basel III recommendations in some areas. Notably, the Commission draft allows 'silent participations', i.e. state loans that make up a significant part of the capital of many EU banks, including the publicly owned German Landesbanken. The Commission's draft also limits the role of the leverage ratio designed to limit risk-taking by banks. The almost unique reliance on the risk-weighted Core Tier 1 ratio in the Commission's draft CRD IV, which was in line with what agreed in Basel III, was criticized for inadequately representing the health of the European banking sector (*Financial Times,* 30 Jan. 2012). On liquidity, the Commission adopts the less prescriptive definition of liquid assets: the Liquidity Coverage Ratio includes 'transferable assets that are of extremely high liquidity and credit quality' and 'transferable assets that are of high liquidity and credit quality'. The Commission's draft lacks a firm commitment to implement the Net Stable Funding Ratio by 2018 called for in Basel III. This was a major concern for French banks (Howarth and Quaglia 2013a).

Whereas Basel III banned the double counting of capital, the implementing legislation drafted by the Commission allowed it, at the insistence of French policy-makers. A ban would hit the three large French commercial banks particularly hard because of the long-standing feature the French banking system of *bancassurance,* in which insurance companies (often subsidiaries of banks) make use of banks to market their products. Given French exposure, it is not surprising that the French Banking Federation considered the BCBS proposal of reduction of insurance capital from Core Tier 1 capital as 'completely unacceptable' (Fédération Bancaire Française 2010: 5).

[17] This and the following three paragraphs are drawn from Howarth and Quaglia 2013a.

The use of a regulation, which once approved is directly applicable without the need for national transposition, is designed to ensure the creation of a single rulebook in the EU. The regulation will eliminate a key source of national divergence. In the CRD II, more than 100 national discretions (differences in national legislation transposing the EU directive) remained. Yet, the Commission's draft regulation also proposes a maximum capital ratio which was opposed by many who argued in favour of EU standards that exceed the Basel minimum because of prevailing balancesheet uncertainties in the EU, the lack of EU-wide resolution arrangements, and the lack of a fully unified fiscal backstop.

Several EU member states, the European Parliament (EP), and even the Commission itself called for 'European specificities' to be taken into account in incorporating the Basel III rules into the CRD IV, reopening some of the issues that had caused friction within the BCBS. Of particular concern has been the fact that, in the US, the Basel III accord would be applied only to financial institutions with over $50bn (US) in assets, whereas the new rules would be applied to all banks in the EU, as in the case of Basel I and Basel II (European Parliament 2011). Both the Commission and the EP have emphasized competition concerns and the need to ensure an 'international level playing field'.

All in all, in the downloading of the Basel accords into EU legislation, three features are noteworthy. First, there was a reopening of some of the issues that had been discussed in the BCBS where these issues were important for the authorities of the member states and/or their financial industries. Examples in the case of Basel III abound, from the use of silent participations and counting of *bancassurance* capital, to the definition of liquid assets. Second, new policy actors, other than banking regulators gathered in the BCBS, entered the regulatory process, although for reasons of space this section could not delve into the details of the EU regulatory process. Hence, the discussion of capital rules in the EU (and the US) were more politicized than in the BCBS.

Third, the EU's preferred tools for downloading the Basel accords were directives, which had to be transposed in the domestic legislation of the member states, leaving some 'national discretion' (i.e. flexibility) in the domestic implementation of the Basel accords across the EU. In the case of the Basel III accord, with a view to creating a single rulebook and minimizing national discretion, the EU also made use of a regulation which does not need to be transposed in national legislation, and is intended to leave very limited room for national discretion.

The Financial Industry and Global Banking Regulation

The EU and the US have a very large banking market (see Table 3.2). Some international political economy scholars have pointed out the influence of

Table 3.2. EU–US market size in banking (values are in billions)

		2008	2009	2010	2011	Sources
Assets	**US ($)**	**12,321**	**11,665**	**11,957**	**12,441**	Federal Reserve
	US ($)	**12, 308**	**11, 822**	**12, 066**	**12,648**	FDIC
	EU (€)	**37,770**	**34,847**	**34,637**	**35,901**	ECB
	Germany	10,009	7,767	7,896	7,995	ECB
	France	7,150	6,101	6,384	6,674	ECB
	Italy	2,757	2,474	2,764	2,794	ECB
	UK	8,559	7,299	10,187	11,142	ECB
Liabilities	**US ($)**	**11,118**	**10,414**	**10,582**	**11,077**	Federal Reserve
	US ($)	**11,154**	**10,514**	**10,701**	**11,227**	FDIC
	EU (€)	**35,937**	**33,090**	**32,826**	**34,107**	ECB
	Germany	9,716	7,490	7,590	7,684	ECB
	France	6,882	5,801	6,066	6,357	ECB
	Italy	2,443	2,274	2,547	2,606	ECB
	UK	8,232	6,944	9,697	10,600	ECB

Note: The Federal Reserve and the FDIC produce monthly data on US banks; data given here correspond to end of Dec. values.

the financial industry over international banking regulation, in particular the big transnational players, which have considerable resources to invest in lobbying and easy access to policy-makers, either at the national level or in international regulatory fora. The empirical account of the negotiations of Basel I suggests that industry was not a main player in its own right and it mainly directed its lobbying efforts towards the national authorities represented in the BCBS. The BCBS had not yet introduced the practice of direct consultation with industry. By contrast, in the Basel II and III accords the main private-sector actors and industry associations in the main jurisdictions as well as international associations, such as the IIF, were very proactive.

Lall (2012: 609) argues that Basel II and Basel III were 'the product of regulatory capture by large international banks in G10 countries'. On the one hand, the main transnational players were rather successful in having some of their preferences incorporated into the Basel II accord, for example, in the use of an internal risk model (Tsingou 2008; Underhill and Zhang 2008). The financial industry also succeeded in watering down the Basel III accord, in particular through long transition periods, although banks' influence was weakened (at least temporarily) by the global financial crisis. On the other hand, Young (2012: 663) qualifies the extent of 'regulatory capture' in Basel II, arguing that while private-sector lobbyists had easy access to the regulatory process, this 'access' did not always mean 'influence' over the outcome. He also points out divisions within the different parts of transnational financial industry, which sometimes resulted in 'stronger' rather than 'weaker' rules in the accord.

Several considerations are in order. To begin with, on some important issues the financial industry had diversified preferences. Often divisions ran along national lines. An example in Basel II was the use of credit ratings for risk-weight assessment, which was opposed by continental European countries and banks that do not have a rating tradition. By contrast, it was advocated by US regulators and their financial industry. An issue that was particularly important for German policy-makers in Basel II was the risk weighting of commercial mortgages, which in the Basel I accord were granted special treatment. German policy-makers were keen to preserve a lower risk weight for commercial mortgages in Basel II. Moreover, German mortgage banks issue the *pfandbriefe*, a special bond with only a 10 per cent risk weighting.

The division along national lines was very marked in the Basel III accord: undercapitalized banks in several EU member states, and in particular in Germany and France, were in favour of less stringent capital rules in Basel III in order to maintain their competitiveness. Proportionately, the Basel ban on hybrids would hit the German banking system hardest, and in particular the Landesbanken (see Howarth and Quaglia 2013a). It is no wonder that the peak association of the German banking system asked the BCBS for a grandfather clause[18] of 'at least 30 years' for own funds instruments (Zentraler Kreditausschuss 2010: 3). Subsequent to the Basel III agreement, in negotiations on the EU's capital requirements legislation, the Germans demanded the inclusion of the one form of hybrid on which all their Landesbanken relied to meet the Core Tier 1 ratio: 'silent participations'.

Strong French and German opposition to the use of a leverage ratio reflected the higher leverage ratios of most large banks in France and Germany (compared to the UK) and in particular the difficult situation facing German Landesbanken and French mutual banks having to respect a new leverage ratio given their lack of equity capital. For example, the Zentraler Kreditausschuss rejected the concept of the leverage ratio (2010: 30) and the Fédération Bancaire Française wanted to limit the use of the leverage ratio to Basel Pillar 2 (2010: 2). The largest French bank, BNP Paribas, argued that the 'leverage ratio... has proven failures [sic] or flawed definitions wherever it has been applied, in particular in the US. Application should be based at most on a pillar 2 approach' (2010: 2).

Comparatively well-capitalized banks, including several in the UK, were less concerned about higher capital requirements. For example, in its response to the BCBS consultation, Barclays (2010a: 2) argued that 'we... have pre-empted the anticipated change by increasing our capital ratios in 2008–9... whilst also lowering our leverage and improving our liquidity positions'. In the case of the proposed liquidity rules, UK banks had substantially increased the resilience of their funding positions because the UK had introduced restrictive liquidity rules in 2009, on which the Basel III rules were largely modelled. British banks thus had a head start on liquidity (Howarth and Quaglia 2013a). The main British bank, HSBC, welcomed the BCBS liquidity rules, arguing that these were similar to those already applied throughout the HSBC group (2010: 1; see also Barclays 2010b).

Besides the structure and the competitive position of the national banking industry, bank–industry ties were also of concern to continental banks and policy-makers, in particular the flow of credit to small and medium-sized enterprises. Continental policy-makers opposed the use of a 'crude' (their words) leverage ratio, which could force the banks to cut credit to industry. By contrast, US banks were already used to operating with a leverage ratio, and because of loose bank–real economy ties, US and UK policy-makers were less worried about the potential reduction of banks' funding to the real economy. The long-standing close relations between banks and industry in several

[18] A *grandfather clause* is a provision in which an old rule continues to apply to some existing situations, while a new rule will apply to future cases.

continental European countries reinforced these concerns. In Germany, the relational (*hausbank*) banking effectively shaped the preferences of both banks and regulators on capital requirements, despite changes in recent years (Deeg 2010). French small and medium-sized enterprises were more dependent upon bank credit than their British counterparts (Howarth and Quaglia 2013a).

Sometimes divisions ran across national lines, i.e. within national industries, especially in countries that have a federal structure (with a dual banking system, as in the US) and a segmented banking sector, such as the three-pillar system in Germany. In the US, the tensions between local banks and main international banks emerged in the implementation of the Basel II accord. Local banks feared that the Basel II rules would benefit the biggest international banks at their expense and lobbied their political constituency in the Congress to delay the domestic implementation of the accord (*The Banker*, Dec. 2005; *Financial Times*, 31 Mar. 2006). In the negotiation of the Basel III accord, German policy-makers were very sensitive to the low capitalization of German public banks, and the difficulties they would encounter in raising new capital.

These examples also suggest that the less internationalized players can have good access to national policy-makers, at least in federal countries, such as the US and Germany. The German banking system was divided on Basel III but the regulators tended to support the position of the public banks and savings banks that were potentially the most negatively affected by the proposed rules. These banks had a sympathetic hearing from national policy-makers, especially at the local and regional level, given the ongoing importance of regional and local government funding (through 'silent participations' or shareholdings). Some commercial banks also relied upon 'silent participations' but they were in a better position to replace these with equity.

Policy-makers did not always give in to industry, either in the BCBS or at the national level. On certain issues, such as the leverage ratio, British policy-makers disregarded the preferences of industry, which would have preferred to do without a binding limit despite the comparatively low leverage ratios of the four largest British banks. Various public statements and interviews with financial-sector representatives indicate that British banks (like most banks) would have preferred lower levels of capital and less rigid liquidity rules. Similar considerations apply to the US regulators and US banks. Overall, the financial industry was more successful in influencing international standards in the case of Basel II than in Basel III, which was negotiated after the global financial crisis, when there was a public backlash against the financial industry and politicians became more attentive to financial regulation.

To sum up, international rules have differentiated effects across national financial sectors, creating competitive advantages and disadvantages for various parts of the industry (Genschel and Plümper 1997). The financial industry located in a given jurisdiction (be it the US or the EU) generally has a vested interested in supporting the uploading of (national or regional) rules to the international level, so as to minimize the costs of complying with international standards and to prevent regulatory arbitrage to their disadvantage. Hence, the industry-lobby explanation can be linked to the explanation based on regulatory templates in given jurisdictions.

Conclusion

Preliminary results from the congruence procedure largely confirm the empirical expectations derived from the analytical framework set out in Chapter 2. In the late 1980s, a combination of weak EU regulatory capacity and strong(ish) US regulatory capacity led to the uploading of US rules into Basel I, and the downloading of these international rules by the EU. Particularly important was the presence of a risk-based regulatory template in the US and the UK—which gave these countries a first-mover advantage in shaping international standards—and the lack of an EU regulatory template on capital adequacy, due to intra-EU divisions.

The temporal dimension is important: the sequencing between the development of domestic regulatory capacity, to be precise the setting in place of robust domestic or regional regulatory templates and international standards, creates a process of path-dependence. Once robust international standards have been developed in a given sector or activity, the EU and the US are likely to download the updated version of these international standards, as in the case of the Basel II and III, albeit while retaining some room for manœuvre in the domestic implementation of international rules. The EU has taken into account 'European specificieties' in its capital requirements legislation and the US did not implement Basel II.

The combination of strong EU and US regulatory capacities resulted in the uploading and downloading of rule elements by these jurisdictions in Basel III. Despite the fact that the EU and the US had downloaded Basel I and Basel II (only the EU) into their domestic legislation, their respective regulatory templates retained some distinctive features, such as the leverage ratio in the US; a broad definition of capital in the EU, including silent participation (in Germany); a broad definition of liquid assets, other than government bonds (France); liquidity rules being introduced in the midst of the crisis in the UK, etc. Some of these domestic rules were uploaded into Basel III, as in the case of leverage ratios from the US and liquidity rules from the UK. But the EU, as such, did not have rules to upload.

Many international political economy works consider the US as the dominant player in the making of rules for global finance because of its market size. When the Basel I accord was negotiated, the US banking sector (and hence US market power) was bigger than those of the individual European members—banking integration and regulation in Europe were not advanced enough for the EU to be considered as a 'single market'. By the 2000s, the aggregate size of the banking sector of the EU rivalled the US. However, market size is a necessary but not sufficient condition in shaping rules for global finance. A large banking market, like that of the EU, is a potential source of power in international financial regulation. But this potential capability will not translate into real influence if the EU lacks a common position.

Despite the remarkable size of the EU banking market, the EU did not project a unified, common position during the Basel negotiations. Whereas this might have been expected for Basel I, it is more surprising in the case of Basel II and III, when banking integration and regulation had advanced significantly in Europe. In the making of Basel III, the EU was almost as divided as it had been more than two decades earlier. This is explained by the persistent differences across the financial (banking) sectors of the member states and their links to the real economy.

4

The EU and Global Securities Markets Regulation

The regulatory capacity of the EU in securities markets was relatively weak until the late 1990s because of the different (mainly protectionist) preferences of the main member states. It was substantially enhanced by the Lamfalussy reform and the adoption of four 'Lamfalussy Directives', following the Financial Services Action Plan (FSAP). Yet certain entities or activities in securities markets remained unregulated until the outbreak of the crisis, due to disagreements amongst the member states, which had different interests at stakes, and the less active stance of the first Barroso Commission.

The US has a strong regulatory capacity in securities markets, which is a federal competence. Prior to the global financial crisis, the US had robust regulatory templates concerning securities trading. However, rating agencies, hedge funds, and over-the-counter derivatives were lightly regulated or unregulated because of effective lobbying from industry and division amongst regulators. In the wake of the financial crisis, the US, like the EU, extended the scope of regulation to these financial activities.

The main international standard-setting body, the International Organization of Securities Commissions (IOSCO), never developed the international status and expertise of its counterpart in banking. Under the aegis of the US, the IOSCO focused on the development of bilateral or multilateral memoranda of understanding designed to facilitate information sharing and enforcement across jurisdictions. It also developed standardized templates for securities trading. After the global financial crisis, the IOSCO revised the code of conduct for rating agencies, issued general principles concerning hedge funds regulation, and produced some documents on the regulation of over-the-counter derivatives.

Having developed its regulatory capacity in the 2000s, the EU was better positioned to actively cross-load some of its rules to the US, or at the very least to resist the passive cross-loading of US rules. After the strengthening of EU and US regulatory capacity on rating agencies, hedge funds, and over-the-counter derivatives, these two jurisdictions have actively and passively cross-loaded parts of their regulatory templates.

Prior to the crisis, the financial industry had resisted national and international regulation on rating agencies, hedge funds, and over-the-counter derivatives, pointing out the advantages of self-regulation. After the crisis, the financial industry was no longer able to prevent the extension of the regulatory perimeter to these activities and lobbying from the financial firms directly affected by the new rules focused on preventing the most burdensome aspects of the new rules.

The Regulatory Capacity of the EU in Securities Markets

The regulatory capacity of the EU in securities markets developed later than in banking and insurance (see Table 4.1) because of domestic political economy factors (Story and Walter 1997). Indeed, the EU very much lagged behind the US in the development of securities markets legislation. There have been two turning points in the development of EU regulatory capacity in securities markets over the past decade—the FSAP and the Lamfalussy reform; and the global financial crisis, followed by the so-called de Larosière reform. These turning points combined the reform of the institutional framework for financial regulation with new regulatory templates in securities markets in the EU.

The Institutional Framework for Securities Markets Regulation in the EU

As part of the Lamfalussy reform, which was initially proposed with reference to securities markets regulation,[1] the European Securities Committee was established in 2001. It is composed of high-level representatives from the national treasury or finance ministry, or in some cases, from the central bank and/or the supervisory authority. Like the European Banking Committee and its counterpart in insurance, the European Securities Committee is a so-called 'level 2' committee: it assists the Commission in the adoption of level 2 implementing measures for EU legislation agreed at level 1 and provides advice on policy issues concerning securities markets. The European Securities Committee operates by qualified majority voting, and the voting weight is the same as in the Council of Ministers.

[1] The European Securities Committee and Committee of European Securities Regulators were explicitly mentioned in the so-called Wise Men Report on the Regulation of European Securities Markets, chaired by Baron Alexandre Lamfalussy (Committee of Wise Men 2001).

Table 4.1. The building up of EU regulatory capacity in securities markets in the 2000s

Policy entrepreneur	Preferences of the large member states	Industry preferences	Regulatory templates - content
Commission, UK	Similar preferences, but some controversial issues in Prospectus and Markets in Financial Instruments Directives (continental vs UK)	Similar preferences of transnational players, but some controversial issues in Prospectus and Markets in Financial Instruments Directives (banks vs exchanges)	*Lamfalussy Directives (2003–5) on securities trading:* – *Transparency* – *Market abuse* – *Prospectus* – *markets in financial instruments* – mostly maximum harmonization – passporting
Commission, France and Germany	Pre-crisis: UK opposed EU rules (rating agencies in London, use of ratings in the City); France and Germany supported EU rules Post-crisis: UK support EU rules	Pre-crisis: rating agencies opposed rules Post-crisis: agencies lobby against burdensome aspects	*Credit Rating Agencies regulation (2009)* – downloading IOSCO code – compulsory registration – rules on conflict of interests – equivalence clauses
Commission, France and Germany	Pre-crisis: UK opposed EU rules (hedge fund industry in the UK); France and Germany supported EU rules Post-crisis: UK accept EU rules	Pre-crisis: hedge funds opposed rules tout court Post-crisis: hedge funds lobby against burdensome aspects	*Alternative Investment Fund Managers Directive (2010)* – legally binding authorization – ESMA supervision – European passport – equivalence clauses
Commission, France, Germany, UK	Pre-crisis: no proposal for EU rules Post-crisis: main countries support EU rules, but some controversial issues, e.g. silos stock exchanges (Germany), location CCPs (UK)	Pre-crisis: OTC derivatives industry opposed rules Post-crisis: industry lobby against burdensome aspects	*European Market Infrastructure regulation (2011)* – reporting obligation for OTC derivatives to trade repositories – clearing obligation for standardized OTC derivatives through CCPs, – common rules for CCPs and trade repositories – equivalence clauses

The Committee of European Securities Regulators, whose forerunner was the Forum of European Securities Commissions,[2] was established in 2001 in Paris (see Coen and Thatcher 2008; De Visscher et al. 2008; Quaglia 2008). It had a secretary general, whereas the chair was elected by its members for a period of two years and each member state had a seat in the Committee. The Committee was involved in levels 2 and 3 of the Lamfalussy process. At level 2, it advised the Commission in the drafting of implementing measures voted upon by the European Securities Committee. At level 3, the Committee of European Securities Regulators monitored the implementation of EU legislation across the EU; it facilitated the cooperation and the exchange of views and best practice between supervisory authorities; and it promoted the convergence of supervisory standards.

Decisions by the Committee were taken by consensus. If consensus could not be reached, decisions were taken by qualified majority. In such a case, members that did not intend to apply the decisions had to state the reason for not doing so—the so-called comply or explain procedure. Posner and Véron (2010) highlight how the activity of the Committee of European Securities Regulators strengthened EU regulatory capacity in this field, especially *vis-à-vis* the US. Moreover, membership of the Committee of European Securities Regulators also strengthened securities supervisors in the domestic arena, i.e. *vis-à-vis* the national political authorities (first and foremost, the government). Indeed, one member of the Committee referred to this committee as 'the trade union of securities supervisors' (interview, Paris, 25 Apr. 2007) (Quaglia 2008).

After the global financial crisis and the implementation of the de Larosière reforms, the Committee of European Securities Regulators was transformed into the European Securities Markets Authority in 2011 (see Moloney 2011a, 2011b). This authority, like its counterparts in the banking and insurance sector, has the following tasks: to contribute to the establishment of common regulatory and supervisory standards and practices by providing opinions and by developing technical standards; to contribute to the consistent application of legally binding Union acts, mediating and settling disagreements between competent authorities; ensuring a coherent functioning of colleges of supervisors and taking actions in emergency situations. [3]

The European Securities Markets Authority can address decisions directly to national authorities and supervises certain entities with pan-European reach. For example, the authority is responsible for the registration and supervision

[2] The Forum of European Securities Commissions was set up as late as 1997. It brought together securities regulators in the EU, but had no official status.

[3] <http://europa.eu/rapid/pressReleasesAction.do?reference=MEMO/10/434&format=HTML&aged=0&language=EN&guiLanguage=en> (accessed Apr. 2013).

of credit rating agencies in the EU. It is also to be given new responsibilities in the monitoring of auditing (see Chapter 6). The main decisions are taken by the Board of Supervisors by a simple majority of its members. Each member has one vote. With regard to regulatory and implementing technical standards, the Board of Supervisors takes decisions on the basis of a qualified majority of its members, as defined by the Treaty on European Union.

Regulatory Templates in Securities Trading in the EU

The first attempts to harmonize securities trading rules in the EU were a set of directives on securities listing in the late 1970s and early 1980s. In 1979, the Admissions Directive regulated the admission of debt and equities securities to the official listing of stock exchanges. In 1980, the Listing Particulars Directive established the conditions for listing on an official exchange. In 1989, the Public Offers Directive fixed the conditions for making a public offering.

In the mid-1980s, the EU focused on the regulation of undertakings for collective investment in transferable securities. The first directive adopted in 1985 created a mandatory national authorization for funds investing in transferable securities. Such authorization was to be valid in all member states. However, de facto, different marketing rules in each member state created obstacles to the cross-border marketing of these funds (Story and Walter 1997). In the early 1990s, discussions on a second directive for undertakings for collective investment in transferable securities were abandoned because the member states could not reach an agreement on its content. In 2001, the third directive was eventually agreed (even though there was not a second directive), giving management companies a 'single passport' to operate throughout the EU, and widening the activities which they were allowed to undertake (Story and Walter 1997).

Another important area of EU regulatory activity concerned the authorization for investment firms to operate throughout the EU by using a 'single passport'. The Investment Services Directive issued in 1993 allowed financial firms to conduct business across Europe with the approval of their home authorities. The activities that could be passported were listed in the annexes to the Directive. One of the main bones of contention in the negotiations of this Directive was the 'concentration rule', which prescribed that all securities trading should be carried out through stock exchanges (see Coleman and Underhill 1998; Underhill 1997). This was a priority for France and other Southern European countries, which had this rule in place, whereas the UK allowed trading outside stock exchanges.

Many of the pieces of securities market legislation issued in the 1990s, and in particular the Investment Services Directive and the Directives on Public

Listing, fell short of their objectives (Ferran 2004; Mügge 2010).[4] Hence, EU regulatory capacity remained underdeveloped for three main reasons. First, 'the protectionist impulses of national governments and of the financial industries that their positions mirrored were too strong and irreconcilable' (Mügge 2010: 51). Many continental European countries had a bank-based financial system, and until the early 1990s, some EU countries did not have securities markets regulators, or at any rate the power and resources at their disposal were rather limited, as in the case of Germany or Italy (see Lütz 1998). Second, as Story and Walter note, 'trust between Europe's financial centres was a scarce commodity. Competition prevailed over cooperation. Tax regimes differed. Ideas differed about the role of capital markets' (Story and Walter 1997: 25). Third, securities markets regulation had implications for corporate governance, which was also a controversial issue amongst the member states (see Cernat 2004; Dewing and Russell 2004; Rhodes and Van Apeldoorn 1998).

The FSAP and the Lamfalussy reform gave new momentum to securities markets integration in Europe. Four Lamfalussy Directives were issued in the early 2000s (Quaglia 2010a, 2010b). The Directive on Insider Dealing and Market Manipulation (also known as Market Abuse Directive) (2002) was designed to promote market integrity in the field of financial instruments and to contribute to harmonizing the provisions concerning market abuse in the EU. The Directive on Transparency Requirements with Regard to Information on Issuers Whose Securities are Admitted to Trading on a Regulated Market (the so-called Transparency Directive) (2004) revised and replaced the 2001 Directive on the Admission of Securities to Official Stock Exchange Listing.

The Directive on the Prospectus to be Published When Securities are Offered to the Public or Admitted to Trading (also known as the Prospectus Directive) (2003) allowed capital to be raised throughout the EU on the basis of one set of documents—the prospectus—and gave bond issuers a choice of regulator. It replaced the 1989 Directive. The Prospectus Directive issued in 2004 was similar to the securities trading regulation in the US (Karmel 2007). It contained disclosure standards that were in line with the international disclosure standards approved in 1998 by IOSCO, and that had been adopted by the Securities and Exchange Commission (SEC) in revising its foreign issuer disclosure requirements in 1999. The development of these international disclosure standards by IOSCO, with the cooperation of the SEC and European

[4] E.g. prior to the Prospectus Directive issued in 2004, the two previous Prospectus Directives based on minimum harmonization were largely unsuccessful in facilitating the raising of capital across borders in the EU because of inconsistent interpretations and implementations in member states (Ferran 2004).

securities regulators, was an important step in the convergence of US and EU disclosure standards (Karmel 2007).

Amongst the four Lamfalussy Directives, the Market in Financial Instruments Directive was the most controversial (Macartney 2010; Mügge 2006). It updated the existing Investment Services Directive, which only applied to a specified number of financial instruments and investment services (see Ferran 2004; Ferrarini and Wymeersch 2006). New categories of firm fell within the remit of this Directive, such as investment banks, stock brokers and broker dealers, futures and options firms, commodity firms, and portfolio managers. Investment firms were enabled to process client orders outside regulated exchanges (stock exchanges), which previously had been impossible in some member states.

The FSAP, and in particular the Lamfalussy Directives, were the result of converging or at least compatible preferences of the member states and the most outward oriented part of their financial industry, with the European Commission acting as policy entrepreneur. As Daniel Mügge put it: 'Continental European equity markets moved from the fringes of national economies into the limelight. Banks, which had previously focused on their domestic markets, began to build cross-border investment banking empires. Stock exchanges were transformed from members-only clubs into for-profit companies' (2010: 69). These changes culminated in the FSAP, which was a major step forwards for the completing of the single financial market and put in place a set of harmonized EU rules. As scholars have argued: 'It was promoted by a coalition of firms with international ambitions and the European Commission' (Mügge 2010: 93).

The UK was very influential in shaping the new (market-making) rules (Posner and Véron 2010) because the UK hosted the main financial centre in Europe and the second financial centre worldwide. Hence, British policy-makers had a widely recognized expertise in the financial field and were regarded as providing state-of-the-art regulation, prior to the crisis. The market-making, competition-friendly approach advocated by the UK was regarded as the most successful, providing a competitive model for the EU (Quaglia 2010a, 2010b). Furthermore, the UK is host to a large financial industry, relative to the rest of the economy. Hence, the large financial players had the resources to lobby policy-makers domestically, in the EU and internationally (Baker 2010; Helleiner 2010).

Prior to the Lamfalussy Directives, the EU passively cross-loaded regulatory templates in securities trading from the US in two ways. First, EU investment companies seeking access to the US market had to register with the SEC and comply with most of its rules. Second, in the development of EU regulatory templates, the EU looked at US securities regulation as a model (Karmel 2007). As Karmel (2007) noted, 'the SEC has served as the gold standard of securities regulation'. Three of the four Lamfalussy Directives (the Market Abuse Directive, the Prospectus Directive, and the Transparency Directive) were similar to US securities regulation, although there were some differences at the margins. Once, the EU developed its own regulatory templates, it was better positioned to begin a process of mutual recognition with the SEC.

Having adopted most of the measures listed in the FSAP, the EU agreed to have a regulatory pause (Commission of the European Communities 2005a, 2005b), which was interrupted by the outbreak of the global financial crisis. In the aftermath of the crisis, the EU passed a regulation on credit rating agencies; a Directive on Alternative Investment Funds Managers, including hedge fund managers; and a regulation on market infrastructures. Prior to the crisis, these activities had been left outside the perimeter of EU regulation. The calls for EU rules by some continental policy-makers had been resisted by the UK authorities. The post-crisis reform of financial regulation in the EU was the result of converging or at least compatible preferences of the main member states, whereby the UK shifted its position, downplaying its previous opposition to regulation (Quaglia 2011a). This chapter devotes much attention to these new pieces of legislation because of their links to international and US financial regulation. Moreover, the secondary literature on post-crisis regulatory reform in the EU is rather limited.

The Regulation on Credit Rating Agencies (2009)

Prior to the proposal for a regulation on credit rating agencies, which was put forward by the Commission in the wake of the global financial crisis in November 2008, rating agencies were not regulated either by the member states or at the EU level, despite some short-lived attempts to consider the introduction of EU legislation in the early 2000s. Following the Parmalat scandal, a resolution of the European Parliament (2004a) called on the European Commission to produce an assessment of the need (if any) for legislative intervention in this field. In July 2004, the Commission asked the Committee of European Securities Regulators to provide technical advice on this proposal.

The Committee of European Securities Regulators concluded that, overall, the IOSCO Code of Conduct for Credit Rating Agencies that had been issued in the meantime addressed the issues raised by the Commission's mandate (Committee of European Securities Regulators 2005, 2006). Mügge (2011a) notes that the position of the Committee of European Securities Regulators was influenced by the fact that European regulators had already endorsed the Code of Conduct in the IOSCO. Hence they also did this at the EU level. The Commission asked the Committee of European Securities Regulators to monitor compliance with the IOSCO Code and to report back on an annual basis. Consequently, 'the supervision and regulation of the activity of rating agencies in Europe was effectively left in the hands of their US home-country regulator' (Pagliari 2013: 11).

Prior to the crisis, attempts to build up EU regulatory capacity on credit rating agencies were unsuccessful for several reasons. To begin with, there was not a critical mass of policy-makers supporting them in the Council: whereas certain member states, first and foremost France and Germany, favoured regulating rating agencies in the EU,[5] other member states, led by the UK and comprising Ireland, the Netherlands, and most of the Nordic countries, preferred self-regulation for credit rating agencies, as envisaged by the IOSCO's Code of Conduct (interviews, London, May 2007; Paris, July 2007; Berlin, Apr. 2008). These countries had had a 'light-touch' market-making approach to financial regulation, with a view to providing a competitive environment for their financial industry in Europe. Indeed, the main credit rating agencies are North American, but their prime location in Europe is in London, which is also the main financial centre in Europe where ratings are used. Hence, the UK authorities were worried about the potential repercussions of EU rules on credit rating agencies.

The Commission was lukewarm towards the prospect of regulating credit rating agencies in the EU and hence did not put forward legislative proposals (interviews, Brussels, May 2007). As pointed out during several interviews with policy-makers and stakeholders, the 'better regulation' approach of the (first) Barroso Commission was often translated into 'light touch' regulation, or no regulation at all, as in the case of hedge funds and credit rating agencies (interviews, Brussels, June 2007; Paris, July 2007). Finally, not surprisingly, there was strong opposition to EU rules from the main stakeholders in the private sector, namely the credit rating agencies, which held considerable bargaining power, given the oligopolistic nature of the rating market (Sinclair 2005).

In September 2007, when the subprime scandal in the US was in full swing, the Commission asked the Committee of European Securities Regulators to review the role of ratings in structured finance and re-evaluate regulatory options in this area. The 2008 Committee of European Securities Regulators report on credit rating agencies, like the 2005 report, continued to support market-driven improvement, considering the IOSCO Code, which had been revised, as the key international standard (Committee of European Securities Regulators 2008a).

[5] E.g. the French Autorité des marchés financiers has been issuing an annual report monitoring the activities of CRAs since 2005.

A second report commissioned by the Commission to the European Securities Markets Experts[6] also concluded against the introduction of legislation in the EU. Echoing the concerns of the Committee of European Securities Regulators, the experts concluded that:

> Given the global nature of the business of credit rating agencies and the existing US law, we have doubts as to whether the development of a separate EU law would produce any particular benefits. We think it is important that credit rating agencies are subject to a global approach to their business . . . regulatory cooperation in this sphere is essential to avoid duplication of effort (European Securities Markets Expert Group 2008).

Notwithstanding the negative advice of these two expert bodies, the global financial crisis had tipped the political dynamics in favour of EU legislation on credit rating agencies. The French presidency of the EU in the second semester of 2008 implicitly made EU legislation on rating agencies one of its priorities in elaborating the regulatory response to the global financial crisis (interviews, Paris, May 2009). The European Council called for a legislative proposal to strengthen the rules on credit rating agencies and their supervision at EU level in October 2008 (European Council 2008). Influential members of the European Parliament also supported the regulation of credit rating agencies in the EU (*Financial Times*, 8 July 2008). Indeed, the European Parliament produced two reports that discussed this matter (Rasmussen 2007; van den Burg and Dăianu 2008).

In November 2008, the Commission officially proposed the draft regulation on credit rating agencies, considering the revised IOSCO Code as the 'global benchmark', but arguing that these rules needed to be made more concrete in some cases and to be backed by an enforcement system. According to the regulation eventually approved in almost record time in April 2009, all credit rating agencies whose ratings are used in the EU need to apply for registration through an application submitted to the Committee of European Securities Regulators (now transformed into an authority). Registered credit rating agencies have to comply with rules designed to prevent conflict of interest in the rating process and to ensure the quality of the rating methodology and the ratings. Credit rating agencies operating in non-EU jurisdictions can issue ratings to be used in the EU provided that their countries of origin have a regulatory framework recognized as equivalent to the one put in place by the EU, or that such ratings are endorsed by an EU-registered credit rating agency.[7]

[6] European Securities Markets Expert Group had been set up in April 2006 as an advisory body to the Commission.

[7] <http://europa.eu/rapid/pressReleasesAction.do?reference=IP/09/629&format=HTML&aged=0&language=EN&guiLanguage=en> (accessed May 2012).

The main issue in the EU regulation on credit rating agencies was which authorities would be competent for registration. Moreover, several substantive provisions in the new legislation were seen as too detailed. In this respect, there were some differences between the rules proposed by the Commission, the SEC rules, and the IOSCO Code. On several issues, the EU proposal was judged as not being aligned with the US regulation on credit rating agencies and with the IOSCO Code. Last but not least, there was the issue of the potential extraterritorial effects of EU rules on credit rating agencies located in third-country jurisdictions and the setting up of mechanisms to ascertain the equivalence of rules.

To sum up, in the wake of the global financial crisis, the EU strengthened its regulatory capacity on credit rating agencies. The countries that in the past had opposed the EU's attempts to regulate rating agencies moved in favour of regulation, even though they continued to oppose the most prescriptive features of the proposed EU rules. On the controversial issue of equivalence, the old divide between the UK and the continental coalition re-emerged. The US was also involved in this particular aspect, given the fact that EU rules would have cross-loading effects in the US.

A controversial issue during the negotiation of the Directive was the allocation of power of authorization and oversight of credit rating agencies. The British authorities in particular opposed granting this power to the Committee of European Securities Regulators. Since the main rating agencies operating in Europe are located in London, the British Financial Services Authority wanted to have the main role in supervising their activities in the EU. Furthermore, the UK has traditionally been wary of strengthening EU institutions, including the Lamfalussy committees (see HM Treasury 2007).

Nonetheless, when the regulation on credit rating agencies was to be implemented, it became clear that a different supervisory arrangement was needed in order for the new rules to be applied uniformly across the EU. In May 2011, the regulation on credit rating agencies was amended, entrusting the European Securities and Markets Authority with exclusive supervisory powers over credit rating agencies registered in the EU, in order to centralize and simplify their registration and supervision at the EU level. Brummer and Loko (forthcoming) note that, by giving the European Securities Markets Authority this power, 'it is at least possible that Europe will be able to export European policy preferences in future through everyday territorial oversight'.

The sovereign debt crisis renewed the political interest in the regulation of credit rating agencies in the EU. During the crisis, credit rating agencies downgraded to junk bonds the ratings of sovereign debts in the periphery of Europe, worsening the crisis and attracting blame from some politicians as well as regulators. The French Internal Market Commissioner Barnier explored different options. Initially, the idea of an EU-run credit rating agency was floated by politicians in Italy and Germany and found some support in the EP, but it was a non-starter (Brummer and Loko forthcoming). An analysis showed that setting up a credit rating agency with public money would be costly, could raise concerns regarding the credit rating agency's credibility—especially if a publicly funded credit rating agency would rate the member states which finance the agency—and put private credit rating agencies at a comparative disadvantage.[8]

The Directive on Alternative Investment Funds Managers (2011)

Prior to the global financial crisis, hedge funds (or fund managers) were not regulated at the EU level. At the national level, hedge fund managers were regulated entities in some member states, though they were not subject to specific legislation concerning hedge fund managers. In other words, they were regulated as 'normal' fund managers. In other countries, such as in France, Italy, Spain, and Germany, the fund itself was a regulated onshore vehicle (IOSCO 2009a), though often it could be domiciled in a third country.

In the 2000s, some member states, most clearly Germany, as well as parts of the European Parliament, had encouraged discussions concerning the regulation of hedge funds at the EU level. Partly to assuage these concerns, the Commission set up a group of experts—the Alternative Investment Expert Group—to discuss the issue. The group issued a report, *Managing, Servicing and Marketing Hedge Funds in Europe*, which concluded against EU legislation on hedge funds (2006). The issue was raised again by the German presidency of the EU in 2007 and during its hosting of the G8 summit (*The Economist*, 26 May 2007). However, at that time there were not many takers for the proposal (interviews, Berlin, Apr. 2008).

Prior to the crisis, one coalition of member states, led by the UK, opposed the building up of EU regulatory capacity on hedge funds regulation, whereas another coalition, led by France and Germany, was in favour of EU (and international) rules on hedge funds. Member states had different preferences rooted in domestic political economy, namely different configurations of the financial system and national varieties of capitalism (Zimmermann 2010). Hedge funds and/or fund managers were already heavily regulated in some continental countries, such as France, Germany, and Italy. Germany and especially France host many assets managers, which on certain business compete with hedge fund managers and were already heavily regulated by EU directives (Woll 2013). Moreover, the activity of hedge funds was regarded as challenging corporate governance arrangements on the continent (Quaglia

[8] <http://europa.eu/rapid/press-release_MEMO-13-13_en.htm> (accessed May 2013).

2011a). The UK is host to four-fifths of hedge fund managers in the EU, hence it was keen to retain a light-touch approach to hedge funds regulation, avoiding EU rules on the matter. The Commission—notably the Commissioner for the Internal Market, Charles McCreevy—ruled out EU legislation on hedge funds, in line with its better regulation approach.

The attempt to regulate hedge funds in the EU was given new momentum by the financial crisis. The European Parliament became particularly vocal on this, producing two reports: the 'Rasmussen' report and the 'Lehne' report (European Parliament 2007, 2008a). A Resolution of the European Parliament issued on 23 September 2008 requested the Commission to submit a legislative proposal or proposals covering all relevant actors and financial market participants, including hedge funds and private equity.

In June 2009, the European Commission presented its proposal for the Draft Directive on Alternative Investment Fund Managers, which includes managers of hedge funds, private equities funds, and real estate funds, hence covering quite a broad range of financial entities (Commission of the European Communities 2009a). The Commission adopted a 'carrot and stick strategy', as McCrevy put it (*Financial Times,* 14 July 2009). On the one hand, the Commission argued that the cross-border dimension of the risks posed by alternative investment funds called for a coherent EU regulatory framework. On the other hand, it pointed out that an EU framework would remove the legal and regulatory obstacles to the efficient cross-border marketing of alternative investment funds across the EU. Therefore, an alternative investment fund manager domiciled in one member state would be allowed to market alternative investment funds to professional investors in another member state.

The Directive introduced a legally binding authorization and supervisory regime for all alternative investment fund managers in the EU, irrespective of the legal domicile of the alternative investment funds managed. Consequently, alternative investment fund managers will be subject to authorization from the competent authority of the home member state and to reporting requirements of systemically important data to supervisors. For reasons of proportionality, the Directive will not apply to alternative investment fund managers managing portfolios of alternative investment funds with less than a certain amount. The alternative investment fund managers will be required to hold a minimum level of capital and provide a minimum level of information to its (professional) investors (Commission of the European Communities 2009a).

The proposed Directive sets up a European passport for alternative investment fund managers. Thus, an alternative investment fund manager authorized in its home member state will be entitled to market its funds to professional investors in other member states. Member states will not be permitted to impose additional requirements on alternative investment fund managers domiciled in another member state. After a three-year transition period, the proposed Directive will allow alternative investment fund managers in the EU to market alternative investment funds located in third-country domiciles only if certain equivalence provisions are satisfied. Equivalence provisions and comparable access to third-country markets also apply to non-EU alternative investment fund managers that apply for authorization in the EU. In all cases, decisions on the equivalence of the relevant third-country legislation and comparable market access are taken by the Commission.

The parts of the Directive that were more problematic for industry and some member states, such as the UK, were: the imposition of a leverage cap on hedge fund activities; the requirement for alternative investment fund managers to use an external depositary, namely a custodian bank, which was seen as a way of safeguarding investors but which would increase the operational costs of hedge funds because banks would charge for the service provided; and the arrangements for the passporting of non-EU funds, which has significant implication for the cross-loading of EU rules on hedge fund managers to third countries. The final compromise was close to the preferences of the UK on several of these issues (Buckley and Howarth 2011).

All in all, the EU developed regulatory capacity on hedge funds and/or fund managers relatively late, and only after the global financial crisis. Following the financial crisis, the UK moved closer to continental coalition, supporting EU rules on alternative investment fund managers, but trying to limit the most prescriptive provisions of the Directive—i.e. those that would have been particularly burdensome for the hedge funds industry. This was because the British authorities were keen to maintain London as the primary location for alternative investment fund managers outside the US. For this reason, British policy-makers were concerned about the equivalence provisions in the Directive, in particular with reference to the US. The US was also heavily involved in this particular aspect, given the fact that equivalence provisions had implications for funds and managers located in the US.

By contrast, France and Germany saw the new legislation as an opportunity to deal with some of their long-standing concerns, amongst which were the implications of hedge funds activities for corporate governance, the competition between hedge fund and asset management funds for certain segments of market activity, and access to the EU market of funds based in low tax jurisdictions. It is noteworthy that, in their responses to alternative investment fund managers consultation, France and Germany argued that 'Europe should play an instrumental role in shaping a global regulatory regime for hedge funds through the creation of a "European label". An EU framework could serve as a reference for global regulation of alternative investment management activity' (Commission of the European Communities 2009b: 8). In comparison, the British authorities were concerned about potential regulatory arbitrage, and the relocation of part of the hedge fund industry outside the EU.

The European Market Infrastructure Regulation (2012)

Unlike in the case of rating agencies and hedge funds, prior to the global financial crisis there were no attempts in the EU to regulate over-the-counter derivatives. These are derivatives that are not traded on stock exchanges or through central counter parties, but are instead traded directly between two parties. The initial response of the European Commission and the European Central Bank (ECB) to the global financial crisis was to encourage industry to set up central counterparties in Europe for credit default swaps (CDSs),[9] which are a special type of over-the-counter derivative that caused so much damage during the global financial crisis. Subsequently, the EU authorities began discussing legislation, albeit at a slower pace than the US, because the EU began its regulatory response to the crisis with the other pieces of legislation mentioned.

In September 2010, the Commission proposed the European Market Infrastructure Regulation. This regulation was considered a critical piece of legislation by the Commission and member states in order to meet the G20 commitments taken at the September 2009 Pittsburgh summit. It was driven by the Commission, with general support from the German and French governments, although the Germans presented determined opposition to a core element of the Commission's draft regulation. The British government was broadly in favour, but also opposed specific institutional elements of the Commission's draft.

The European Market Infrastructure Regulation generally mirrored reforms enshrined in the Dodd Frank Act to shift derivatives on to exchanges and other types of trading platforms (*Financial Times,* 9 May 2011: 16). Unlike the Dodd Frank Act, the Brussels proposal did not deal with how over-the-counter derivatives should be traded, which was an issue tackled separately in the review of the Markets in Financial Instruments Directive, which was also under way. The European Market Infrastructure Regulation was initially conceived by the Commission as a 'directive', but it quickly changed to a 'regulation'. This distinction is important, as regulations are enacted into law with immediate effect in EU member states, with no discretion over their interpretation.

The legislation aimed to ensure the transparency of over-the-counter derivatives transactions and to reduce the risks associated with these products where possible by shifting over-the-counter derivatives trading to central counterparties. These central counterparties reduce risks because they act as intermediaries between sellers and buyers of derivative products. They ensure the solvency of their participants by requesting deposits and margin calls. The regulation also involved the creation of harmonized rules for central counterparties and

9 A credit default swap is a financial swap agreement whereby the seller of the swap will compensate the buyer in the event of a loan default or other credit event.

EU supervision of trade repositories. The reporting of all transactions was made mandatory with a view to providing supervisory authorities with the full picture of these markets.

Despite the broad consensus about the two main pillars of the European Market Infrastructure Regulation—that is, the need for central clearing and reporting (*European Voice*, 10 June 2010)—there were a handful of controversial issues in the negotiation of the European Market Infrastructure Regulation. These issues were mainly related to different configurations of national financial systems and competitiveness concerns across the EU, as well as outside it.

First, there were disagreements as to the scope of the regulation and whether it should refer only to over-the-counter derivatives (i.e. derivatives not traded on a regulated market), as mandated by the G20 and as maintained by Germany, or to all derivatives, including those traded on stock exchanges, as argued by the United Kingdom (*Financial Times*, 13 May and 4 Oct. 2011). The question of scope was linked to the issues of access and interoperability. According to the open-access provisions, exchanges would have to allow clients to access any central counterparty, while clearing houses would be obliged to accept any trade executed at another venue. This presupposed 'interoperability' in terms of compatible technical requirements, as well as compatible processes, business practices, and fees.

Germany's Deutsche Börse, which was a major player in trading and clearing derivatives, operated a 'vertical silos' structure, as did the Polish stock exchange, and unlike other exchanges in Europe, including the London Stock Exchange. In a vertical structure, the stock exchange incorporates trading and post-trading services of clearing and settlement. The Deutsche Börse, therefore, had most to lose from open-access provisions because these changes would split its vertical model. Not surprisingly, German and Polish policy-makers opposed open access, arguing that the extension of the scope was not in line with G20 commitments. They also saw it as an attack on the successful business model of their national stock exchanges (*Financial Times*, 4 Oct. 2011; *Risk Magazine*, 29 Sept. 2011). British policy-makers, supported by the Dutch and Scandinavians, were in favour of open access, arguing that it would allow independent central counterparties to compete with those that were tied to an exchange. The London Stock Exchange could gain market share from any breakup in the vertical silos models, even though the British authorities claimed that they advocated open access with a view to closing potential loopholes in the legislation and ensuring end-user choice (*Risk Magazine*, 12 Mar. 2011).

The initial Commission proposal only covered the over-the-counter market, but in a hearing before the Parliament, Patrick Pearson, head of the Financial Markets Infrastructure Unit at the Commission, argued for the scope to be extended to all derivatives. The Council of Ministers considered the possibility of expanding the scope of new market infrastructure legislation to include exchange-traded derivatives, but the German representative in the Council and German members in the European Parliament resisted this (Buckley et al. 2012). The Commission backed down, agreeing to address the issue in later legislation, and the proposal eventually limited the scope of clearing to over-the-counter derivatives. It covers all segments of the over-the-counter derivatives market (interest rates, credit, equity, foreign exchange, and commodities) and there are some exemptions from clearing and reporting requirements for non-financial firms. An article on the access of central counterparties to venues of executions was included in the final draft, giving access rights of central counterparties to transactions traded on a venue of execution. However, this provision did not imply the implementation of interoperability arrangements between those central counterparties.[10]

The second controversial issue in the European Market Infrastructure regulation concerned the location of central counterparties and their access to central bank liquidity. The ECB and some regulators—notably the French[11]—believed that central counterparties clearing over-the-counter derivatives should have access to central bank liquidity in the same currency as the product being cleared (Buckley et al. 2012). They linked the liquidity issue to the question of where central counterparties should be physically located. In other words, a central counterparty would have to be located in the euro-zone and clear euro-denominated products in order to access ECB liquidity.

The British authorities opposed this view because it would be to the detriment of clearing houses located outside the euro-zone—first and foremost those currently operating in the London over-the-counter markets: LCH. Clearnet and Ice Clear Europe. These clearing houses argued that they did not need access to central bank liquidity to ensure their resilience. Central banks were reluctant to provide such support (*Risk Magazine,* 10 Jan. 2012). The final text established that central counterparties' access to liquidity could result from access to a central bank or to creditworthy and reliable commercial bank liquidity, or a combination of both.

The issue of the so-called 'location policy' for central counterparties re-emerged in the summer of 2011, when the ECB issued a policy paper requiring clearing houses to be based in the euro-zone if they handle more than 5 per cent of the market in a euro-denominated financial product. The

[10] <http://europa.eu/rapid/pressReleasesAction.do?reference=MEMO/12/232&format=HTML&aged=0&language=EN&guiLanguage=en> (accessed Sept. 2012).

[11] This ECB position was especially supported by the Banque de France: 'If eurozone central banks are going to provide liquidity to central counter parties, they will require direct oversight of these institutions, hence the request for such infrastructures to be located within the eurozone' (Philippe Troussard, head of payments and market infrastructures oversight at the Banque de France, cited in *Risk Magazine,* 10 Jan. 2012).

ECB's concern was that if a central counterparty failed, or malfunctioned, it could cause systemic liquidity problems, or defaults, that the central bank would be unable to remedy without direct oversight of the clearing house (Buckley et al. 2012).

The issue was complex, as it involved the safeguard of ECB independence and financial stability, but also competitiveness concerns across the member states, and the central counterparties they host. The ECB location policy would severely damage multi-currency clearing houses, such as LCH.Clearnet's SwapClear service, based in London, which clears euro-denominated credit default swap (CDS) contracts. According to UK government figures, 40 per cent of global over-the-counter derivatives trading and 75 per cent of European trades currently take place in London (*Daily Telegraph,* 14 Feb. 2012). Other central counterparties potentially affected because they were located outside the euro area were Nasdaq OMX, which runs a Stockholm-based interest rate swap clearing service, and CME, which clears euro-denominated interest rate swap contracts from Chicago (*Risk Magazine,* 10 Jan. 2012). Other central counterparties, such as the Frankfurt-based Eurex Clearing—which planned to relaunch its over-the-counter services and was already able to access the Bundesbank's financing window to get collateralized cash if the need arose, were to benefit from the ECB location policy, hence supported it. So did French industry associations—including France's banking association.

The British government brought a legal case against the ECB, arguing that the ECB's policy restricted the free movement of capital and infringed on the right to establish cross-border businesses in the EU (*Financial Times,* 14 Sept. 2011). The issue then reached the highest political level, and made the headlines when the British Prime Minister, David Cameron, refused to sign up to a series of EU treaty changes in December 2011. Cameron had tabled six demands in return for UK support, one of which was exemption from the ECB location policy.[12] The French President and the German Chancellor opposed these requests at the EU summit. Hence, the British government decided to pull out of the treaty negotiations (Buckley et al. 2012).

The third issue concerned the powers of European Securities Markets Authority, but this is not of primary importance for the topic of this book. Members of the European Parliament wanted to give this newly created authority significant powers. By contrast, some member states, including the United Kingdom and Germany, were reluctant to do so and had a blocking minority in the Council (*Risk Magazine,* 12 Feb. 2012). The final compromise largely preserved the powers of the European Securities Markets Authority

[12] <http://www.out-law.com/en/articles/2012/february/treasury-files-second-legal-challenge-to-ecb-clearing-house-location-policy> (accessed Mar. 2012).

outlined in the Commission's original draft regulation. The fourth issue, concerning third countries, is discussed in a later section.

Overall, the EU developed regulatory capacity on over-the-counter derivatives only after the financial crisis. Unlike in the case of rating agencies and hedge funds, there had not been previous attempts to do so in the EU (although there had in the US). The crisis and the G20 statements post-crisis brought the issue into the spotlight. Despite the broad agreement of the member states to regulate over-the-counter derivatives, the main disagreements concerned the specific contents of the new rules that could have competitive implication for the national financial industry.

The Regulatory Capacity of the US in Securities Markets

The US has a strong regulatory capacity in securities markets, which is a federal competence. Prior to the crisis, regulatory templates were mainly developed with reference to securities trading in the US. Other financial activities or instruments related to securities markets remained unregulated or lightly regulated. After the global financial crisis, the perimeter of regulation in the US (as in the EU) was extended to these activities.

The Institutional Framework for Securities Markets Regulation in the US

The SEC was set up by the Securities Exchange Act (1934) in the wake of the stock market crash in 1929. It holds primary responsibility for enforcing federal securities laws and regulating securities markets and stock exchanges. Central to its mandate is investor protection and the integrity of capital markets. Prior to the global financial crisis, the Commission mainly focused on full and fair disclosure of financial information by companies with publicly traded securities and the regulation of accounting industry, discussed in Chapter 6 (Khademian 2002). The second pillar of the SEC regulatory approach is the rigorous enforcement of securities law, which explains why the SEC was keen to promote the use of memoranda of understanding sponsored by the IOSCO (Bach and Newman 2010). The SEC has a reputation for technical expertise (which, admittedly, has been tarnished by the crisis) and despite budgetary constraints attracts high-quality legal staff (Khademian 2002; see also Khademian 1992).

The Commodity Futures Trading Commission was set up in 1974 as an independent agency with the mandate to regulate commodity futures and option markets. It replaced the Commodity Exchange Authority, previously set up by the Commodity Exchange Act (1936), which established federal regulation of all commodities and futures trading activities and required all futures and commodity options to be traded on organized exchanges. On regulatory issues that are of competence for both the SEC and the Commodity Futures Trading Commission (such as certain aspects of derivatives regulation), there has been some bureaucratic turf fighting between these agencies (Partnoy 2001), as will be explained with reference to derivative regulation.

The following discussion of US regulatory templates focuses on activities and entities in securities markets that are relevant for the EU rules discussed in the opening section and the international rules discussed later.

Regulatory Templates for Securities Trading in the US

The US had developed relatively early robust regulatory templates concerning securities trading, which are based on the principles of disclosure and enforcement (Khademian 2002). The Securities Act (1933) was the first major federal legislation to regulate the offer and sale of securities. It was followed by the Investment Company Act (1940) and the Investment Advisers Act (1940). The Sarbanes-Oxley Act (2002), which was issued in the aftermath of major accounting and corporate scandals, including Enron and WorldCom, introduced important changes concerning corporate governance, auditing, and accounting and is therefore discussed in Chapter 6.

In the 1990s, European companies were eager to enter the US capital markets. In order to do so, they mainly formed US subsidiaries and registered them as broker-dealers with the SEC (Karmel 2007). European issuers could access US capital markets, opting out of certain provisions of US securities law. There were special accommodations for foreign private issuers accessing public US markets (for example, they did not have to comply with federal proxy rules and quarterly filings of financial data required for domestic issuers) (Jackson and Pan 2001). The SEC also developed informal procedures for foreign issuers, such as special scheduling and confidential treatment of filings that would normally be public for domestic companies. The SEC regulation afforded even more favoured treatment of foreign issuers seeking access to private US capital markets. Rule 144A allowed foreign private issuers to sell securities to qualified institutional investors without having to comply with disclosure and liability rules applicable to companies accessing the public markets (Jackson and Pan 2001).

During the 1990s, the SEC refused to agree to European demands for mutual recognition. One of the reasons adduced by the US authorities, beside their national mandate to secure investors protection in the US, was that the EU legislation was not sufficiently harmonized across member states and was less advanced than in the US (Posner 2009a). In the EU, US financial companies established affiliates that were regulated by one national regulatory regime—generally British law—and in principle could operate in any other EU national market (Posner 2009a). However, in practice, given the incomplete state of the EU financial market and EU regulation, many national (regulatory) barriers remained.

The issue of mutual recognition of certain aspect of securities markets law in the US and the EU was given new momentum in the mid-2000s. In 2007, the SEC Director of the Office of International Affairs, Ethiopis Tafara, coauthored an academic paper that outlined a blueprint for a mutual recognition regime between the US and the EU, even though he used the term 'substituted compliance' (Tafara and Peterson 2007). His blueprint for bilateral substituted compliance was based on four steps: (1) a petition from a foreign entity to the SEC seeking an exemption from registration; (2) a discussion between the SEC and the entity's home regulator to determine the degree to which the trading rules, prudential requirements, and other securities regulatory requirements are comparable; (3) a dialogue between the entity and the SEC which would include an agreement to submit to SEC jurisdiction for anti-fraud laws; and (4) public notice and an opportunity for comment on the petition. The proposal also envisaged collaboration between the SEC and an entity's home jurisdiction, including the signing of a memorandum of understanding and their ability to share enforcement-related information (Tafara and Peterson 2007).

As a response, in December 2007,[13] Commissioner McCreevy pointed out a window of opportunity concerning an agreement for mutual recognition between the SEC and the EU. This was to take place on the basis of: a gradual approach based on a political understanding by the SEC and EU regulators; a multilateral process; equality of criteria in determining access to markets and firms established overseas; no extraterritoriality. In 2008, the SEC signed a joint statement with the European Commission declaring that the implementation of mutual recognition would be intensified.[14] In 2007, the US and the EU leaders adopted the Framework for Advancing Transatlantic Economic Integration, including the goal of mutual recognition in securities regulation[15] (Verdier 2011).

What can account for the changed US stance on mutual recognition with the EU? There were several factors. First, in the late 1990s European issuers were turning away from US public capital markets because of private access to US capital, the offshore presence of US institutional investors,

[13] Testimony before the European Parliament Committee for Economics and Monetary Affairs.

[14] SEC Press Release 2008–9.

[15] *Framework for Advancing Transatlantic Economic Integration, US–EU*, annex 6, 30 Apr. 2007, available at <http://www.eeas.europa.eu/us/docs/framework_trans_economic_integration07_en.pdf> (accessed Mar. 2014). The Framework also provided for the establishment of a Transatlantic Economic Council to oversee regulatory cooperation efforts.

and unsatisfactory trading performance of European issuers that obtained US public listing in the early 1990s (Jackson and Pan 2001). Hence, there was the desire to make the US regulatory environment more welcoming for European issuers. Second, there were other important market developments taking place, in particular, transatlantic exchange mergers. The merger between the New York Stock Exchange and Euronext in 2007 created the largest stock exchange in the world, but different regulation applying to its US and European operations prevented full efficiencies from the merger (Schammo 2008).[16] In order to facilitate this merger, the SEC and the College of Euronext Regulators in Europe negotiated a comprehensive arrangement to facilitate cooperation in market oversight.[17] Third, the centralization of regulatory authority in the EU, political pressure from the EU, and the need for the US to deal with the new wave of EU securities markets legislation adopted between 2004 and 2006 (the Lamfalussy Directives) softened the stance of the SEC (Posner 2009a).

The US programme for mutual recognition was set aside during the global financial crisis and its aftermath.[18] Nonetheless, the regulatory response to the crisis in the US and the EU raised a new set of regulatory issues concerning the cross-loading of EU–US rules, in particular the provisions on equivalence and substitute compliance in these jurisdictions, which that had to be resolved for a level playing field.

The Regulation of Rating Agencies in the US

In the US, the SEC introduced ratings into the regulatory system in 1975, creating the concept of 'nationally recognized statistical rating organizations', whereby corporate bond ratings were used to help set minimum capital requirements for brokers-dealers (Coffee 2011). The nationally recognized statistical rating organizations were not legally defined by the SEC rules and were traditionally recognized as such by SEC staff through the no-action letter process (Sinclair 2005).

Although the SEC had the power to grant nationally recognized statistical rating organization status, it lacked a robust monitoring capacity and the ability to regulate credit rating agencies. Thus, the agency's leverage *vis-à-vis* the industry was mainly upfront, by acknowledging a given rating agency

[16] NASDAQ also pursued several merger possibilities in Europe, including the London Stock Exchange, but its bid failed.

[17] More generally, various players in the financial markets were also pressurizing the SEC to change its policies. Finally, the development of strong capital markets in Asia and South America has also influenced the SEC and the EU to cooperate in the international securities regulatory sphere.

[18] Mutual recognition was not mentioned in later releases of the Transatlantic Economic Council.

as 'nationally recognized'. It has been argued that 'Afterwards, the SEC was largely irrelevant' (Brummer and Loko forthcoming). Moreover, there was relatively little guidance about what a credit rating agency needed to do to qualify as a nationally recognized statistical rating organization. The SEC did some work in order to develop these rules, but for decades progress was slow, and no statutory rules were issued.

Prior to the 2006 bill, the SEC had designated only five nationally recognized statistical rating organizations: Moody's, S&P, Fitch, A. M. Best, and Canada's Dominion Bond Rating Service. By contrast, there were 125 credit rating agencies in the US without the recognized status, which hampered their ability to expand. Some credit rating agencies that had applied to the SEC for the status had to wait years for a decision, based on vague criteria such as being 'nationally recognized' (*Financial Times,* 14 July 2006).

Following the Enron scandal in 2002, the Senate Governmental Affairs Committee investigated the activity of rating agencies and concluded that meaningful SEC oversight was needed. The following year, the SEC published its own report, which also found serious problems with credit rating agencies. In June 2003, the SEC issued a concept release seeking comments on possible new regulations. Two years later, in April 2005, the SEC issued a proposed rule (*Financial Times,* 4 Mar. 2005). In the meantime, Congress had decided to intervene, in part due to a 'widespread perception of SEC lethargy about the initiative' (Brummer forthcoming).

The sponsors of the Credit Rating Agency Reform Act of 2006, which was backed by the White House, argued that existing rules and practices had created an 'artificial barrier to entry' in a market that had already oligopolistic tendencies. The new law set up a regulatory framework for credit rating agencies that evaluate corporate and government debt, modifying the system that had been in place since 1975. The bill, which was followed by SEC's regulation in 2007, replaced the SEC's nationally recognized statistical rating organizations designation with a formal registration system and gave the SEC supervisory and investigatory powers.

According to the bill, a credit rating agency was able to register with the SEC if the credit rating agency had been in business as a credit rating agency for at least the past three consecutive years and issued credit ratings certified by at least ten qualified institutional buyers (*Financial Times,* 14 July 2006). The SEC was to grant registration within a certain time frame if the requirements were satisfied. Such requirements did not cover the substance of the ratings or the procedures by which credit rating agencies determined their ratings. Once registered, each nationally recognized statistical rating organization had to certify every year that it complied with the registration criteria. The SEC was authorized by the Act to suspend or revoke the registration in case of non-compliance.

This reform was a compromise in several ways. First, the SEC was not given the authority to regulate the substance of ratings or how nationally recognized statistical rating organizations determine ratings. The issuer-pays business model was left intact. New reporting requirements were introduced for practices and procedures, but some of these documents were already made publicly available by the main credit rating agencies (Brummer and Loko forthcoming). Finally, the big three rating agencies continued to dominate the market.

Credit rating agencies performed poorly during the global financial crisis and were partly blamed for it. The 2010 Dodd Frank Act strengthened the regulatory regime for credit rating agencies in the US. It gave the SEC the power to suspend or revoke a rating agency's registration if warranted, or to penalize individual agency employees for misconduct. It created at the SEC an Office of Credit Ratings with a view to administering regulations and conducting annual examinations. The Act contained provisions for the public disclosure of the assumptions and data used to arrive at each rating, and submission of an annual report on internal controls by each agency; rules to strengthen corporate governance and board independence (see Acharya et al. 2011).

The Dodd Frank Act required the SEC to adopt a number of new rules on rating agencies concerning: internal controls; conflicts of interest; disclosure of performance statistics and credit rating methodologies; consistent application of rating symbols and definitions; and specific and additional disclosure for ratings related to structured financial products. In line with the agreement reached in the G20, the Act removed references to ratings from the Securities Exchange Act and a number of other statutes. In addition, it required federal agencies to modify or remove any reference to or reliance on credit ratings, substituting a standard of creditworthiness determined as appropriate by the agencies (Acharya et al. 2011). Given the fact that the largest credit rating agencies are based in the US but operate worldwide in what resembles an oligopolistic market (Sinclair 2005), the regulation of credit rating agencies in the US has de facto extraterritorial effects in the EU.

The Regulation of Hedge Funds in the US

In the US, prior to the global financial crisis, there were four key pieces of legislation concerning hedge funds: the Securities Act (1933), the Securities Exchange Act (1934), the Investment Company Act (1940), and the Investment Advisers Act (1940). However, hedge funds were deliberately lightly regulated and indeed there were well-established exclusions from the key mandates of these Acts (Sami 2009). Hedge funds were structured in such a way as to take advantage of the various exceptions envisaged by Congress (Horsfield-Bradbury 2008). Many advisers to hedge funds had previously avoided registration with the SEC under the Advisers Act by relying on an exemption for investment advisers with fewer than fifteen clients (with each fund advised counting as only one client);[19] which did not hold themselves out to the public as investment advisers (often referred to as the private adviser exemption), and did not advise a registered investment company (Horsfield-Bradbury 2008).

In late 2004, in a divisive and controversial three-to-two vote for an agency that generally acts unanimously (Paredes 2006), the SEC amended its rules so that hedge fund managers would have to register with the Commission as investment advisers. In particular, a hedge fund manager that advised a 'private fund' could no longer rely on the 'private adviser exemption' if the fund or funds the manager advised had fifteen or more total investors. The new rules required the counting of each investor in the fund as a single client for the purposes of the registration requirement. Accordingly, an adviser would need to register with the SEC if there were fifteen or more investors in the fund. This meant that a hedge fund manager had to file with the SEC, disclosing information about the fund's business practices and the manager's background; deliver to clients basic information about the fund's business practices and the fund manager's background; develop a system of internal controls and compliance procedures; and maintain specified books and records and make them available to the SEC for examination (Paredes 2006).

The requirement that hedge fund managers register was short-lived. In 2006, the US Court of Appeals, District of Columbia DC, overturned the Commission's rule-making in the case of *Goldstein v. SEC*.[20] In its unanimous decision, the Court argued that the SEC had exceeded its statutory authority and that its interpretation of the term client was arbitrary and unreasonable. Subsequently, the SEC staff announced that they would not appeal the Goldstein decision, reverting back to the pre-amended legislation, which exempted hedge funds managers from registration. The SEC allowed those managers who had registered to deregister. Hence, registration with the SEC remained voluntary.

Although hedge funds were not at the epicentre of the crisis, according to some they played a role in worsening it. Moreover, the Madoff scandal in the US renewed the regulators' interest in hedge funds regulation.[21] The Dodd Frank Act in 2010 repealed the private adviser exemption, as the SEC had effectively attempted to do in 2004. It kept a limited exemption from

[19] Hence, a hedge fund with, say, 100 investors counted as a single client of an adviser for the fifteen-client threshold.

[20] Remarks at the Symposium on 'Hedge Fund Regulation and Current Developments' by Commissioner Troy A. Paredes, US Securities and Exchange Commission, 8 June 2011.

[21] Madoff was a hedge fund manger who turned his business into a massive Ponzi scheme, defrauding thousands of investors.

registration for advisers to private funds with less than $150 million in assets under management. The Act directed the SEC to adopt regulations that prohibit incentive-based compensation that could encourage inappropriate risks by a financial institution, including an investment adviser with assets of $1 billion or more (Acharya et al. 2011).

In 2011, the SEC adopted final rules implementing the provisions of the Dodd Frank Wall Street Reform and Consumer Protection Act that amended the Investment Advisers Act 1940. It repealed several of the previous exemptions, amended some registration thresholds, and created new exemptions. In implementing legislation, the SEC required investment advisers to hedge funds, as well as other private funds, to report a significant amount of information to assist the new Financial Stability Oversight Council in assessing systemic risk.[22]

The reform of hedge funds regulation in the US also involved the Commodity Futures Trading Commission because an investment manager of a hedge fund that has one or more US investors may be required to register as a commodity pool operator and/or a commodity trading adviser. Many hedge funds are subject to the futures regulatory framework administered by the Commodity Futures Trading Commission. This is because they are managed by commodity pool operators registered with the Commission and invest in futures contracts and commodity options. In addition, if a fund manager is providing commodity trading advice to other accounts, it may be required to register as a Commodity Trading Advisor with the Commission unless an exemption applies. From 2003 until the aftermath of the global financial crisis, Commodity Pool Operators and Commodity Trading Advisors of funds were largely exempted from registration with the Commission. The Dodd Frank Act and the implementing rules adopted by the Commodity Futures Trading Commission in 2012 rescinded the exemption.

The Regulation of Over-the-Counter Derivatives in the US

Prior to the financial crisis, in the US many classes of derivatives were not regulated at all. This was partly due to the lobby efforts of industry but also to the ineffective way in which responsibilities were allocated between the main regulators. The SEC regulates 'securities' (which include stocks, bonds, and options), pursuant to the 1933 Securities Act and 1934 Securities Exchange Act. The Commodity Futures Trading Commission regulates 'futures' (which include exchange-traded futures on various commodities, instruments, and

[22] Remarks at the Symposium on 'Hedge Fund Regulation and Current Developments' by Commissioner Troy A. Paredes, US Securities and Exchange Commission, 8 June 2011.

indices), pursuant to the Commodity Exchange Act. Many of the conflicts in derivatives regulation stem from the turf battle between the SEC and Commodity Futures Trading Commission created by these two statutory regimes. It is indeed difficult to determine whether a particular instrument is a 'security', a 'future', or neither (Stout 2009).

Derivatives were initially used as hedging instruments, similar to commodities futures, to ensure market participants predictable revenues for agricultural products or revenues in foreign currencies. In 1936, the Commodity Exchange Act prohibited trading in 'off-exchange futures', leaving an exception for over-the-counter trading of 'forward' contracts intended to be settled by actual delivery, which were presumed to serve a hedging purpose. Thus, the Act confined speculative derivatives trading to the organized exchanges (Stout 2009).

These legal restraints on over-the-counter derivatives speculation were dismantled during the 1980s and 1990s. In the 1990s, the volume of mortgage-backed securities and CDSs increased substantially. The year 1994 was especially bad for the reputation of over-the-counter derivatives. Some high-profile cases highlighted the risk posed by the inappropriate use of these instruments. In the US, these financial scandals involved Gibson Greetings and Bankers Trust, Proctor & Gamble (P&G), Bankers Trust, Orange County, and Merrill Lynch.

Consequently, a debate ensued about the need to regulate over-the-counter derivatives. Basically, there were two fields. Those in favour of regulation were led by the Commodity Futures Trading Commission, which in 1998, under the impulse of its chair, Brooksley Born, issued a concept release indicating that it might seek to exercise regulatory authority over financial derivatives. Industry opposed regulation and so did the Treasury secretary Robert Rubin, the chairman of the US Federal Reserve Alan Greenspan, and other regulators. The financial industry lobbied hard on the issue and the regulatory policy community 'stuck together through the common belief in self-regulation as promoted by the G-30 recommendations' (Tsingou 2003). The battle was won by those favouring industry self-regulation: Congress enacted legislation to limit the Commodity Futures Trading Commission's rule-making authority over over-the-counter financial derivatives.

It is noteworthy that there were links between regulatory developments in the UK (the other main international centre for derivatives trading) and in the US. The UK Financial Services Act (1986) made all financial derivatives, whether used for speculation or not, legally enforceable in the UK (Stout, 2009: 3). This left US derivative traders at a potential competitive disadvantage compared with those based in the UK, hence the former were eager to make over-the-counter derivatives legally enforceable in the US. In the period up to 1998, debate grew in the USA about how to resolve this situation (Morgan 2010).

The Commodity Futures Modernization Act (2000) was the solution, as it legally prevented the Commodity Futures Trading Commission (or any other federal regulator) from regulating off-exchange derivatives (Woolley and Ziegler 2012). It gave 'legal certainty' to speculative trading by 'eligible contract participants', namely banks, corporations, mutual funds, pension funds, and wealthy individuals for the first time in US history (Stout 2009). The Act excluded most financial derivative transactions from the Commodity Exchange Act and its ban on off-exchange trading, and it was followed by an exponential growth in the over-the-counter derivatives market. Brooksley Born resigned from her Commodity Futures Trading Commission position.

In the aftermath of the global financial crisis, the Dodd Frank Act categorizes the derivatives transactions as either 'swaps', which are subject to primary regulation by the Commodity Futures Trading Commission, 'security-based swaps', which are subject to primary regulation by the SEC, or 'mixed swaps', which are subject to joint regulation by the Commodity Futures Trading Commission and the SEC (D'Souza et al. 2009). Title VII of the Dodd Frank Wall Street Reform and Consumer Protection Act reverses the Commodity Futures Modernization Act and restores legal constraints on over-the-counter financial derivatives by requiring that non-hedging (speculative) transactions be done either on an exchange or via an approved 'derivatives clearing organization' that performs the same contract guarantee function as an exchange.

Like the old Commodity Exchange Act, the Dodd Frank Act provides an exemption from the clearing requirement if one of the two parties to the swap 'is using swaps to hedge or mitigate commercial risk', leaving it to the Commodity Futures Trading Commission to define 'commercial risk', specifying however that 'financial entities' cannot rely on the 'commercial risk' hedging exemption to escape the clearing requirement. Hence, hedging transactions remain both legal and legally enforceable on the over-the-counter markets. Purely speculative trading in derivatives, however, is confined to clearinghouses. The Dodd Frank Act also tasked the Fed with the supervision and regulation of systemic market infrastructures and with financial stability. As with other parts of the Act, many details of the new regulatory regime relating to swaps are left to the secondary regulators to determine through rule-making (Acharya et al. 2011).

What accounts for the changed US stance on over-the-counter derivatives regulation? Helleiner and Pagliari (2010) noted that an ideational shift took place amongst US officials, from a light-touch regulatory approach to prescriptive regulation, not just with reference to over-the-counter derivatives. As the former chairman of the US Federal reserve pointed out, in his testimony before the Congress, 'those of us who have looked to the self-interest of lending institutions to protect shareholders' equity (myself especially) are in a state of shocked disbelief. Such counterparty surveillance is a central pillar of our financial markets' state of balance. If it fails, as occurred this year, market stability is undermined' (*Wall Street Journal,* 23 Oct. 2008).[23] The issue was also domestically politicized because derivatives had made the headlines in the US and elsewhere. It was no longer perceived simply as a 'technical' matter. Industry, for example, the powerful International Swaps and Derivatives Association (ISDA), accepted the need for regulation but set out to avoid heavy-handed rules by responding to policy-makers' requests to develop central counterparties.

The IOSCO and International Standard-Setting in Securities Markets

The IOSCO is the main international regulatory forum for securities markets. The IOSCO issued standards for securities markets trading in the 1990s, but it failed to issue prudential rules (capital requirements) for investment firms. In the 2000s, most of the IOSCO's activity focused on carrying out studies and issuing general principles concerning new financial products or institutions, such as derivatives, hedge funds, rating agencies, etc. After the crisis, it became more active in these areas.

The International Institutional Framework for Securities Markets Regulation

The IOSCO, like the International Association of Insurance Supervisors (IAIS), has 'universal' membership, composed of more than 100 national securities markets regulators. Some self-regulatory organizations, such as national stock exchanges, are affiliate members without voting power. Unlike the BCBS, the IOSCO and the IAIS meet at the very senior level only once a year. Since the IOSCO has a much larger membership than the BCBS, most of the high-level technical preparatory work is generally carried out by the Technical Committee, which is composed of fifteen agencies that regulate some of the world's largest securities markets. However, the work done by the Technical Committee needs to be endorsed by the General Assembly for it to be adopted by the IOSCO. In the IOSCO, there was no EU representative, the argument being that the European Commission does not have supervisory powers. In 2011, the European Securities Markets Authority joined the IOSCO as an associate member.

[23] <http://blogs.wsj.com/economics/2008/10/23/greenspan-testimony-on-sources-of-financial-crisis> (accessed Jan. 2011).

The US is represented by the SEC, whose influence has been predominant in the IOSCO over the past decades because of its strong domestic regulatory capacity and cutting-edge expertise.[24] Within the IOSCO, the SEC encouraged the signing of bilateral and multilateral memoranda of understanding for information exchange, which are instrumental for the enforcement of US rules (Bach and Newman 2010). The US also played an important role in the IOSCO discussions on accounting standards. Indeed, in the 2000s, the IOSCO cooperated with the International Accounting Standards Board (IASB) in the discussion on international accounting standards, as explained in Chapter 6.[25]

IOSCO Regulatory Templates for Securities Markets Trading in the 1990s

In its early years, the IOSCO mainly promoted the development and exchange of memoranda of understanding amongst its members (Bach and Newman 2010). Therefore, *Principles of Memoranda of Understanding* (MOUs) were issued by the IOSCO in 1991 with a view to providing a blueprint for the MOUs amongst its members. As the document clarifies 'MOUs are statements of intent which do not impose legally binding obligations on signatories... The strength of MOUs, however, is that they facilitate the exchange of information by accommodating the differences between regulators and by responding to changing legal environments.' Following the terrorist attack of September the 11th, the IOSCO produced a multilateral MoU in 2002.

In the 1990s, the IOSCO promoted regulatory harmonization concerning securities trading with a view to fostering market integration (Underhill 1995). This served the interests of investment bankers and institutional investors operating in the saturated US markets and keen to expand in Europe and in fast-growing economies (Underhill and Zhang 2008). In 1998, the IOSCO produced a comprehensive set of 'Objectives and Principles of Securities Regulation', which are recognized as the international regulatory benchmarks for securities markets, and which reduced the risks and costs to major firms engaged in cross border securities trading (Underhill and Zhang 2008). These IOSCO standards are part of the twelve policy areas standards designated by the Financial Stability Board as key for sound financial systems.[26]

The activities of the IOSCO expanded substantially in the 2000s. In the 1990s, it produced an average of ten policy documents per year. In the 2000s,

[24] E.g. whenever a new idea comes up in the IOSCO discussions, the SEC usually has a well prepared dossier on it.

[25] In 2005, the IOSCO also cooperated with the BCBS to draft the trading book review that became part of the Basel 2 accord, discussed in ch. 3.

[26] <http://www.financialstabilityboard.org/cos/key_standards.htm> (accessed Mar. 2014).

this number almost doubled, reaching its peak after the financial crisis. The post-crisis documents mainly concerned instruments and activities previously unregulated or subject to private-sector governance, such as rating agencies, hedge funds, and over-the-counter derivatives.

The IOSCO Code of Conduct Fundamentals for Credit Rating Agencies

Amongst international regulatory fora, the IOSCO took the lead for the discussion of rating agencies regulation, because in the US, where the largest credit rating agencies are based, the SEC, not the Federal Reserve, had been the lead regulator of credit rating agencies since the 1970s (Sinclair 2005). In the early 2000s, a series of significant corporate failures, such as the collapse of the US energy group Enron, and subsequently of the Italian dairy group Parmalat, drew policy-makers' attention to the activity of credit rating agencies, which had failed to spot problems in these companies.

In September 2003, the IOSCO issued the *Principles Regarding the Activities of Credit Rating Agencies* (IOSCO 2003). The principles, which outlined high-level objectives, were designed to be a tool for securities regulators, rating agencies, and other interested parties wishing to regulate the activity of credit rating agencies. Following the publication of the principles, some commentators, including a number of credit rating agencies, suggested that it would be useful if the IOSCO could develop a more specific and detailed code of conduct, giving guidance on how the principles could be implemented in practice (IOSCO 2004).

In 2004, the IOSCO issued a voluntary Code of Conduct Fundamentals for rating agencies (IOSCO 2004). The IOSCO Code was meant to be applied by rating agencies of all sizes and business models and in every jurisdiction—it was a market-driven compliance mechanism. As with the principles that preceded them, the Code fundamentals were developed out of discussions among IOSCO members, credit rating agencies, representatives of the BCBS, the IAIS, issuers, and the interested public. The Code contained rules that drew upon the substance of the principles, namely: the quality and integrity of the rating process; credit rating agencies' independence and the avoidance of conflicts of interest; and credit rating agencies' responsibilities to the investing public and issuers (IOSCO 2004: 3).

As explained by Philippe Richard, the secretary general of the IOSCO in a letter to the *Financial Times* (7 Jan. 2005: 14):

> it was always intended that the code fundamentals should be sufficiently flexible to accommodate the wide variations that exist between the legal and market circumstances that apply in different jurisdictions. Indeed, the advantage of this flexibility is that any jurisdiction that has the power and the need to do so may

supplement the code fundamentals with additional regulatory measures or incorporate it into its own regulatory requirements.

The Code works on a 'comply or explain' basis—i.e. credit rating agencies are expected to incorporate all the provisions of the IOSCO Code into their own internal codes of conduct. Where they choose not to do this, they must explain how their code nevertheless gives effect to the provisions of the IOSCO Code. The compliance of credit rating agencies with the Code has been monitored in the EU by the Committee of European Securities Regulators.

In the aftermath of the global financial crisis, a revision of the IOSCO Code was deemed necessary. The IOSCO issued a revised Code of Conduct Fundamentals for credit rating agencies in May 2008 (IOSCO 2008). The amendments to the IOSCO Code concerned the following measures: the strengthening of rules designed to avoid or limit conflicts of interests (for example, prohibiting analysts from advising on the design of structured finance products rated by the agency); enhancing the transparency of credit rating agencies' methodologies and ratings (for example, prescribing the use of a separate set of rating symbols for structured finance products); and improving the quality of rating (for example, ensuring that the data used for the rating are of a sufficiently good quality and the refusal of ratings if sufficient quality data are not available or the structured product is too complex).

The IOSCO Code provided the benchmark for the Commission's draft regulation on credit rating agencies (Commission of the European Communities 2008a, 2008b), which indeed contained most of the provisions of the Code, even though it was more detailed in some respects. At the same time, the revisions of rules concerning credit rating agencies took place in another key jurisdiction, the US. The US law was also largely based on the IOSCO Code. The main difference between the IOSCO Code on one side and the US and EU legislation on the other is that the former is not (nor could it be) legally binding, whereas national and EU laws are legally binding. The US and EU laws also prescribe processes of registration for credit rating agencies in their respective jurisdictions,[27] unlike the IOSCO rules, which do not envisage the registration of credit rating agencies.

Overall, prior to the crisis, the US had a weak domestic regulatory template for credit rating agencies. Thus, it was not in a position to upload its rules internationally. In contrast, the rating industry was well positioned to advocate self-regulation at the international and national levels. The EU did not manage to push for international standards on credit rating agencies other

[27] It should also be noted that discussions amongst regulators at the IOSCO were instrumental in facilitating the settlement of the issues raised by the potential extraterritorial impact of the proposed EU rules.

than the voluntary Code of Conduct because member states were divided on this issue and the EU did not have its own regulatory template to upload.

The main European countries had different preferences on this issue because of different regulatory approaches, but also because of the configuration of the rating industry, with the main European subsidiaries of US rating agencies being located in London. Moreover, divisions also ran between the regulators, gathered in the IOSCO and the Committee of European Securities Regulators, which initially opposed EU rules, and some (mainly French and German) politicians in the European Parliament and national capitals, who unsuccessfully called for EU rules prior to the crisis. After the crisis, there was a realignment of preferences within the EU, in particular by the UK and some Nordic countries. The rating industry was not in a position to lobby hard to oppose EU legislation, though they did try to prevent the most burdensome parts of it (and partly succeeded). In parallel, the US also strengthened its regulation of credit rating agencies.

The IOSCO Principles on Hedge Funds Regulation

Prior to the global financial crisis, some research and fact-finding exercises on hedge funds had been undertaken by international financial regulatory fora, generally following policy failures. After the Asian financial crisis and the collapse of the hedge fund LTCM in the US, a set of policy documents were issued by BCBS (1999b, 1999c), IOSCO (1999), and subsequently by the newly created FSF (2000, updated in 2007). The US also conducted its own review through the President's Working Group on Financial Markets (1999). Basically, all these documents concluded in favour of indirect regulation of hedge funds, which was subsequently strengthened. Indirect regulation means the regulation of the financial institutions (in particular the prime brokers) through which hedge funds operate in the securities markets and banks (in particular investment banks) investing in or lending to hedge funds.

In policy discussions in international fora, two different approaches could be detected, one in favour of regulating hedge funds, championed by Germany and France, whereas the US and the UK opposed regulation (interviews, Basel, Nov. 2008). In 2007, German officials used their presidency of the EU and of the Group of Eight (G8) to push for regulation, receiving some backing from the Financial Stability Forum (FSF), which the G8 charged with studying the issue.[28] At the outset of the global financial crisis, the German Finance Minister Peer Steinbrück called for a formal code of conduct for hedge funds.

[28] Previously, in July 2005, the then-Chancellor of Germany, Gerhard Schröder (Social Democrat) had pressed for tighter controls on hedge funds at G7 Summit in Britain, where it was blocked—as Schröder himself revealed—by 'Wall Street and London' (*Independent*, 16 June 2005).

The US opposed a code of conduct, while the US Treasury Secretary Henry Paulson Jr supported a set of principles that informed investors, leaving them to monitor risk (*International Herald Tribune*, 23 Apr. 2007; *Bloomberg News*, 23 Apr. 2007). An impasse followed and no action was taken to deal with the problems posed by hedge and private-equity funds.

In the aftermath of the global financial crisis, the split over how to regulate hedge funds re-emerged, as it became evident in preparation for the April 2009 G20 summit. Several European countries, led by France and Germany—as suggested by Sarkozy and Merkel's joint letter (2009)—with the support of Italy (Italian Treasury Minister Giulio Tremonti had vociferously called for the regulation of hedge funds),[29] pushed for a tougher regulatory regime for hedge funds and wanted the funds to be overseen similarly to banks (*Financial Times*, 23 Feb. 2009). In comparison, the US and UK authorities favoured more disclosure over more regulation, proposing instead that funds be required to register with the government and disclose more information with a view to increasing transparency (*Wall Street Journal*, 14 Mar. 2009). European leaders also wanted to clamp down on tax havens.

In February 2009, the German Chancellor Angela Merkel hosted a summit of German, French, Italian, Spanish, Dutch, and British leaders in Berlin. The purpose of the gathering was to prepare a common EU policy in advance of London's G20 summit in April 2009. In relation to hedge funds, the press statement issued after the meeting pointed out that 'all financial markets, products and participants must be subject to appropriate oversight or regulation, without exception and regardless of their country of domicile. This is especially true for those private pools of capital, including hedge funds, that may present a systemic risk.'[30]

The consensus reached was seen as a victory for France and Germany, which championed the need for a comprehensive regulatory architecture in the face of resistance from the UK, where many hedge funds are based (*Financial Times*, 23 Feb. 2009). Reportedly, at the meeting Gordon Brown agreed to restrictions on hedge funds in order to clear the way for an overall accord, which included the call to strengthen the International Monetary Fund (IMF) and endow it with more resources (*Daily Telegraph*, 23 Feb. 2009).

A letter sent jointly by President Nicolas Sarkozy and Chancellor Angela Merkel (2009) to Mirek Topolanek, Prime Minister of the Czech Republic, and

[29] The Italian Treasury minister Giulio Tremonti argued that the rewriting of financial market rules should target 'absolutely crazy bodies, like hedge funds which have nothing to do with capitalism' and are 'dark and opaque'. He fell short of proposing the abolition of hedge funds and faced a backlash from the industry concerned (*Reuters*, 11 Oct. 2008).

[30] <http://www.diplo.de/diplo/en/WillkommeninD/D-Informationen/Nachrichten/090224-1.html> (accessed May 2009).

Jose Manuel Barroso, President of the European Commission, in preparation for the G20 Summit in April 2009, reiterated that:

> The first priority is to build a new global financial architecture. The European Union must assert a common position and take the lead on this.... On the basis of the achievements of the Berlin preparatory summit in February we are determined to obtain at the London summit concrete results on strengthening international financial regulation.... The European Union must propose that all hedge funds and other funds presenting a potential systemic risk be subject to appropriate registration, regulation and oversight.

After protracted negotiations, the G20 in London in April 2009 agreed that:

> hedge funds or their managers will be registered and will be required to disclose appropriate information on an ongoing basis to supervisors or regulators, including on their leverage, necessary for assessment of the systemic risks that they pose individually or collectively. Where appropriate, registration should be subject to a minimum size. They will be subject to oversight to ensure that they have adequate risk management. (G20 2009a)

The G20 agreement, which was followed by the expansion of the IOSCO perimeter of regulation to hedge funds (and other previously unregulated or self-regulated activities, such as credit rating agencies), could be seen as evidence of EU influence. However, the US had also switched position in favour of hedge funds regulation for domestic political reasons, namely the public backlash against financial institutions and the politicization of financial regulation (Helleiner and Pagliari 2010).

In the IOSCO, the Task Force on Unregulated Financial Entities, co-chaired by the Italian securities markets authority and the British Financial Services Authority, decided to focus its work on hedge funds. The task force was chaired by two regulatory agencies embracing very different domestic regulatory models about hedge funds. The report *Hedge Funds Oversight* was published for consultation in March 2009. The *Final Report* published in June 2009 recommended six high-level principles. Amongst the most important: 'Hedge funds and/or hedge fund managers/advisers should be subject to mandatory registration'; 'Hedge fund managers/advisers which are required to register should also be subject to appropriate ongoing regulatory requirements'; 'Hedge fund managers/advisers and prime brokers should provide to the relevant regulator information for systemic risk purposes' (extracts from IOSCO 2009a).

The report is a rather bland document. Indeed, it is deliberately ambiguous on the rather crucial issue of whether certain provisions should apply to hedge funds or hedge fund managers. Regulators in Italy, Germany, and France, where hedge funds, and not only hedge fund managers, are subject to registration and/or supervisory oversight were in favour of regulating the hedge fund, not just the fund manager. They also called for more prescriptive prudential requirements, somewhat akin to those for banks or regulated funds. By contrast, the UK and the US (and the hedge funds industry) wanted to limit the application of the IOSCO principles to hedge fund managers, and opposed certain prudential requirements.

The reason why the EU lacked a cohesive position on the content of the IOSCO standards is that in the same period the EU was negotiating, but had not yet agreed, the Directive on Alternative Investment Fund Managers. This Directive, which mainly targets hedge fund managers and private equities managers, was proposed by the European Commission in April 2009 and was eventually agreed in November 2010. The scope of the Directive was broader than the scope of the work of the IOSCO Task Force: it had the objective of creating a comprehensive and effective regulatory and supervisory framework for alternative investment fund managers in the EU. It contained provisions on the leverage employed by hedge fund managers, and imposed minimum capital requirements, as well as valuation and depository requirements.

Intra-EU negotiations on the Alternative Investment Fund Managers' Directive were contested because the main European countries had different preferences on issues such as third-country access to the EU market and prudential requirements. Some divisions amongst European regulators, for example, on prudential requirements, emerged in the EU as well as the IOSCO. In the end, European regulators in the IOSCO were unable to get key provisions of the Alternative Investment Fund Managers' Directive into the IOSCO high-level principles.

Overall, the record of EU influence in international standards for hedge funds was mixed. Prior to the crisis, the EU lacked a regulatory template to upload and member states had competing preferences on this issue. Whereas some continental policy-makers called for hedge funds regulation, the UK and the US successfully opposed any attempt to directly include hedge funds (or fund managers) in the perimeter of international regulation. The US did not have a robust domestic regulatory template to upload internationally. Industry was very active in promoting self-regulation, rather than public regulation.

After the crisis, there was a realignment of preferences within the EU, which reached a cohesive position on the principle of regulating hedge funds. Under the aegis of France and Germany, the EU was highly influential in getting hedge funds into the international regulatory agenda. This outcome was facilitated by the changed regulatory preferences of the US (a less market-friendly approach) and its somewhat weakened position after the global financial crisis, which originated in the US. In the wake of the crisis, the US also revised its hedge funds regulation.

When the international standards were negotiated by the IOSCO, the EU was in the process of building up its regulatory capacity in the sector, which most likely weakened its influence in IOSCO. The EU lacked a cohesive position on the specific content of regulation (intra-EU negotiations were ongoing), hence its influence in shaping the content of the IOSCO standards was limited. The EU as such was not represented in IOSCO, where the European Commission, which proposed the Alternative Investment Fund Managers Directive, was not a member.

International Over-the-Counter Derivatives Regulation

In the early 1990s, over-the-counter derivatives became widely used. In the absence of international rules on the matter, a private-sector body, the Group of Thirty (G30 1993) issued a series of recommendations, *Derivatives: Practices and Principles,* that de facto became an international standard and largely reflected the interests of the derivatives industry (Tsingou 2003). The G30 put forward twenty-four recommendations, mostly directed at dealers and end-users, addressing the main types of risk and proposing risk management procedures. The G30 recommendations were adopted and promoted by the public authorities at the national and international levels. Tsingou noted that 'Having succeeded in offsetting regulation and legislation, both internationally, and in the US, the [G30] study was also instrumental in helping the private sector use over the counter derivatives' (Tsingou 2003). In the US, the G30 recommendations were instrumental in preventing additional regulation on derivatives that was being debated at that time.

Internationally, following the policy failures concerning derivatives trading, and the Barings scandal in the UK,[31] which also involved derivatives, the IOSCO and the BCBS discussed the issue. However, none of these international regulatory bodies recommended that national authorities directly regulate derivatives markets. Instead they called for better self-regulation, endorsing the G30 standards, and emphasized the need for disclosure and risk management (see, for example, the BCBS and IOSCO 1995a, 1995b). The joint paper issued by the BCBS and the IOSCO explicitly recognized that the 'Two committees are aware of the potential costs associated with requests for additional information on derivatives activities and recognise that additional information requirements should only arise where there is a clear supervisory need' (1995a: para. 14).[32]

[31] In the collapse of Barings Bank in 1995, a single trader at the bank carried out a series of disastrous derivatives trades (Tickell 2000).

[32] See *Framework for Supervisory Information about the Derivatives Activities of Banks and Securities Firms* (BCBS and IOSCO, 1995a).

Prior to the crisis, the US and UK authorities vetoed the regulation of over-the-counter derivatives because of a competitiveness concern and because they shared a light-touch regulatory paradigm. Lobbying from the financial industry was also intense. The US authorities passed a bill in 2000 that prevented domestic regulation of over-the-counter derivatives, despite Warren Buffett calling derivatives 'weapons of mass destruction'. Alan Greenspan (1998), chairman of the Federal Reserve Board, argued that:

> There appears to be no reason for government regulation of off-exchange derivative transactions between institutional counterparties. Private market regulation appears to be achieving public policy objectives quite effectively and efficiently... Participants in these markets have been savvy enough to limit their activity to contracts that are very difficult to manipulate. Institutional participants in the off-exchange derivative markets also have demonstrated their ability to protect themselves from losses of fraud and counterparty insolvencies.

After the global financial crisis, the US switched position on this issue because of domestic politics (the attempt by US politicians to be seen as taming the power of the financial industry) and became one of the main advocates of over-the-counter derivatives regulation. In the preparation for the G20 Pittsburgh summit, the US secretary called for efforts to reduce the systemic risk of CDSs and to strengthen the infrastructure for over-the-counter derivatives (US delegation to the G20, 2008, cited in Woolley and Ziegler 2012). The day before the G20 summit in November 2008, the US approved a set of objectives for the regulation of over-the-counter derivatives markets, some of which ended up in the G20 statement, and others went beyond it (President's Working Group 2008). In May 2009, the US made further commitments that went beyond the G20 commitment: the mandatory use of central counterparties for all standardized over-the-counter derivatives and registration for all trade; mandatory trade on exchange for standardized contracts (US government 2009, cited in Helleiner and Pagliari 2010).

In September 2009, G20 leaders agreed in Pittsburgh that:

> All standardised over the counter derivative contracts should be traded on exchanges or electronic trading platforms, where appropriate, and cleared through central counterparties by end- 2012 at the latest. Over-the-counter derivative contracts should be reported to trade repositories. Noncentrally cleared contracts should be subject to higher capital requirements. We ask the FSB and its relevant members to assess regularly implementation and whether it is sufficient to improve transparency in the derivatives markets, mitigate systemic risk, and protect against market abuse. (G20 2009b)

The G20 summit in London in April 2009 called for the setting up of CCP, subject to official regulation:

> We will promote the standardisation and resilience of credit derivatives markets, in particular through the establishment of central clearing counterparties subject to effective regulation and supervision. We call on the industry to develop an action plan on standardisation by autumn 2009; and we will each review and adapt the boundaries of the regulatory framework regularly to keep pace with developments in the financial system and promote good practices and consistent approaches at the international level.[33]

The Dodd Frank Act in the US and the European Market Infrastructure regulation in the EU put into legally binding legislation these G20 commitments. Their potential cross-loading effects will be discussed later.

Overall, the record of EU influence in international standards for over-the-counter derivatives is very thin. Not only did the EU not have a pre-crisis regulatory template to upload, but also, unlike in the case of hedge fund and rating agencies, there were no European voices calling for over-the-counter derivatives regulation prior to the crisis. The US, like the EU, had no regulatory template on over-the-counter derivatives, despite some domestic policy discussions on this issue. After the crisis, the US strengthened its regulatory capacity on over-the-counter derivatives and, with EU support, pushed this issue in international regulatory fora. Unlike in the pre-crisis period, the derivatives industry was not in a position to oppose regulation, though they did try to prevent the most burdensome parts of it (and partly succeeded).

The Post-Crisis Cross-Loading of Securities Markets Regulation from the EU to the US

The post-crisis rules adopted by the US and the EU differ in certain respects, creating potential obstacles to cross-border financial activity, with the risk of latent protectionism. In several areas, the Dodd Frank Act requires US regulators to assess the existence of adequate home state regulation. The EU has also made use of equivalence clauses in the legislation on credit rating agencies, hedge funds, and over-the-counter derivatives. Verdier (2011) notes that 'in the aftermath of the global financial crisis, transatlantic mutual recognition should no longer be seen solely as a market liberalization initiative, but as

[33] *Global Plan Annex: Declaration on Strengthening the Financial System*: <http://www.g20.utoronto.ca/2009/2009ifi.html> (accessed June 2011).

a means to maintain the openness of international financial markets as the United States and the EU concurrently ramp up their regulation of the financial industry'.

Credit Rating Agencies

The EU regulation on credit rating agencies contains equivalence clauses concerning rating agencies located in third countries. Indeed, one of the rationales of this Directive was to ensure that US rating agencies operating in the EU would not escape the supervision of European authorities (Pagliari 2013). The then French Finance Minister, Christine Lagarde, argued that it was not possible only to have US regulation for financial institutions producing 'collateral effects from financial instruments and products', as the way of selling those products was 'completely extraterritorial' (quoted in Pagliari 2013). Chancellor Angela Merkel and French President Nicolas Sarkozy supported the creation of a European rating agency as a way to challenge the hegemony of US rating agencies in Europe *(Financial Times*, 10 June 2008).

According to the initial Commission's proposal, credit rating agencies with headquarters outside the EU but which wanted to operate in the Community were required to set up a subsidiary in the EU which could then be registered by the competent authority. A credit rating agency registered in one member state could issue credit ratings anywhere in the EU, de facto setting in place a passport for credit rating agencies across the EU. However, many policy-makers, especially the British authorities, were worried about the negative effects that this could have for the financial instruments traded in the City of London (House of Lords 2009). They felt that a mechanism was needed to recognize third-country regulation of credit rating agencies as 'equivalent' to the EU, so that the ratings issued by credit rating agencies located outside the EU could be used in the EU.

In the end, the regulation indicated two ways through which credit rating issued outside the EU can be used in the EU for regulatory purposes. 'Certification' (Article 5 of the EU Regulation) allows a third-country credit rating agency, whose activities are not considered to be of systemic importance to the financial stability or integrity of the financial markets of one or more member states, to be used in the EU for regulatory purposes. A positive equivalence decision is necessary to enable a third-country credit rating agency to apply for certification. The second method is 'endorsement' (Article 4) through which third-country agencies can have their ratings endorsed by a European subsidiary. This provision safeguarded the position of London as the main location for the European activity of the main US rating agencies (Pagliari 2011).

In July 2012, the European Securities Market Authority and the SEC signed a Memo of Understanding on the supervision of credit rating agencies, concerning consultation, cooperation, and exchange of information concerning cross-border regulated agencies, described in the Annex. These agencies were: Standard and Poor (US, UK, Italy, and France), Moody's (France, Germany, Italy, UK, Spain, and the US), Fitch (US, UK, Italy, France), DBRS (UK, US), and A. M. Best (UK, US).[34] In October 2012, following the advice of the European Securities Market Authority,[35] the European Commission adopted a decision on the recognition of the legal and supervisory framework of the US, Canada, and Australia as equivalent to EU regulation.[36]

Hedge Funds

During the negotiations of the Alternative Investment Fund Managers' Directive, some controversial issues concerned the term of access of third-country funds and third-country fund managers to the EU. In a nutshell, a coalition led by France, with some support from Germany, sought to make the terms of access to EU market of non-EU funds and fund managers more restrictive than the ones initially proposed by the European Commission (Pagliari 2013). They argued that such an approach was necessary to prevent Europe from becoming 'the Trojan horse for offshore funds', as the French Treasury minister put it (*European Voice,* 29 Apr. 2009). Many Members of the European Parliament (MEPs), especially the Socialists, were in favour of similarly tough rules.

The UK and the hedge fund industry regarded these rules as protectionist. The British authorities were keen to safeguard the status of London as the main location for hedge funds in the EU and its capacity to attract funds based in the many British Crown dependencies that act as offshore financial centres (Pagliari 2013). Many British alternative investment fund managers ran funds based outside the EU for tax purposes. The British sought a regime whereby non-EU fund managers and non-EU funds would be able to operate across the EU, provided the jurisdiction in which they were based had 'equivalent' regulatory standards, with a relaxed set of criteria to determine 'equivalence'. Ireland, the Czech Republic, Malta, Sweden, and Austria adopted a similar position (Buckley and Howarth 2011).

[34] <http://www.esma.europa.eu/content/MOU-supervision-CRAs-ESMA-and-SEC> (accessed Feb. 2013).

[35] <http://www.esma.europa.eu/content/Technical-advice-CRA-regulatory-equivalence-US-Canada-and-Australia> (accessed Mar. 2013).

[36] <http://ec.europa.eu/internal_market/securities/agencies/index_en.htm> (accessed Mar. 2013).

The US administration made public its opposition to the 'third-country' provisions of the proposed Directive. The US SEC stated that it would be unlikely to be able to comply with the equivalent criteria suggested in the alternative investment fund managers draft, which would have closed the EU market to US-based funds (Harris 2010). Timothy Geithner, the US Secretary of the Treasury, sent a letter to Michel Barnier, the Commissioner for Internal Market and Services, and to the Spanish chair of the Council of Economic and Financial Affairs (ECOFIN Council) in March 2010.

> I believe we agree that [it] is essential to fulfil our G 20 commitment to avoid discrimination and maintain a level playing field. In this context, we are concerned with various proposals that would discriminate against US firms and deny them the access to the EU market that they currently have. We strongly hope that the rule that you put in place will ensure that non-EU fund managers and global custodian banks have the same access as their EU counterparts. You will see that our approach in the US maintains full access for EU fund managers and custodians to our market. (*Financial Times*, 11 Mar. 2010)

Subsequently, Geithner sent another letter to the UK Chancellor of the Exchequer Alistair Darling and the German, French, and Spanish Finance Ministers (*Financial Times*, 6 Apr. 2010). The US administration argued that, if the third-country rules of the Directive were not significantly changed, EU-based fund managers could face reprisals in the US Congress. The British Labour government joined forces with the Obama administration to water down the demands imposed on third-country funds (Buckley and Howarth 2011).

The issue of 'equivalence' concerned non-EU hedge funds and non-EU hedge fund managers (for an in-depth discussion, see Ferran 2011). In the end, it was agreed that alternative investment fund managers would be able to market non-EU funds through national placement regimes, and after a period of three years, they would be able to market throughout the EU through the 'third country passport'. In order for their fund to be eligible for the EU passport, third countries should allow European funds to be sold there, they should comply with international standards on anti-money laundering, terrorist financing, and tax cooperation, and their authorities should sign supervisory agreements with European regulators (Pagliari 2013). Non-EU hedge fund managers should comply with certain aspects of the AIFM Directive in order to be able to operate in the EU.

Over-the-Counter Derivatives

The debate on the third-country regime under the European Market Infrastructure Regulation was especially complex. The key issues were: to guarantee legal certainty; to avoid over- or underlaps with similar legislation in third-country jurisdictions; to ensure an international level playing field for EU central counterparties and trade repositories; and to abide by World Trade Organization (WTO) obligations. During the negotiations, some parties, especially French policy-makers, called for reciprocal provisions—for example, concerning access to data held in repositories outside of a regulator's geographic jurisdiction. Others, including the British, objected to the concept of reciprocity with a view to ensuring open markets. They also argued that it could jeopardize EU commitments under the WTO (interviews, Washington, Aug. 2011).

As for central counterparties (CCPs), the crucial issues for the EU concerning the location of CCPs were to avoid over-reliance on US CCPs and the ability to access central bank money. The ECB and the Commission wanted at least one central counterparty to be located and regulated in the EU, to avoid European dependence on over-the-counter derivatives clearing in the US (Buckley et al. 2012). Moreover, the ECB insisted on a central counterparty to be located in the euro area because of access to central bank liquidity. The City and the ISDA preferred global clearers, which were considered more efficient from the point of view of industry. Some of these global clearers are located in London and in the US. The final text of the regulation established that recognition of a third-country central counterparty by the European Securities Market Authority would first require an equivalence decision by the Commission. The European Securities Market Authority should also establish cooperation arrangements with the third-country competent authorities.

As for trade repositories, two issues were at stake for the EU in their location: the treatment of confidential data and market competition (interview, Washington, Aug. 2011). First, after the failure of Lehman brothers, European regulators had been denied access to trade repositories data in the US on the basis of the confidentiality of these data. The Dodd Frank Act mandated that American-based swap data repositories obtain indemnification from foreign regulators before sharing information. For all these reason, European policy-makers were keen to establish European trade repositories (interview, Brussels, Mar. 2011). Market competition was also at stake. For example, the American authorities argued in favour of one trade repository per asset class because the Depository Trust and Clearing Corporation (an American post-trade group) was to launch an interest rate swap data repository in London in late 2012 and had another planned for commodities and foreign exchange (*Financial Times*, 25 Aug. 2011).

According to the European market infrastructure legislation, authorities were to be granted access to the data of trade repositories (owned by private companies). Recognition of a third-country trade repository was subject to equivalence decisions by the Commission. In addition, there was to be an international agreement in place between the Commission and that third country with regard to mutual access to data and exchange of information on over-the-counter derivatives contracts held in trade repositories, in order to address the issue of confidentiality (*Financial Times*, 10 Oct. 2011).

What is remarkable about European Market Infrastructure Regulation (EMIR) and its third-country treatment is that it applied clearing obligations, not only to transactions between EU counterparties, but also to transactions between two entities established in one or more third countries that would be subject to clearing obligations if they were established in the EU, provided that the contract has a direct substantial and foreseeable effect within the EU, or where such an obligation was necessary to prevent the evasion of any provisions of the EU legislation. This wording was a reaction to a similar wording in the US implementation of over-the-counter products reform in the Dodd Frank Act. This created tensions between the EU and the US, as it was impossible to clear the same contract in two locations (interview, Washington, May 2013). Hence, rules for EU–US cooperation needed to be established and are currently under negotiation.

The Financial Industry and Global Securities Markets Regulation

The financial industry has been a powerful lobbyist in securities markets legislation. It is somewhat easier to find evidence of its activity at the national or EU levels than at the international level, given the fact that only recently and selectively has the IOSCO begun to publish responses to consultations. Moreover, the IOSCO mostly issues general principles, which are non-legally binding, hence industry has limited incentive to lobby on the IOSCO output, with some exceptions, such as the robust contributions of the financial industry to the discussion on rules on rating agencies, hedge funds, etc.

Three main features of the financial industry's influence on international securities markets regulation stand out. To begin with, changes in the configuration of financial markets have altered the preferences of the financial industry as well as the preferences of regulators in several jurisdictions. In the EU, partly as a result of previous regulatory reforms, continental equities markets developed substantially in the 1990s, the main banks in the core countries (the UK, France, Germany, and the Netherlands) aggressively engaged in cross-border investment banking, and stock exchanges were demutualized and turned into profit-making companies (Mügge 2010). All this paved the ground to the EU regulatory changes of the early 2000s: it affected the negotiations for the completion of the single financial market and the content of the Lamfalussy Directives. The mergers between European and US stock exchanges in the 2000s created an incentive for US regulators to consider the possibility (previously ruled out) of mutual recognition with the EU.

The second feature is that, outside 'traditional' securities trading, certain entities or instruments, such as credit rating agencies, hedge funds, and over-the-counter derivatives, were subject to self-regulation (or private-sector governance) prior to the global financial crisis. Self-regulation was also an effective way to prevent public (legally binding) regulation (Pagliari 2011). Prior to the global financial crisis, credit rating agencies were regulated by the voluntary code of conduct issued by IOSCO in 2004 on the comply-or-explain basis. In 2007, the FSF called on the hedge fund industry to develop a code of best practice. In response to a call by the FSF, several standards on hedge funds were issued by private-sector bodies located in different jurisdictions. The Hedge Fund Working Group/Hedge Fund Standards Board, based in the UK, issued standards (2008) which managers could decide to sign up to. Standards were also issued by the Managed Funds Association based in the US (2007). Finally, the Alternative Investment Industry Association, based in the UK, issued a guide to sound practice for hedge fund valuation (2007). Basically, all these recommendations tended to cover issues related to sound practices for hedge fund governance, transparency, processes, and methodology related to the valuation of hedge fund portfolios.

Over-the-counter derivatives were also subject to extensive self-regulation. The ISDA, set up in 1985, was the de facto trade association of the global over-the-counter derivatives industry, representing approximately 800 member dealers. It contributed to the development of over-the-counter derivatives markets by developing standardized documentation concerning legal and operational issues (Flanagan 2001). Since 1987, the ISDA has produced standardized 'master' agreements for a broad range of over-the-counter derivatives transactions. In 1994, as a response to the document produced by the G30 and at the suggestion of the SEC, the Derivatives Policy Group was set up by major American banks and investment firms to formulate a code of conduct for trading in derivatives (Mügge 2009). The report *A Framework for Voluntary Oversight of the OTC Derivatives Activities of Securities Firms Affiliates to Promote Confidence and Stability in Financial Markets* (Derivatives Policy Group 1995) took on the G30 recommendations and produced concrete guidelines of practice and disclosure.

The third feature is that the initial reaction of the financial industry to the global financial crisis was to continue to rely on self-regulation by improving existing practices. Subsequently, their lobbying focused on preventing or modifying the most burdensome parts of the new rules. Internationally, in the midst of the crisis, credit rating agencies called for a revision of the IOSCO Code of Conduct, which took place in 2008. In their initial response to consultation about EU rules on credit rating agencies, the main credit rating agencies argued that it would be unduly burdensome for credit rating agencies to maintain different policies and procedures only within the EU to reflect variations made to the IOSCO language. Moreover, differences between EU and IOSCO rules would de facto create new barriers because the main credit rating agencies are based in North America (Committee of European Securities Regulators 2008a).

Afterwards, the main credit rating agencies (Standard and Poor, Moody's, Fitch, A. M. Best) lobbied to exclude provisions that in their opinion would restrict the analytical independence of the credit rating agencies. In their response to consultation,[37] they argued that EU rules should not regulate the substance of credit ratings and the methodology used by credit rating agencies, but rather the principles and processes that a credit rating agency follows to generate a proper rating. This was also stressed by the British and Dutch finance ministries. The criticism concerning the prescriptive nature of the Commission's proposal was also shared by several members of the Committee of European Securities Regulators, regardless of their nationality, because national supervisors were worried about the practical implementation and enforceability of the rules proposed (Committee of European Securities Regulators 2008b).

In the wake of the crisis, under the aegis of the IOSCO, industry associations worked together to produce a single summary standards document—the Hedge Fund Matrix.[38] Hedge fund managers based in the US undertook a process of developing new industry standards under the auspices of the President's Working Group, which had two separate committees: the Asset Managers' Committee, which comprised institutional alternative asset managers whose first task was to develop guidelines that define best practices for the hedge fund industry (Asset Managers' Committee 2009); and the Investors Committee.

Hedge funds managers initially opposed their inclusion within the perimeter of EU legislation. They argued that they had themselves been negatively affected by the crisis, which had been caused by other financial (regulated) institutions, such as banks and mortgage lenders. If anything, hedge funds had been part of the solution and not the problem (Alternative Investment Management Association 2008). Afterwards, they focused their lobbying on the issue of equivalence between EU and US rules, third-country access, and international harmonization. Industry associations echoed the concern raised by the American Treasury Secretary with reference to the third-country

[37] <https://circabc.europa.eu/faces/isp/extension/wai/navigation/container.isp> (accessed Mar. 2014).

[38] <http://www.hedgefundmatrix.com> (accessed Aug. 2009).

provisions, pointing out the potential protectionist effects of EU rules and the risk of retaliatory action in non-EU jurisdictions (*Financial Times*, 13 May 2010). According to the Alternative Investment Management Association, the 'directive makes it so difficult and costly for non-EU funds and managers to access the EU market that it is clearly protectionist in effect, if not in intent' (Alternative Investment Management Association 2009). The uncertainty also hit offshore centres, such as the Cayman Islands. For the first time, the Channel Islands of Jersey and Guernsey established a diplomatic mission in Brussels to articulate their concerns to EU policy-makers (Pagliari 2013).

In the market for over-the-counter derivatives, in April 2009, ISDA adapted its Master Agreement, introducing the 'Big Bang protocol' with the objective of improving contractual standardization within CDS markets. The Big Bang protocol built into the Master Agreement used by all the ISDA members the compulsory requirement that parties to certain types of CDS contracts should engage in the auction process if a credit event occurs on the basis of a specified timetable, whereby the final settlement would take place within 120 days (Morgan 2010).

Furthermore, when European regulators requested from market participants improved infrastructure in over-the-counter derivatives credit markets, Eurex clearing[39] announced the creation of a European over-the-counter central counterparty, with initial focus on credit derivatives. The European over-the-counter central counterparty was to deliver central clearing services for credit index products that were bilaterally over-the-counter traded so far and registered in the Depository Trust and Clearing Corporation's trade information warehouse (Eurex Clearing 2008). Afterward, when the momentum in favour of regulation was clear, industry focused its lobbying on specific aspects of regulation in the EU and the US. For example, in the US, the financial industry claimed that 'It supports the aims of Dodd-Frank; it opposes only some details of the law and the rules being crafted to implement it.'[40]

Last but not least, there were diversified preferences in the financial industry, not so much along national lines, as in the case of banking, as amongst different categories of actors. In particular, the financial entities or instruments directly affected by the new rules were far more concerned than other (indirectly affected) financial players. The negotiations on the Market for Financial Instruments Directive pitted stock exchanges (which had much to lose from the abolition of the 'concentration' rule) against systematic

[39] It is one of the largest clearing houses in Europe. Eurex Clearing is a wholly owned subsidiary of Eurex Frankfurt AG and is jointly operated by Deutsche Börse AG and SIX Swiss Exchange: <http://deutsche-boerse.com/dbag/dispatch/en/kir/gdb_navigation_other_languages/ru/trading/20_clearing/50_eurex_clearing> (accessed May 2011).

[40] <http://www.bloomberg.com/news/2012-04-17/derivatives-lobby-has-u-s-regulators-on-the-run.html> (accessed May 2012).

internalizers, i.e. large investment banks. However, even stock exchanges and investment banks did not form two coherent blocs (see Mügge 2010).[41] In the case of hedge funds in the EU, Undertakings for Collective Investment in Transferable Securities were eager to extend the perimeter of regulation to alternative investment funds managers, which competed with them for some business (Woll 2013).

The European Market Infrastructure regulating opened a dispute between 'silos exchanges' and their competitors, which attempted to seize this opportunity to push through interoperability requirements. The 'location policy' of central counterparties in the EU also divided the industry, pitting the central counterparties located outside the euro-zone, in particular in the UK, against those in the euro-zone. Regulators became involved in this dispute and the UK government brought the ECB before the European Court of Justice. The *Financial Times* reported 'ferocious lobbying' from securities exchanges, investment banks, and companies that use over-the-counter derivatives to be excluded from clearing requirements (13 Sept. 2010). Companies on both sides of the Atlantic argued that being forced to use clearing would drain cash and prevent legitimate hedging of business risk.[42]

All in all, prior to the crisis, rating agencies, hedge funds, and over-the-counter derivatives managed to escape national or international rules. Industry self-regulation was in line with the prevailing regulatory approaches in the main financial jurisdictions, first and foremost in the US and the UK. Those who supported regulation were divided on the specific content of the new rules. After the crisis, at least in the short term, the financial industry was on the back foot, and so were the jurisdictions where the crisis originated (the US) or that were badly hit by the crisis (the UK had by far the largest banking rescue plan in Europe). Financial regulation became politicized, attracting considerable political attention. Industry was no longer able to prevent regulation in the US and the EU, though in the medium term it successfully opposed the most prescriptive (i.e. costly) parts of the new regulation. Industry also tried to minimize divergences between EU and US rules that would have increased compliance costs and unlevelled the playing field (of course, except when the unlevelled playing field was in their favour, as in the case of exemptions from derivatives clearing).

[41] E.g. the Federation of European Stock Exchanges was unable to reach a cohesive position and so was the European Banking Federation.

[42] Bloomberg warned that the derivatives industry was 'squeezing Washington like a python' with a view to controlling the tone and thrust of derivatives regulation: <http://www.bloomberg.com/news/2012-04-17/derivatives-lobby-has-u-s-regulators-on-the-run.html> (accessed Jan. 2013).

Conclusion

Preliminary empirical results from the congruence procedures largely support the theoretical predictions put forward in Chapter 2. Until the 2000s, the EU had a weak regulatory capacity in securities markets. In that period, the EU mostly downloaded the IOSCO principles and passively cross-loaded US regulatory templates in securities trading. With the Lamfalussy Directives, the EU reformed its regulation of securities trading. Afterwards, it was better able to resist passive cross-loading from the US, for example settling EU–US regulatory disputes on more favourable terms for the EU than in the past (Posner 2009a). Despite the completion of the FSAP, certain financial activities remained unregulated in the EU, and were included within the perimeter of EU regulation only after the global financial crisis.

The US had a strong regulatory capacity in securities trading. Hence, it was able to upload some of its regulatory templates to the IOSCO in the 1990s. However, prior to the global financial crisis, the US had weak (or no) regulatory templates on rating agencies, hedge funds, and derivatives. Lacking domestic regulatory templates on these activities, neither the US nor the EU were able to upload their domestic rules as international standards. Industry self-regulation prevailed prior to the global financial crisis.

The temporal dimension—i.e. the sequencing between domestic and international standard-setting—is important in several ways. In the case of securities trading, the US enjoyed a first-mover advantage. The content of several IOSCO documents in the 1990s were mostly uploaded by the US, which also cross-loaded its securities trading template to the EU. Only in the 2000s was the EU able to achieve significant concessions from the SEC, including the prospect of mutual recognition. On rating agencies, hedge funds, and over-the-counter derivatives, neither the US nor the EU enjoyed a first-mover advantage prior to the crisis. After the crisis, the EU seemed to be keen to reap the benefits of first mover, shaping the emerging international rules according to EU templates. US regulators were also spurred into action. Therefore, the EU and US competed and to some extent cooperated in the shaping of global financial rules after the crisis.

The US–UK alliance on several issues weakened the EU position in international fora. Regulators from the US and the UK shared a light-touch regulatory approach to financial services. Opposition from the UK was an important factor in slowing down the development of EU regulatory templates on rating agencies and hedge funds. The UK was instead fully supportive of the Lamfalussy Directives with a view to promoting market integration.

Market power, i.e. the size of the domestic or regional market, is a background factor that provides the EU with potential influence in shaping the rules for global finance. In the 2000s, the SEC could no longer take a unilateralist approach to securities regulation because its market power was declining (see Table 4.2):

Table 4.2. EU–US market size in securities trading (values are in billions)

	2008	2009	2010	2011	2012	Sources
US ($)	**70,085**	**46,735**	**47,953**	**48,242**	**39,225**	WFE
US ($)	**1,194,791**	**840,825**	**1,025,926**	**1,121,306**	**849,791**	WFE*
EU (€)	**647,226**	**528,371**	**509,135**	**568,963**	**655,259**	FESE*
EU (€)	**36,922**	**28,907**	**35,500**	**40,275**	**35,701**	ECB
Germany	3,737	1,985	2,066	1,868	1,302	ECB
France	2,041	1,148	1,229	1,281	928	ECB
Italy (total)	2,634	2,354	2,510	2,444	2,120	ECB
Borsa Italiana SpA	1,325	1,010	1,069	1,013	902	ECB
TLX SpA	25	65	n/a	n/a	n/a	ECB
MTI Wholesale Market (government securities)	873	728	880	868	568	ECB
MTI BONDVISION	396	549	560	561	644	ECB
UK	11,643	7,610	7,858	6,667	7,711	ECB

* Figures of the World Federation of Exchanges (WFE) and Federation of European Stock Exchanges (FESE) correspond to the value of trades in equities, bonds, and other securities, including derivatives.

Note: The ECB figures do not include derivatives trading.

Table 4.3. EU–US market size in derivatives

Instrument	Measure	Euro share (%)	US share (%)	Source
Interest rate swaps	Notional amounts outstanding	36	34	BIS
	Gross market value	27	56	BIS
OTC equity derivatives[a]	Notional amounts outstanding	45	23	BIS and ECB
	Gross market value	40	23	BIS and ECB
Credit default swaps (CDS)	Market turnover	39	59	CLS and ECB
OTC FX derivatives	Notional amounts outstanding	21	42	BIS
	Gross market value	20	40	BIS
Repo market[b]	Repo contracts outstanding	47	45	Federal Reserve, Bank of New York, ECB, ICMA

[a] These numbers are based on an imperfect estimate using the euro area share of EU stock market capitalization. In general, derivatives contracts on European equities can in principle be written in non-European currencies. In the absence of better data, these are the best available estimates (ECB 2009).

[b] Only the repo markets for the US dollar, the pound sterling, and the euro are included (ECB 2009)

Nominal or notional amounts outstanding are defined as the gross nominal or notional value of all deals concluded and not yet settled on the reporting date. Nominal or notional amounts outstanding provide a measure of market size and a reference from which contractual payments are determined in derivatives markets. However, such amounts are generally not those truly at risk. Gross market values provide a more accurate measure of the scale of financial risk transfer taking place in derivatives markets.

US investors bought significant amounts of foreign securities and foreign issuers no longer sought offerings in the US in order to raise capital (Karmel 2007). In contrast, the EU was in the process of completing its single financial market.

The market size for credit rating agencies is hard to define because the US is home to the main credit rating agencies, but the ratings of these agencies are used worldwide. In the EU, the main US-headquartered credit rating agencies operate with subsidiaries mainly based in London. The market size for hedge funds is also difficult to determine because the US hosts the majority of alternative investment fund managers, but the funds are domicilated overseas, and many of them are active in Europe (see Table 4.4). About half of over-the-counter credit derivatives amounts (48 per cent) and over-the-counter equity derivatives amounts (59 per cent) are traded in Europe (see Table 4.3), whereas in the US 41 per cent of over-the-counter credit derivatives amounts and 21 per cent of over-the-counter equity derivatives amounts are traded. London is by far the main centre for over-the-counter derivatives trading in the EU.

Overall, market power is a necessary but not a sufficient condition for EU influence in global standard-setting in securities markets. In rating agencies, hedge funds, and over-the-counter derivatives, the EU had a considerable

Table 4.4. Mapping of the hedge fund industry by domicile and location of managers (end 2004)

	Domicile of hedge funds									
	% of total					Capital under management, % of total				
Location of hedge fund managers	EU	US	Offshore centres	Other	Total	EU	US	Offshore centres	Other	Total
EU	7	1	16	.	23	8	.	18	.	27
US	1	33	21	.	54	1	23	29	.	53
Offshore centres	1	.	13	.	14	1	.	12	.	13
Other	1	.	5	2	8	1	.	6	1	7
Total	9	34	55	2	100	11	24	64	1	100

Source: Garbaravicius and Dierick (2005), Table 5, 17.

Notes: The shaded areas refer to the shares of EU hedge funds. Only funds with reported (estimated) capital under management. The term 'EU hedge funds' refers to funds based (domiciled) in the EU and/or with manager residing in the EU, which may not necessarily invest exclusively in the EU markets. This definition excludes only hedge funds that are managed from outside the EU and not domiciled in the EU. In this way, the definition also captures funds that are domiciled in the EU but managed from outside the EU, which might therefore be labelled as non-European funds (Garbaravicius and Dierick (2005), 11).

market but no regulatory templates to upload or actively cross-load prior to the crisis. After the EU increased its regulatory capacity in these fields, it was better positioned to negotiate *vis-à-vis* the US. At any rate, as some European policy-makers put it, they were keen to regulate these activities on one of the two largest markets worldwide, as a first step towards international regulation.

5

The EU and Global Insurance Regulation

The regulatory capacity of the EU in insurance was limited until the early 2000s. Following the FSAP, the EU set in place common regulatory templates for reinsurance and solvency requirements without waiting for international standards. Unlike in banking and securities markets, the US did not have a strong regulatory capacity in insurance, which is a state competence, not a federal competence. Hence, the US authorities have been less well equipped to influence global insurance regulation.

The main international standard-setting body is the International Association of Insurance Supervisors (IAIS), which was established later than its counterparts in banking and securities. Embryonic international solvency requirements began to be discussed in the 2000s and the process is ongoing. In these international negotiations, the EU was able to upload some of its regulatory templates because its member states had already reached an agreement at the EU level on the Reinsurance Directive and the Solvency II Directive. In bilateral negotiations with third countries, especially the US, the EU attempted to cross-load parts of these pieces of legislation.

The Development of EU Regulatory Capacity in Insurance

In the EU, prior to the FSAP, insurance markets were mostly fragmented along national lines and regulatory harmonization was limited (Story and Walter 1997). After the Plan and the Lamfalussy reform, the EU substantially strengthened its regulatory capacity in insurance (see Table 5.1). The European Commission, and the main member states, first and foremost the UK, were the main promoters of this leap forward.

Table 5.1. The building up of EU regulatory capacity in insurance in the 2000s

Policy entrepreneur	Preferences of the large member states	Industry preferences	Regulatory templates—content
UK, Commission	Similar preferences on EU rules (large member states are home to reinsurers)	Reinsurers in the main member states support EU rules	*Reinsurance (2002)* - single passport - no collaterals - equivalence (potential cross-loading)
UK, Commission	Similar preferences on EU rules (large member states are home to large insurance groups) NB small member states oppose group provisions	Support of large insurance groups in the main member states No opposition from small insurers (exemptions)	*Solvency II (2007)* - single passport - solvency requirements - equivalence clauses - some uploading and cross-loading

The Institutional Framework for Insurance Regulation in the EU

The Insurance Committee, created in 1992, was an advisory body to the European Commission, but it never acquired a high profile, unlike the Banking Advisory Committee. In 2004, as part of the Lamfalussy reform, this committee was replaced by the European Insurance and Occupational Pensions Committee, a level 2 committee in the Lamfalussy architecture. The members of the European Insurance and Occupational Pensions Committee are appointed from the insurance supervisory and regulatory authorities of the member states.

The level 3 Lamfalussy committee, the Committee of European Insurance and Occupational Pensions Supervisors, was established in 2004 in Frankfurt. In 2012, it was transformed into the European Insurance and Occupational Pensions Authority. The Committee (later the Authority) is composed of high-level representatives from the insurance and occupational pension supervisory authorities of member states.[1] In the Committee, each member state had the same number of voting rights as in the Council of Ministers. Decisions were taken by consensus, except when giving advice to the Commission. In that case, if no consensus could be reached, decisions could be taken by qualified majority, identifying and elaborating the opinion of the dissenting individual members. With the transformation of the Committee into an Authority, the Board of Supervisors has become the main decision-making body, composed of representatives of the supervisory

[1] In countries where insurance undertakings and pension funds are supervised by separate authorities, two members may be designated, one from each authority.

authorities of the member states.[2] The decisions of the Board of Supervisors are taken by a simple majority of its members and each member has one vote. Regulatory standards are adopted by the Board of Supervisors on the basis of a qualified majority of its members, as defined in the Treaty on European Union.

Regulatory Templates in Insurance in the EU

The 'first generation' of EU directives on insurance, which dated back to the early 1970s, took a sub-sectoral approach, focusing on life insurance, non-life insurance, motor insurance, reinsurance, etc. Not until 2007 did the Solvency II Directive eliminate this sub-sectoral approach, setting solvency requirements for all types of insurers. The directives issued in the 1970s and early 1980s dealt with the taking up and pursuit of the insurance business, and the abolition of restrictions on freedom of establishment, subject to host-country control. The 'second-generation' insurance directives issued in the second part of the 1980s permitted cross-border insurance business, subject to host control. The 'third-generation' insurance directives issued in the 1990s established the single licence for insurance companies, subject to home country control, coupled with mutual recognition of 'technical provisions',[3] which varied considerably amongst member states (Story and Walter 1997: 265).

The FSAP envisaged two main pieces of legislation dealing with issues that had been deliberately left outside the scope of EU rules in the past, namely reinsurance and solvency requirements. Financial conglomerates, including insurance businesses, were regulated by the Financial Conglomerates Directive issued in 2002.

The Reinsurance Directive

Reinsurance is 'insurance for insurers', i.e. the practice whereby an insurance company (the insurer) transfers a portion of its risks to another (the reinsurer). The main reasons for the lack of a harmonized regulatory framework for reinsurance at the EU level prior to 2005 were three-fold. First, reinsurance business takes place between insurance companies, and does not directly involve consumers (policy-holders). Hence, the assumption was that professional insurers were less in need of EU legislative protection than the customers of direct insurers. Second, the regulation of reinsurance varied considerably

[2] The board also includes the chairperson of the European Insurance and Occupational Pensions Authority, representatives of the European Commission, the European Systemic Risk Board, the European Banking Authority, and the European Securities Markets Authority.

[3] 'Technical provisions' are the amounts that an insurer needs to hold in order to meet its expected future obligations on insurance contracts.

across the EU. Until the early 2000s, professional reinsurers were not subject to any supervision in Belgium, Ireland, and Greece. Germany, France, and the Netherlands applied elements of their direct insurance supervisory regime to reinsurers. A reduced licensing regime existed in Austria, Italy, Spain, and Sweden, where only the latter two imposed solvency requirements. Only in the UK, Denmark, Finland, and Portugal were reinsurers subject to the comprehensive regulation and supervision applied to direct insurers, including licensing and ongoing financial supervision (Commission of the European Communities 2002). Third, any EU regulation of reinsurers was hampered by the fact that there was no agreement on international accounting standards in the insurance sector (interview, Basel, 28 Nov. 2008).

The Reinsurance Directive adopted by the EU in 2005 changed the status quo, setting in place a harmonized EU regime for the regulation of reinsurers. The Directive had three main rationales. The first objective was to establish a 'single passport' for reinsurance companies, whereby they would be supervised by the competent authorities in their 'home' country, setting harmonized EU rules for supervision. The lack of a harmonized EU regulatory framework created barriers to cross-border reinsurance services. For example, collateral requirements for outstanding claims against reinsurers were compulsory in some member states, such as France, but not in the majority of member states. Moreover, reinsurers had to comply with different administrative burdens in member states and this represented an additional cost for the industry.[4]

Second, the Directive was intended to contribute to reinforcing international financial stability—an issue of significant concern in international fora. For example, the International Monetary Fund (IMF) used its Financial Sector Assessment Programme reviews of member states to reiterate the need for legislation in this field (Commission of the European Communities 2004a). Amongst other things, international bodies pointed out that the regulation of insurance and reinsurance worldwide had not kept pace with financial and technological innovation, such as the increasing use of derivatives and other complex hedging instruments.

Third, the Directive was expected to strengthen EU bargaining power in international fora and *vis-à-vis* the US. To begin with, the IAIS, of which the member states of the EU and the Commission were members, was in the process of undertaking a project concerning the regulation of reinsurance. Hence, the Reinsurance Directive was expected to enable the EU member states to present a unified voice in international fora, in particular shaping

[4] <http://europa.eu/rapid/pressReleasesAction.do?reference=IP/04/513&format=HTML&aged=0&language=EN&guiLanguage=en> (accessed June 2012).

the international regulatory framework under discussion (Commission of the European Communities 2002). The EU also had an outstanding issue about the regulation of EU reinsurers in the US. New EU legislation in this field could provide the EU with extra bargaining power *vis-à-vis* the US.

The Reinsurance Directive built on the regime introduced by the third-generation insurance directives. It basically extended to reinsurance companies the system for the authorization and supervision of an insurance undertaking by the member state in which it had its head office, so-called 'home country control'. Such authorization represented a true 'single passport', which enabled reinsurers to carry out their business anywhere in the EU, either by establishing themselves in other member states, or by providing services directly from their home or another member state. This had long been the case for primary insurers.[5]

In order to implement such 'home country control' while ensuring adequate EU-wide protection of reinsurance customers (who are mostly direct insurers), the Directive set out essential provisions for the supervision of reinsurance to be applied by all the member states. The Directive outlined a licensing regime for reinsurance undertakings and the conditions that reinsurers had to meet before a licence could be granted. It also set out prudential rules for the supervision of reinsurance undertakings, including rules on the establishment of technical provisions and rules on the investment of assets covering those technical provisions (Norton Rose Fulbright 2007). One of the most important and controversial aspects was the abolition of national regimes that obliged a reinsurer to pledge assets (collaterals) to cover unearned premiums and outstanding claims provisions of an insurance undertaking.[6] This regime was in place in some countries.

France and Portugal prescribed these collaterals in the form of letters of credit or bonds in their national legislation. Such requirements were viewed in France as a critical means of exercising insurance supervision. In contrast, the industry and the Commission reiterated that the purpose of the Directive was to introduce effective direct supervision at the EU level and therefore to eliminate the need for costly statutory collateral requirements, at least within the EU. The industry also argued that the collateral requirement tied up capital without justification (*Reinsurance Magazine*, 2005). In the end, the European Parliament and the member states in the Council agreed that such requirements should be phased out as part of the Reinsurance Directive (*Financial Times*, 30 Mar. 2005).

[5] <http://europa.eu/rapid/pressReleasesAction.do?reference=IP/04/513&format=HTML&aged=0&language=EN&guiLanguage=en> (accessed June 2012).

[6] <http://europa.eu/rapid/pressReleasesAction.do?reference=IP/04/513&format=HTML&aged=0&language=EN&guiLanguage=en> (accessed May 2012).

The Commission officially put forward the legislative proposal in 2004, and the European Parliament and the Council of Ministers approved it at first reading in late 2005. The fact that this piece of legislation was adopted in less than two years suggests that the main member states and the Parliament were happy with the draft. The UK, which hosts Lloyds, one of the largest reinsurance markets in the world, was the main sponsor of the Directive. Indeed, in the European Parliament, the rapporteur for the Directive was the British Member of the European Parliament (MEP), Peter Skinner. The other large member states, which also host thriving insurance industries, supported the harmonization of EU rules and the creation of a single passport. Of the world's largest eight reinsurers, three are based in Germany, one in France, and one in the UK. Only two are American.

The Solvency II Directive

The Solvency II Directive was one of the main outstanding items of the FSAP. The solvency margin is the amount of capital that an insurance undertaking is required to hold against unforeseen events. Such requirements have been in place in the EU since the 1970s and were amended for life insurers by the Solvency I Directive in 2002, which raised the minimum guarantee fund. The Solvency II Directive had a much wider scope: it applied to all life and non-life insurance undertakings and reinsurance undertakings, albeit small mutual undertakings and some small (non-mutual) insurance undertakings were exempted.

The main objective of the Solvency II Directive was to set appropriate requirements for solvency margins, taking into account the true risk profile of (re)insurance undertakings, with a view to ensuring adequate policyholder protection in all EU member states. The Directive also aimed to increase regulatory harmonization and the convergence of supervisory tools and powers.[7] It was designed to streamline EU legislation, replacing fourteen existing directives regulating insurance services with a single directive.

The new approach was articulated across three pillars, which resemble those of the Basel II accord in banking (see Chapter 3). According to the first pillar of the Solvency II Directive, insurers are required to hold capital against market risk, credit risk, and operational risk. All these types of risk potentially affect insurers' solvency, though they were not covered by the Solvency I legislation. Pillar 1 outlined two capital requirements, which had different purposes and were calibrated accordingly: the Solvency Capital Requirement, which enabled an institution to absorb significant unforeseen losses; and the

[7] <http://europa.eu/rapid/pressReleasesAction.do?reference=IP/07/1060&format=HTML&aged =0&language=EN&guiLanguage=en> (accessed June 2011).

Minimum Capital Requirement, below which supervisory action was triggered (Commission of the European Communities 2004b). The former could not be lower than the latter. Subject to supervisory approval, insurers could use their own internal model to calculate capital requirements.

These concepts were similar to those introduced in the UK by the domestic reform of insurance regulation in 2004 (the so-called 'Tiner reform'). Indeed, the UK was the main promoter of the Solvency II Directive and to some extent was able to upload its domestic insurance templates to the EU level (Quaglia 2011b). Even the terminology used in the UK and EU legislation was the same, with the difference that in the UK the Solvency Capital Requirement is called 'Enhanced Capital Requirement'. This slight change in terminology was introduced during the drafting of the Solvency II Directive for political reasons, i.e. so as not to look too similar to the text of the British legislation (interview, London, 30 Sept. 2008, 23 July 2008).

The second pillar of the Solvency II Directive, consisted of a supervisory review process of the overall financial position of insurance undertakings. Depending on the outcome of the review, supervisors could require additional capital. The scope of the second pillar also related to the harmonization of supervisory activities. The third pillar outlined requirements concerning the disclosure of information, with a view to imposing market discipline on insurance undertakings.

Overall, the reform of the EU framework for insurance regulation and supervision adopted a risk-based, principle-based approach to prudential rules for insurance companies. This approach represented a major change to the domestic regulatory framework for the vast majority of member states, with the notable exception of the UK, which had already adopted a similar framework domestically, without waiting for EU rules. Indeed, the UK, which hosts the largest insurance industry in Europe, was the main promoter of the new Directive, although it was supported also by the other large member states.

The most controversial issue in the Solvency II Directive was the creation of group support and supervision. According to group supervision, a single authority was to be appointed with coordination and decision powers for each insurance group. The group supervisor was given primary responsibility for key aspects of group supervision (group solvency, intragroup transactions, etc.), to be exercised in cooperation and consultation with host supervisors (Commission of the European Communities 2007). Group support concerned capital management by groups, which allowed, under certain conditions, a parent undertaking to use declarations of group support to meet part of the Solvency Capital Requirement of its subsidiaries.

The UK is widely credited for being the crafter of the relevant provisions on group supervision and group support, articulated in a draft document produced by Her Majesty's Treasury and the Financial Services Authority (FSA) in November 2006, and subsequently taken on board by the Commission in its official legislative proposal presented in July 2007 (interviews, Brussels, 9 Apr. 2008; London, 23 July 2008). The other large member states, namely, France, Germany, and Italy which, like the UK and the Netherlands, were home to several large insurance groups (see Comité Européen des Assurances (CEA) 2005), also supported the proposal, as did the main players in the insurance sector.

By contrast, twelve member states, led by Poland and Spain and encompassing several new member states, which mainly hosted subsidiaries and branches of insurance groups, disagreed with the proposed approach (*Financial Times*, 10 June 2008; interviews, Brussels, 9 Apr. 2008; Frankfurt, 10 Sept. 2007). The argument used by those opposing the new regime was that group supervision would substantially reduce the power of the supervisory host authorities to control what happened in their jurisdictions. It was feared by the host countries' authorities that they would be 'left to pick up the pieces if local problems emerged' (*Financial Times*, 19 Mar. 2008). Towards the end of the negotiations, the outcome moved towards the inclusion of group supervision, though with strong limitations on group support.

Although the Commission began a review of insurance regulation in 1999, it proposed the draft legislation in April 2005, outlining three legislative approaches (Commission of the European Communities 2005c). Subsequently, the UK authorities proposed a unified legislative approach, i.e. a single piece of legislation, rather than three pieces as initially proposed by the Commission. The proposal for a unified approach was then followed by the Commission (House of Lords 2008: Ev. 36). The final stage of the negotiations was very much based on trade-offs and horse trading (*Financial Times*, 10 June 2008), whereby provisions for group support and supervision were scaled down.

The Solvency II Directive was expected to have an important external dimension, especially in the US. The Commission and the European Parliament were keen to use it to exert some leverage over US regulators in order to change the way in which EU reinsurers operating in the US were regulated. The main request was the abolition of collateral requirements for 'alien' insurers, which had already been advocated when the Reinsurance Directive was agreed. In this respect, it is worth reporting the key passage of the European Parliament (2008b: 43) report on the Solvency II Directive, prepared by the (British) rapporteur Peter Skinner:

> The proposal will introduce rules on the equivalence of third country solvency regimes, which will have consequences for groups with subsidiaries in or outside of the EU. Equivalence can only be agreed with sovereign Nation States and not parts of such Countries. . . . The Commission shall decide whether the third country solvency regime is equivalent.

The EU model for solvency requirements embodied in the Solvency II Directive was largely uploaded from the national level in the UK to the EU level. It differs widely from the regulatory model in place in the US. EU legislation adopted the concept of 'Enterprise Risk Management' and relied on market valuation of assets and liabilities, whereas in the US the valuation of assets and liabilities was based on principles and rules. Unlike in the US, the EU envisaged the use of the internal models of insurers to calculate capital requirements. Similarly, the EU relied on targeting solvency capital to specific confidence levels; it was not so in the US. EU legislation established group supervision, to be performed by colleges of supervisors, whereas in the US there was no group calculation of solvency requirements or group supervision.[8]

To sum up, the UK and the Commission acted as policy entrepreneurs in the development of the regulatory capacity of the EU in insurance. The main member states shared similar preferences because the configurations of their national insurance industries were similar. In particular, the big insurance players in the main member states were deemed to benefit from the new reinsurance provisions and solvency requirements set by the EU in the 2000s. The smaller insurers got some exemptions, as will be discussed. Smaller member states were appeased by concessions concerning the power of the home supervisory authorities, mostly located in the large member states.

The Regulatory Capacity of the US in Insurance

Domestically, the US has weaker regulatory capacity in insurance than in securities markets and banking because insurance is a state competence in the US, not a federal competence. Moreover, US templates in insurance are in need of modernization. The US has a large domestic insurance market, with limited presence of foreign companies (except for reinsurers), and few US insurers are active abroad. Hence, the US authorities have relatively limited capability and little incentive for international cooperation in this sector.

The Institutional Framework for Insurance Regulation in the US

In the US, each state has an insurance commissioner or an insurance department and insurers are licensed on a state-by-state basis. Generally, an insurer must obtain a licence in any state where it wants to write policies. The National Association of Insurance Commissioners (NAIC) brings together senior state

8 <https://www.kpmg.com/US/en/IssuesAndInsights/ArticlesPublications/Documents/solvency-II.pdf> (accessed Jan. 2010).

officials of the departments that regulate insurance companies, but it is not a federal regulatory body. Indeed, the NAIC, as well as representatives from the US state insurance departments, sit in the IAIS.

The NAIC is often unable to project a unified US position in the IAIS[9] and cannot guarantee uniformity and consistency in the domestic implementation of internationally agreed rules (Singer 2007). By contrast, in securities markets and banking, federal regulators, such as the Securities and Exchange Commission (SEC) and the Federal Reserve, muster a considerable degree of expertise and carry considerable weight (Kapstein 1989; Simmons 2001; Singer 2007). The recent reforms introduced as part of the Dodd Frank Act in Title V 'Insurance', Subtitle A 'Federal Insurance Office', aimed to address some of these shortcomings through the establishment of a Federal Insurance Office, headed by a director appointed by the Secretary of the US Treasury (interview, Washington, Aug. 2011). However, the role of this office is mainly to share information; it does not have regulatory power.

Regulatory Templates in Insurance in the US

While state insurance laws vary, most are based on model laws and regulations developed by the NAIC. Insurance regulation in the US is rather outdated. For this reason, in 2008, the NAIC launched the Solvency Modernization Initiative as a critical self-examination of the United States' insurance solvency regulatory framework.[10] Amongst other things, the modernization programme looked at the IAIS principles to which the NAIC had signed up. 'There are significant linkages between IAIS principles and Solvency II, with NAIC specifically considering enhanced governance, Own Risk Solvency Assessment, supervisory colleges, sharing of information with other regulators, and recalibration of the Risk-Based Capital standards.'[11]

Of particular interest for the EU and EU–US regulatory relations are the provisions for alien (i.e. non-US-headquartered) insurers. The reinsurance capacity in the US can only be satisfied by allowing non-US insurers to assume reinsurance business in the US. In fact, nearly half of US reinsurance premiums are reinsured outside of the US, mostly in Europe (the EU and Switzerland), which has the largest reinsurance industry in the world.[12]

[9] According to the IAIS statute, the NAIC does not have a right to vote; and it may, at any one time, designate up to a maximum of fifteen of its members who may exercise their rights to vote (art. 6.4).

[10] <http://www.naic.org/index_smi.htm> (accessed June 2012).

[11] <https://www.kpmg.com/US/en/IssuesAndInsights/ArticlesPublications/Documents/solvency-II.pdf> (accessed May 2011).

[12] According to the NAIC, more than 4,000 reinsurers from more than 100 countries either assumed premiums or owed recoverables to US insurers in 2004, <http://www.worldmedialaw.com/resources-a-links/29-credit-for-reinsurance-rules> (accessed June 2010).

The main barrier faced by EU reinsurers keen to expand their already significant presence in the US was the requirement to post collateral for the value of their commitments in the markets (US states) where they conduct business (Singer 2007). While each state had a 'credit for reinsurance' law, nearly all were based on the NAIC's Credit for Reinsurance Model Law. The amount of such collateral for the US market was estimated at $50 billion by the Comité Européen des Assurances (European Federation of Insurers) in 2002 (Commission of the European Communities 2004c). Moreover, since insurance regulation is a state competence in the US, EU insurers operating in several US states were subject to different states' rules and procedures for authorization. This regime for non-US reinsurers was seen by foreign companies as putting them at a disadvantage, but was regarded by the US authorities as instrumental to safeguarding the solvency of foreign reinsurers operating in the US.

At the insistence of the EU and after years of deliberation, in 2011 the NAIC amended its Credit for Reinsurance Model Law, permitting the reduction of collaterals posted by 'certified reinsurers' based outside the US (i.e. alien reinsurers). Under the Model Law, the amount of collateral required of certified reinsurers depends on a 'rating' assigned to the reinsurer by a state insurance commissioner. Although the NAIC amended its Model Law, such amendments are not automatically effective in any state. They need to be enacted by the states. Some states, such as New York, Florida, New Jersey, and Indiana, where the activity of foreign reinsurers is relatively high, have amended their laws to allow for reduced collateral. Others have not, and this remains an open issue in the EU–US regulatory relations in insurance.

International Standard-Setting in Insurance

The main international regulatory forum concerning insurance is the IAIS, which was set up in 1994 and has a small secretariat hosted by the Bank for International Settlements (BIS). Unlike its counterparts in banking and securities markets, the IAIS began to issue insurance rules only as late as the 2000s.

The Institutional Framework for International Standard-Setting in Insurance

The IAIS has members from over 190 jurisdictions. In the IAIS, the US is represented by the NAIC and fifty-six jurisdictions. The member states of the EU sit in the IAIS and the Commission participates as observer. Unlike the Basel Committee on Banking Supervision (BCBS), the IAIS hardly ever meets at senior level and does not enjoy the same status as its counterpart in banking. Unlike central bankers and banking supervisors, insurance supervisors do not form a cohesive group with a common professional culture. In some countries, insurance supervision is still carried out by the ministry of finance (or even social affairs), not by an independent (or semi-independent) regulatory agency. Some countries, such as the UK prior to the reform agreed in 2012, have a single supervisory authority for all financial services. In other countries, such as Italy, two insurance supervisory authorities exist, one dealing with insurance and the other specializing in pensions.

International Insurance Regulation: IAIS Standards

Initially, the IAIS was mainly a forum where insurance regulators met to discuss best practice. In 2003, the IAIS adopted the Insurance Core Principles (core principles were also adopted in banking and securities markets, see Chapters 3 and 4). These principles represent a globally accepted framework for the regulation and supervision of the insurance sector and provide the basis for evaluating insurance legislation and supervision across countries. Indeed, they are included amongst the twelve 'Key Standards for Sound Financial Systems' designated by the Financial Stability Board (FSB). The IAIS 'principles', 'standards', and 'guidance papers'[13] elaborate various aspects of the core principles. Since 2007, the IAIS has promoted the signing of a Multilateral Memorandum of Understanding on cooperation and information exchange amongst insurance supervisors. More than thirty supervisory authorities, including ten EU member states and two US states, have signed the memorandum.

In the mid-2000s, the IAIS commenced a major project designed to formulate qualitative and quantitative benchmarks to assess insurer solvency. Three standards on solvency were adopted in October 2008. 'Standard No. 2.1.1 on the structure of regulatory capital requirements', 'Standard No. 2.2.6 on enterprise risk management for capital adequacy and solvency purposes', 'Standard No. 2.2.7 on the use of internal models for regulatory capital purposes'. These documents were subsequently included in the revised 'Insurance Core Principles, Standards, Guidance and Assessment', issued in 2012.[14]

It is remarkable that key topics of the IAIS regulatory agenda from the mid-2000s onwards—namely, 'Enterprise Risk Management', 'structure of regulatory capital'; 'use of internal models'; 'group supervision'; 'mutual

[13] The IAIS website explains that 'principles' deal with fundamental areas of supervision, 'standards' focus on specific issues, and 'guidance papers' are designed to assist supervisors and are an addition to principles and standards.

[14] These standards can be found on <http://www.iaisweb.org/index.cfm?pageID=40> (accessed Dec. 2010).

recognition of supervisory regimes'—very much reflect EU priorities and perspectives, not the US regulatory model. Key concepts of the Solvency II approach (such as enterprise risk management; market valuation of assets and liabilities; technical provisions; calibration of solvency capital to specific confidence levels; choice of internal model or standardized model; group supervision) found their way into IAIS standards and guidelines. The IAIS's guidance paper on principles of group-wide supervision borrowed from the group regime painstakingly negotiated in the Solvency II Directive (*Financial Times*, 10 June 2008).

The IAIS paper on mutual recognition (2008a) provided guidance on cross-border recognition of reinsurance supervision with a view to convincing the US to abolish its regime for alien (non-US) insurers. The purpose of the IAIS guidance was 'to allow a supervisor to recognize the value of the supervision exercised by another jurisdiction and thus remove significant amounts of unnecessary regulatory and supervisory requirements for reinsurers' (2008a: 1). Reportedly, the Commission and the UK representatives were instrumental in pushing this issue onto the IAIS agenda, given the fact that the main international reinsurers are headquartered in the EU, first and foremost in London.

The IAIS standards agreed in late 2008 contained rules—such as the prescribed capital requirement and the minimum capital requirement, the enterprise risk management framework, the own risk and solvency assessment; the use of an internal model for regulatory capital purposes—which were deliberately lifted from the Solvency II framework, even though some of the names were slightly changed in order not to look too similar to the EU legislation (IAIS 2008b). For example, 'Prescribed Capital Requirement' was used in the IAIS standards instead of 'Solvency Capital Requirement', a term that is used in the Solvency II Directive (interviews, London, 30 Sept. 2008). Moreover, a guidance paper on principles of group-wide supervision was also issued by the IAIS in October 2008 (IAIS 2008c). The paper was a first step in the IAIS's work on the development of global standards and guidance on group-wide supervision and it borrowed from the group regime proposed and painstakingly negotiated in the Solvency II Directive. Some of these provisions were also included in the core principles issued in 2012 (IAIS 2012).

The European Commission actively participated in the preparation of the rules for the new international regime for capital requirements in the insurance sector. Together with the EU member states participating in the work of the IAIS, the Commission weighed in to make sure that the new framework would resemble as much as possible the Solvency II regime being introduced in the EU (interviews, Frankfurt, 10 Sept. 2007; Brussels, 9 Apr. 2008). Moreover, certain European policy-makers, in particular the British, played an important role in chairing and driving discussions forward in the relevant IAIS subgroups (House of Lords 2008: Ev. 8–9).[15]

The US did not oppose the new solvency regime in the IAIS. However, it was not a strong supporter either because the proposed regulatory framework was different from that already in existence in the US. The negotiating position of the US was complicated, and somewhat weakened, by the fact that there was no federal supervisory authority able to represent it (interviews Basel, 19 Nov. 2008; Singer 2007; see also US Senate Committee on Banking 2008a). Moreover, the US regulatory templates were outdated: not only did they not provide suitable models for international rules, but the US authorities were seeking ways to modernize them.

The Cross-Loading of Insurance Regulation Between the EU and the US

In insurance, there has been a long-standing dispute between the EU and the US concerning the treatment of 'alien'[16] (i.e. non-US) insurers in the US. One of the reasons put forward by the US for the maintenance of collateral requirements for EU reinsurers operating in the US was that there was no harmonized EU legislation on this and some EU member states did not regulate the reinsurance business at all (US Senate Committee on Banking 2008a). At the same time, US reinsurers operating in the EU could not benefit from a single passport to conduct business throughout the EU and had to comply with different national legislation.

Many European associations and member states, in particular those that are home countries of large reinsurers operating in the US, first and foremost, Germany, the UK, and France,[17] believed that harmonized EU rules could give European reinsurers a strong negotiating tool for persuading foreign regulators (for example, the US) that they should be considered adequately supervised (*Financial Times,* 30 Mar. 2005). This move, however, encountered stiff resistance from regulators and industry in the US. Besides the somewhat protectionist undertones of the US rules on alien insurers, another problem was that, as argued by the Reinsurance Association of America, the US reinsurance industry was reluctant to support any proposal that would permit

[15] Interviews, Frankfurt, 10 Sept. 2007; Brussels, 28 Mar. 2007; Brussels, 9 Apr. 2008; London, 23 July 2008; Rome, 23 June 2008; Rome, 27 July 2008.

[16] Whereas 'foreign' insurers are subsidiaries or branches of a US insurer domiciled in another state.

[17] In the EU, Germany has a dominant position in reinsurance with companies such as Munich Re, Hannover Re, and Allianz Re. Lloyds is the largest UK writer of reinsurance, and SCOR together with Axa Re are the largest French reinsurers (Commission of the European Communities 2004d).

non-US reinsurers to assume reinsurance risks from US cedants on the basis of a single licence through mutual recognition, while US reinsurers continued to be constrained by a fifty-state regulatory system (Reinsurance Association of America 2000). The problem was the lack of mutual recognition between US states. These issues were often discussed in the Reinsurance Subcommittee of the IAIS.

During the negotiation of the Reinsurance Directive, the Council of Ministers unanimously decided that there was no need to introduce specific rules on the treatment of non-EU reinsurers operating in a member state through a branch or on a cross-border basis. The Council agreed with the proposal put forward by the Commission that third-country reinsurers should not be granted more favourable treatment than domestic ones. This meant that each member state would be free to impose a different set of regulatory requirements to third-country reinsurers. EU-based subsidiaries of non-EU insurers, however, would be able to fully benefit from the EU passport (Norton Rose Fulbright 2007).

The hope was that the new EU regime for reinsurers would put pressure on the US to drop the collateral requirements imposed on non-American reinsurers.[18] The European Commission had made this point on several occasions, but its position was undermined by the fact that, prior to the Reinsurance Directive, France and Portugal imposed similar requirements nationally (*Financial Times*, 30 Mar. 2005). The Reinsurance Directive harmonized EU rules in this crucial respect.

When the Reinsurance Directive was adopted, the European Commission was urged by some MEPs, first and foremost the rapporteur of the Reinsurance Directive, to bring the case before the World Trade Organization (WTO) and if necessary to seek trade sanctions against the US if the latter did not abolish the collateral requirements for foreign (including EU) reinsurers operating in the US (*Financial Times*, 23 May 2005). The elimination of the collateral requirement was a key request that the EU pursued in the WTO Doha Development Agenda negotiations on financial services and this issue has regularly been raised by the EU in the WTO context.[19]

The EU also used the issue of equivalence under the Solvency II Directive to put pressure on the US to change its regime on 'alien' insurers, subsidiaries, or branches of non-US insurers (interviews, Brussels, 28 Mar. 2007; *National Underwriter*, 6 Aug. 2007, *Reactions*, July 2005; see also the letter by the MEP

[18] Some industry experts estimate that as much as $40 billion (€32 billion, £22 billion) is deposited in the US by European reinsurers (*Financial Times*, 23 May 2005). Lloyds, the London reinsurance market, has $7 billion (£3.8 billion) of collateral tied up in the US (*The Times*, 24 May 2005).

[19] <http://madb.europa.eu/madb/barriers_details.htm?barrier_id=060127&version=6> (accessed Sept. 2011).

Peter Skinner, the rapporteur of the Solvency II Directive, *Financial Times*, 9 Nov. 2007). Solvency II rules on third countries stipulate that:

> The supervisory authorities concerned shall verify whether the insurance and reinsurance undertakings, the parent undertaking of which has its head office outside the Community, are subject to supervision, by a third-country supervisory authority, which is equivalent to that provided for in Solvency II... The verification shall be carried out by the supervisory authority which would be the group supervisor... unless the Commission had concluded previously in respect of the equivalence of the third country concerned.... (Council of the European Union and European Parliament 2009)

In the absence of equivalent supervision, member states shall apply to insurance and reinsurance undertakings Solvency II provisions on a solo basis, not as part of a group. Hence, foreign insurers would not be able to benefit from lower solvency requirements deriving from being part of an insurance group. In this respect, there were two open issues for the US, the first being the possibility that the entire fifty-state system in the US would not be deemed 'equivalent' to the one-stop approach based on a passport system for insurance companies operating in the EU (*Wall Street Journal,* 16 Apr. 2008). The second issue was the disadvantageous treatment of alien (EU) insurers in the US, which was not equivalent to the EU treatment of reinsurers.

The Commission developed a transitional regime for Solvency II equivalence for third countries which either have a risk-based regime similar to Solvency II or are willing and committed to move towards such a risk-based regime over a predefined period. In February 2012, the Commission wrote to the European Insurers and Occupational Pension Authority, indicating the list of third countries with which it had informally discussed a potential transitional regime for third-country equivalence under Solvency II, namely Australia, Chile, Hong Kong, Israel, Mexico, Singapore, South Africa, plus Brazil, China, Turkey (Faull 2012). The inclusion in the transitional regime was subject to a Commission Decision to be taken in 2013.

In 2012, the EU and US set in place a regulatory dialogue in insurance involving the European Commission, European Insurance and Occupational Pension Authority, the US NAIC, and the Federal Insurance Office of the US Department of the Treasury. Prior to that date, the US had felt no need for such a dialogue with the EU, further evidence that EU regulatory templates in insurance had important implications for the US. The official objective of the project was to gather a better understanding and identify important characteristics of insurance regimes in the US and the EU.[20] The (unstated) objective

[20] <http://ec.europa.eu/internal_market/insurance/solvency/latest/index_en.htm> (accessed Sept. 2011).

was to facilitate the decision on equivalence of US insurance regulation to be taken by the EU, or, to be precise, by the Commission, following the advice of the European Insurance and Occupational Pension Authority.

The Insurance Industry and Global Insurance Regulation

Two main features are noteworthy concerning the preferences and lobbying of the insurance industry in international insurance regulation. In the EU, industry preferences, in particular those of the big insurers and reinsurers headquartered in the large member states, were rather similar. These insurers were deemed to benefit from the Reinsurance Directive and the Solvency II Directive (CEA 2007; *Financial Times,* 4 June 2008) and this facilitated reaching an agreement on these rules at the EU level and the uploading and cross-loading of these rules internationally. This is not to say that there were no conflicts of interest within the EU insurance industry.

The main division was between the Comité Européen des Assurances (CEA), which represents the European insurance and reinsurance industry through national insurance associations on one side and, on the other side, the Association Internationale des Sociétés d'Assurances Mutuelle and Association of European Cooperative and Mutual Insurers, which represents mutual insurers and co-operative insurance companies. Despite the different characteristics of their members, which cover different segments of the insurance market (in the reinsurance markets there are only big players), the EU was able to avoid open conflicts and/or standstill through exemptions, proportionality clauses, and similar legislative provisions.

Another intra-EU division that concerned regulators, not so much industry, was between countries that were home supervisors of large insurance groups[21] and the host supervisors, mostly located in the new member states. The concept of group supervisor was heavily backed up by large international insurance groups, such as Aviva, Axa, Allianz, Generali, Fortis (*Financial Times*, 10 June 2008), which have headquarters in the large member states and in the Netherlands and Belgium. Policy-makers in member states in which these big players were located therefore supported the new EU rules.

Lobbying from the insurance industry, more precisely the big EU players, was instrumental in the cross-loading of EU rules to the US, which would produce immediate tangible effects for these companies. Several European insurers are active in the US and mostly dominate the reinsurance market

[21] The largest European insurance groups and their turnover (€ billions) in 2006 were: (1) Allianz (DE) 91; (2) Axa (FR) 75; (3) Prudential (UK) 74; (4) Generali (IT) 64; (5) Aviva (UK) 60; (6) ING (NL) 55; (7) Aegon (NL) 49; and (8) Legal & General (UK) 48 (CEA 2007).

internationally.[22] Since 1999, Lloyds and the London market have been lobbying for the NAIC to revisit this issue.[23] European reinsurance leaders such as Hannover Re and Swiss Re spoke out against the collateral requirements and so did the CEA, with backing from the International Underwriting Association.[24]

In the US, reinsurers favoured the status quo, as reflected in the position of the Reinsurance Association of America. This Association argued that state regulators cannot be expected to know the intricacies of accounting systems and regulatory schemes used throughout the world to determine the financial strength of non-US insurers (the president of the Association, Frank Nutter, presented these arguments to Congress in June 2002).[25] However, US insurers that used EU-headquartered insurers stood to benefit in terms of lower reinsurance costs from the abolition of US collateral rules.[26] Moreover, US insurers operating in Europe were concerned about potential counter-measures by the EU. Lobbying from these US insurers as well as from EU-based insurers provided extra ammunition to the EU.

On solvency requirements, the EU and US insurance industries were subject to different regulatory models, hence they did not share the same preferences about the most suitable approach for international solvency standards. The solvency framework based on the template elaborated by the EU Directive was seen as state of the art, giving 'European companies a head start in the global economy', whereas the US 'was stuck with highly fragmented insurance regulation' (*Financial Times,* 11 July 2007). According to the European Commission the new rules would allow large insurance groups to save up to 40 per cent of their solvency requirements, freeing vast sums up for profitable investments (*Financial Times,* 11 July 2007), so there were concerns about the competitive impact of Solvency II for US insurers (*National Underwriter,* 27 Oct. 2008). For some policy-makers and industry participants in the US, the new EU prudential regime provided a convincing regulatory template

[22] The main world reinsurers ranked by gross premiums written in 2010 are as follows (US$ billions): (1) Munich Reinsurance Company 31; (2) Swiss Reinsurance Company Limited 24; (3) Hannover Rueckversicherung AG 15; (4) Berkshire Hathaway Inc. 14; (5) Lloyds 12,977; (6) SCOR S.E. (French) 8; (7) Reinsurance Group of America Inc. 7; (8) Allianz S.E.5: <http://www.insurance-networking.com/news/Swiss_re_reinsurance_munich_re_a_m_best_premiums-28767-1.html> (accessed May 2011).

[23] <http://www.worldmedialaw.com/resources-a-links/29-credit-for-reinsurance-rules> (accessed June 1012).

[24] <http://www.reactionsnet.com/Article/2149727/The-collateral-battle.html> (accessed Sept. 2011).

[25] <http://worldmedialaw.com/resources-a-links/29-credit-for-reinsurance-rules.html> (accessed June 2012).

[26] <http://www.worldmedialaw.com/resources-a-links/29-credit-for-reinsurance-rules> (accessed June 2012).

for potential reforms in the US (*Reactions*, July 2008).[27] Thus, it is not surprising that they were well disposed towards its inclusion in international insurance standards, being aware that this would also facilitate the reform of the domestic regulatory system in the US through the domestic downloading of international rules.

The EU's adoption of a new prudential regime in insurance was seen by some of the main market players and federal policy-makers as calling for a regulatory response in the US in order for the US insurance industry to remain competitive in the global economy and to settle the issue of equivalence with the EU (*Wall Street Journal*, 31 Mar. 2008; see also US Senate Committee on Banking 2008a). Some of the regulatory changes proposed by the reform coalition in the US had been fruitlessly advocated during domestic reform attempts in the past. Large insurers in the US had long complained about the 'inefficient patchwork of state regulation', arguing that 'they would be better off with a single federal regulator so as to better compete in a global market place' (*Wall Street Journal*, 15 May 2006). However, the majority of state insurance commissioners and insurance agents had opposed this option (*Wall Street Journal*, 15 May 2006).

Conclusion

In insurance, until the 2000s, the EU and US had weak regulatory capacities. In these jurisdictions the regulation of insurers was mostly a state competence, not a federal or EU competence. In the 2000s, the EU beefed up its regulatory capacity through the Reinsurance Directive and the Solvency II Directive. It was therefore better placed to upload parts of its new regulatory templates into the IAIS standards, which, however, are not as developed as the Basel accords in banking. This process was facilitated by weak US regulatory capacity in this field, its fragmented system of external representation in the IAIS, and the participation of the European Commission in this forum. The EU has also engaged in a transatlantic cross-loading with a view to resolving existing controversies with the US in the regulation of reinsurance.

Unlike in the regulation of banking and securities markets, the UK often sided with continental countries on insurance regulation, promoting EU regulatory templates in the IAIS. Within the EU, division amongst the main member states largely faded away in the making of the directives issued in the

[27] E.g. in June, the NAIC in the US adopted a 'solvency modernisation work plan' to analyse the international solvency standards and propose US regulatory reforms. The work plan was also to analyse the potential impact that adopting the Solvency II Directive would have on capital requirements of US insurers (*Reactions*, July 2008).

Table 5.2. EU–US market size in insurance (values are in billions)

Total gross premiums (life and non-life)	2008	2009	2010	2011	Sources
US ($)	**2,039**	**2,029**	**2,035**	**2,154**	OECD
US ($)	**1,166**	**1,149**	**1,239**		sigma
EU ($)	**1,559**	**1,315**	**1,288**	**1,376**	OECD*
EU (€)	**1,060**	**1,061**	**1,103**	**1,072**	CEA
Germany	164	171	178	178	CEA
France	183	199	207	190	CEA
Italy	92	117	125	110	CEA
UK (€)	247	205	206	206	CEA

* EU 15 countries.

2000s. Whereas in the past the EU was largely a collection of national insurance markets, the regulatory reforms of the 2000s not only strengthened EU regulatory capacity but also promoted the completion of the single market in insurance. As a result of this, the EU and US have almost the same market size in insurance, as reported in Table 5.2.

6

The EU and International Accounting and Auditing Standards

The regulatory capacity of the EU in accounting was very limited until 2002, when the EU decided to adopt international accounting standards, rather then develop its own rules. However, it set up an endorsement process for downloading these international standards into EU legislation. In contrast, the US had a strong regulatory capacity in accounting and was therefore able to cross-load some of its domestic standards to EU companies over the 1990s.

The main international (private) standard-setting body is the International Accounting Standards Board (IASB), which in 2001 succeeded the International Accounting Standards Committee (IASC). International accounting standards, which began to be issued in the late 1970s, spread worldwide after the EU's decision to adopt them for publicly listed companies by 2005. The governance structure of the IASB and most of its accounting standards were initially uploaded by the US.

Following a process of convergence between international and US accounting standards, in 2007 the US authorities decided to remove the reconciliation requirement that they had imposed on non-US firms listing in the US. This convergence process was, however, halted by the global financial crisis, when accounting standards concerning financial instruments were revised in the US and internationally. New public monitoring mechanisms were set up under the auspices of the US and the EU.

The regulatory capacity of the EU in auditing was very limited until the 2000s, but it subsequently built up. The 8th EU Company Law Directive issued in 2006 introduced the public oversight of auditors in the EU. After the global financial crisis, the Commission proposed new legislation, whereby member states were required to use international auditing standards. Unlike in accounting, an EU-level process for the downloading of international auditing standards was not set up.

Prior to the Sarbanes-Oxley Act, the regulatory capacity of the US in auditing was weak: auditing was subject to industry self-regulation, as in the EU. The Sarbanes-Oxley Act (2002) strengthened the US regulatory capacity by introducing the public oversight of auditors. Certain provisions of the Act had extraterritorial effects, but the EU resisted their cross-loading to EU firms by beefing up its own regulatory capacity through the 8th Company Law Directive.

The main international private standard-setting body, the International Auditing and Assurance Standards Board (IAASB), began to issue auditing standards in the late 1970s. However, they never acquired the same prominence as the international accounting standards. In light of the EU's decision to adopt international auditing standards, the governance structure of this private standard-setting body was reformed. The IAASB also embarked on the so-called 'clarity' project, so as to make its standards better suited for adoption in the EU as well as worldwide.

The accounting profession and the big auditing firms played an important role in shaping international accounting and auditing standards, as well as in the governance of private standard-setting bodies. However, their influence has declined following the global financial crisis, as the public authorities in the US and the EU have become more involved in monitoring private standard-setting bodies. The financial industry has also been active in the debate on accounting standards, whereas in auditing standards the auditing profession was most involved.

The Regulatory Capacity of the EU in Accounting

The regulatory capacity of the EU in accounting developed relatively late, despite early efforts by the European Commission (see Table 6.1). The EU bodies set up over time mainly advised the Commission on the national implementation of EU rules and later on assisted the Commission in the adoption of international standards.

The Institutional Framework for Accounting Standards in the EU

The Contact Committee, which was established by the 4th Company Law Directive (1978) and still exists, comprises representatives from member states and is chaired by the European Commission. The main task of the Committee is to facilitate the harmonized application of accounting directives across the member states. It also advises the Commission on amendments to these directives. From 1995 onwards, the Committee has liaised with the IASC and later the IASB in order to channel EU views to these private standard-setting

Table 6.1. The building up of EU regulatory capacity in accounting and auditing in the 2000s

Policy entrepreneur	Preferences of the large member states	Industry preferences	Regulatory template content
Commission UK	Different preferences on core issues (historical vs fair value; creditors vs investors protection), due to different accounting systems and varieties of capitalism (continental vs UK)	Some different preferences along national lines, but support for accounting harmonization in the EU	*International accounting standards regulation (2002)* – downloading international accounting standards – European 'specificities' – cross-loading international standards to the US
Commission	Similar preferences	Support from financial industry; auditing profession resisted some points	*8th Company Law Directive on Statutory Audit (2006)* – public oversight of auditors – possibility of adopting ISA – mutual reliance for third county auditors
Commission	Similar preferences	Opposed by audit industry, in particular by the big players	*Regulation on quality of audits and Directive on Single Market for Statutory Audits (proposed)* – rotation for auditors – rules on non-audit services – passport for auditors – compliance with international standards

bodies (van Hulle 2004). The meetings of the Contact Committee take place together with meetings of the Accounting Regulatory Committee.

The Accounting Regulatory Committee, which was set up in accordance with the International Accounting Standards regulation issued in 2002, advises the Commission on the adoption of international accounting standards. This regulatory committee is composed of representatives from member states and is chaired by the European Commission. The 2002 regulation also stated that the European Commission should seek 'advice from a technical committee' prior to endorsing international auditing standards.

The European Financial Reporting Advisory Group, set up in 2001, fulfils the role of a technical committee, bringing together representatives from the main European associations interested in financial reporting.[1] After the global financial crisis and with a view to strengthening the EU 'voice' in international standard-setting, the European Commission launched a review of

[1] As of 2012, members of the Group are: the European Business Federations, the Federation of European Accountants, the European Insurance and Reinsurance Federation, the European Banking Federation, the European Savings Banks Group, the European Association of Co-operative Banks, and the European Federation of Accountants and Auditors.

the activities of EFRAG (interview, Brussels, July 2013). The review is ongoing at the time of writing.

Regulatory Templates in Accounting in the EU

There were two turning points in the development of EU regulatory capacity in accounting over the past decade: the EU's decision to endorse international accounting standards for listed companies through the International Accounting Standard Regulation in 2002 and the EU's calls for a reform of international accounting standards after the global financial crisis.

In the 1970s and 1980s, the European Commission dealt with accounting and auditing matters as part of company law. The EU first adopted harmonized accounting requirements for limited liability companies in 1978 through the 4th Company Law Directive on annual accounts. The Directive was hotly debated in the Council, especially after the accession of the UK, Ireland, and Denmark to the EU, because these countries, together with the Netherlands, insisted on the 'true and fair view principle' in accounting, in line with their national regulatory approaches. This principle was not used in continental accounting (Donnelly 2010). In the end, the 4th Company Law Directive required limited liability companies to prepare annual accounts that must show a 'true and fair view'.[2] In 1987, the 7th Company Law Directive on consolidated accounts was approved after prolonged negotiations amongst the member states.

Both Company Law Directives were compromises between different national regulatory templates. They left open the possibility of different national options, i.e. different interpretations of the true and fair principle, especially the 4th Directive (Nobes and Parker 2006). On the one hand, they facilitated the comparability of accounts across member states and permitted mutual recognition for the purpose of listing on securities exchanges throughout the EU (Commission on the European Communities 1995). On the other hand, these EU rules were based on minimal harmonization. At that time, unanimity was needed in the Council of Ministers to pass legislation, which contributed to slowing down and diluting the process of harmonization.

Accounting standards differed widely across countries because these standards were influenced by the national system of corporate governance and corporate finance; financial market structure; and systems of taxation (Perry and Nölke 2006).[3] In liberal market economies, accounting standards were designed to protect and inform investors, providing them with accurate and

[2] It also contained exceptions that member states could introduce for small and medium enterprises.

[3] Hence, accounting standards can be linked to the literature on varieties of capitalism. This literature is vast. For some comprehensive analyses, see Amable 2003; Hancké et al. 2007; Hall and Soskice 2001; Schmidt 2002; and Jackson and Deeg 2008.

up-to-date information (Gebhardt 2000).[4] By contrast, in coordinated market economies, such as Germany, accounting rules were designed to protect creditors, hence they were based on the 'principle of prudence'. In many continental countries, such as France and Germany, accounting standards were used for taxation purposes (Nobes and Parker 2006), whereas in the US financial accounting was separate from tax accounting.

In countries with common law, the details of accounting rules were delegated to regulators, such as the SEC, which, in turn, delegated this task to private standard-setting bodies, such as the Financial Accounting Standards Board (FASB). In the UK, standard-setting in accounting was performed by the profession through the Accounting Standards Board, established in 1990. In countries with code law, such as France and Germany, commercial and tax legislation contained detailed accounting rules. Accounting was part of codified law and could be changed only through legislation (Botzem and Quack 2006). The public authorities in continental countries were keen to retain control of accounting legislation because of its tax implications (Gebhardt 2000). Over time, this function was reluctantly delegated to private standards-setting bodies, following the Anglo-Saxon model.

Over the 1980s and 1990s, the EU did not make much progress in the harmonization of accounting standards due to the resistance of two member states. Germany had problems in implementing the Accounting Directives because small and medium enterprises opposed the disclosure of financial statements. In the UK, the Directives hindered the development of new accounting standards at the national level. Hence, the UK privileged the process of international (rather than EU) accounting harmonization by cooperating with other standard-setters in the so-called Group of Four[5] and by supporting the standards of the IASC (van Hulle 2004).

In 1995, as a way out of the impasse, the Commission issued a communication endorsing the international harmonization process under way in the IASC. Several reasons explain this shift in the Commission's strategy. First, international harmonization based on international accounting standards was preferable for the EU to harmonization based on US Generally Accepted Accounting Principles (GAAP) (Dewing and Russell 2004). As a senior Commission official working on this matter put it: 'American standards had been developed without any European input and were designed to satisfy the needs of the US capital market' (van Hulle 2004: 358; see also Commission of the European Communities 1995).

[4] However, in the UK accounting tended to be principle-based, whereas in the US it was rule-based, due to the widespread culture of litigation in the US; hence the accounting rules (Generally Accepted Accounting Principles—GAAP) were prescriptive and detailed.

[5] The Group of Four (G4) comprised the US, UK, Canada, and Australia, with some representatives of the IASC being present as observers (Camfferman and Zeff 2007).

Second, large EU companies that wanted to raise funds on capital markets faced the problem that international markets did not consider their financial statements, prepared on the basis on national legislation and deriving from the EU Accounting Directives, as providing the necessary information. The real problem for EU global players was access to the US capital market (Posner 2010). Moreover, several member states were in the process of implementing privatization programmes that required access to the US capital market (Commission of the European Communities 1995). Many European companies were listed on the New York stock exchange and Nasdaq, and were subject to the GAAP, under the oversight of the Securities and Exchange Commission (SEC). To no avail the Commission tried to negotiate an agreement on mutual recognition of financial statements with the SEC, with an interesting parallel to the failed mutual recognition of securities trading regulation (see Chapter 4).

Third, the old approach to EU harmonization had proven to be slow and ineffective. It took a long time to agree on each Directive, and in some cases agreement was not reached. Moreover, the Directives left many options open as a result of compromises amongst the member states. Finally, the Directives had to be incorporated into national laws, causing additional delays and cross-country differences (Commission of the European Communities 1995). Basically, as Véron put it (2007: 30), standard-setting remained a national task that was only marginally impacted by the two Accounting Directives.

The creation of a European accounting standards board was considered as an option, but it would have created an additional set of rules between national and international standards (Commission of the European Communities 1995). What is more, the establishment of an EU standard-setting body would have required time and significant funding. 'The Commission saw no need to develop European standards for the sake of having European standards when other solutions were equally satisfactory. It was also clear that a more flexible framework was needed' (van Hulle 2004: 357). It is noteworthy that the communication explicitly acknowledged the EU's attempt to increase its influence in international accounting harmonization. It argued that: 'There needs to be closer cooperation within the Union, through the improved functioning of the existing bodies at EU level which deal with accounting issues, to reach agreed positions on both international and internal accounting issues. This would strengthen the influence of the EU in the international harmonisation debate' (Commission of the European Communities 1995: 2).

The FSAP listed amongst its objectives the move towards a single set of financial statements for listed companies. In 2000, the EU Commission adopted *EU Financial Reporting Strategy: The Way Forward* (Commission of the European Communities 2000), proposing that all EU companies listed on a regulated market (at that time estimated at around 6,700) should be required to prepare consolidated accounts in accordance with international accounting standards. It noted that this was in line with the International Organization of Securities Commissions' (IOSCO) recommendations in 2000. The Commission also pointed out that 'major developments' had taken place within the IASC itself, including its reformed organizational structure.

In 2001, the Commission proposed a regulation on International Accounting Standards (Commission of the European Communities 2001), which was adopted by a single reading by the European Parliament and the Council of Ministers in 2002. It had the support of all the member states, the market, the profession, and users (van Hulle 2004: 368). The regulation established that from 2005 onwards the consolidated accounts of publicly traded companies in the EU should be prepared in conformity with the international accounting standards, adopted in accordance with the procedure laid down in the regulation.[6] It applied to all companies whose securities were admitted to trading on a regulated market in the EU.

Originally, the Commission wanted to apply the regulation to all companies that were required to publish a public offer prospectus, regardless of whether their securities were admitted to trading on a regulated market. This broad scope was not accepted by the member states, which were, however, left free to allow or require unlisted companies to use international accounting standards. The regulation applied only to consolidated accounts. Annual accounts of listed companies (which in some countries provide the basis for the distribution of profits and for taxation purposes) remained subject to national law, derived from the Accounting Directives. Foreign companies, especially US companies listed in the EU, were not required to adopt international accounting standards or reconcile to them. The regulation envisaged an endorsement process for downloading international accounting standards in the EU.

As part of the FSAP, the EU also passed new legislation that contained equivalence clauses on accounting. For foreign firms raising capital or listing securities in regulated markets in the EU, the Prospectus Directive and the Transparency Directive (see Chapter 4) required the use of international accounting standards or the approval that home accounting standards met EU requirements (Posner 2010). European policy-makers used these clauses to put pressure on the SEC to agree to a mutual recognition regime with the EU. In fact, the Commission delayed its equivalence decisions until the SEC agreed to recognize the use of international accounting standards by foreign companies in the US without reconciliation requirements (Posner 2010).

To sum up, the main hindrances to the development of EU regulatory capacity in accounting were the different preferences of the member states.

[6] This regulation includes an option allowing member states to extend the scope of application of the IFRS to the annual accounts of listed companies or to the accounts of non-listed companies.

These were rooted in their domestic political economy, namely their national accounting systems and their link to varieties of capitalism. The UK authorities preferred to work with the FASB in the Group of Four because they shared a similar approach to accounting. Likewise, the British authorities supported the IASC and the IASB, which were private-sector bodies in which the Anglo-Saxon accounting profession was well represented (Camfferman and Zeff 2007).

A process of path-dependence was also at work. Some European multinationals had unilaterally adopted US GAAP or international accounting standards in the 1990s; hence the adoption of a new set of EU standards was unpalatable. Moreover, the European Commission lacked the expertise and the resources to rival international or US accounting standards. When in the early 2000s, the European Commission, with the support of the member states, engineered a major reform of accounting standard-setting in the EU, the EU decided to adopt ready-made international standards, with a view to promoting their worldwide acceptance (interviews, Brussels, July 2013).

The Regulatory Capacity of the US in Accounting

In the US, financial reporting (accounting and auditing) is dealt with by federal securities regulation and applies only to listed companies (Eberle and Lauter 2011). The US has developed strong regulatory capacity in accounting. Indeed, over the 1990s many US accounting standards were uploaded onto the standards issued by the IASC and the IASB. They were also actively cross-loaded to EU firms listed in the US.

The Institutional Framework for Accounting Standard-Setting in the US

The Securities Act (1933), which was issued in the aftermath of the Great Depression, gave the SEC the authority to set accounting standards for reporting financial information. The accounting profession lobbied hard in the 1930s to prevent the SEC from setting accounting standards. At that time, there was no consensus in the profession and even less at the SEC about the content of these standards (Khademian 2002). The SEC decided to delegate its authority to set accounting standards and to monitor the quality of independent audits to the accounting industry with the oversight of the SEC (Mattli and Büthe 2004). In 1973, the FASB was given the task of issuing accounting principles that were widely accepted. It worked together with the SEC to ensure that standards were in the public interest.

Regulatory Templates in Accounting in the US

Since its establishment, the FASB has issued 105 GAAP. Accounting standards in the US are rule-based, rather than principle-based. Hence, they tend to be very detailed. They also privilege the information needs of investors, rather than creditors. Prior to 2007, the US authorities required foreign issuers seeking access to US stock exchanges and securities markets to reconcile their financial statement compiled according to local accountancy rules with US GAAP (Flower 1997). In contrast, in order to attract foreign issuers, several EU member states allowed them to prepare financial statements using US GAAP. Since EU-based issuers were keen to adopt either international accounting standards or US GAAP, some member states (for example, Germany, France, Italy, Belgium) allowed national companies to draft their financial statements according to these rules (Haller 2002). Hence, US accounting rules were actively cross-loaded to these EU countries.

As mentioned in the previous section, in 1995, the European Commission had proposed a mutual recognition regime for accounting standards, whereby EU companies listing in the US would use their own national accounting standards and vice versa (Commission of the European Communities 1995). However, the SEC had little interest in mutual recognition with the EU because financial statements of US companies prepared under the US GAAP were already recognized in all the EU member states (van Hulle 2004). The assumption was that eventually the rest of the world would adopt US standards (Simmons 2001). Moreover, the EU directives did not provide a comprehensive set of standards that would meet the US requirements: there were significant differences across the member states because of the number of options included in the Directives and the national laws implementing the Directives (Commission of the European Communities 1995). The EU's decision to adopt international accounting standards gave new momentum to the international adoption of these standards. Afterwards, the US authorities became more interested in seeking a cooperative solution with the EU and the IASB (interview, New York, Nov. 2011), as discussed in the following section.

International Standard-Setting in Accounting

Unlike the international regulatory fora discussed in the previous chapters, the IASB and its predecessor, the IASC, are not transgovernmental bodies, they are private-sector standard-setting bodies. The indirect influence of the US, and to a lesser extent the UK, have been predominant, first within the IASC and later in the IASB. This was because of their large national securities markets and strong domestic regulatory capacity, including cutting-edge accounting expertise.

The IASC began issuing International Accounting Standards (IAS) in the 1970s and these standards became more detailed over time. In 2001, when the IASC was transformed into the IASB, these standards were renamed International Financial Reporting Standards (IFRS). It was only after their adoption by the EU in 2005 that they were widely adopted worldwide. Subsequently, the IASB and the FASB began a convergence process, leading to the mutual recognition of the IAS/IFRS and the US GAAP in 2007. After the global financial crisis, the governance of the IASB and the content of some of its standards have been revised, but the convergence process has lost momentum.

The Institutional Framework for International Standard-Setting in Accounting

The IASC was established in London in 1973 and comprised representatives from national professional accounting bodies (i.e. private bodies) from nine countries. Its establishment was promoted by the British accounting profession as a counterweight to the EU's policy on accounting. The timing was explained by UK's joining of the EU and the opposition of British accounting bodies to the draft for an accounting directive proposed by the Commission, which mainly reflected continental accounting principles (Hopwood 1994).

The IASC had an international remit, but it was a private-sector body. It was dominated by professional bodies from the UK and other Anglo-Saxon countries, keen to promote their model of accounting, as opposed to the continental one. The SEC's interest in accounting standards led to close links between the IASC and the IOSCO (Camfferman and Zeff 2007), where the SEC had a predominant influence (see Chapter 4). As Véron put it (2007: 27), global accounting was a UK-born idea, which survived thanks to US support.

Some authors have stressed the power of the then Big Six, now Big Four, accounting firms in the IASC and later the IASB. Martinez-Diaz (2005) describes the IASC as an 'epistemic community' of like-minded professionals because its members had shared values and knowledge. They believed that accounting standards should meet the needs of shareholders and investors, not creditors, and that the cross-border comparability of financial statements would promote efficient markets. They also agreed that international standard-setting should be kept in the hands of accountants in the private sector, not in the hands of regulators (Botzem 2012; Martinez-Diaz 2005).

Since its establishment, the IASC managed to fend off competition from other potential international standard-setters, namely the EU and the United Nations. The IASC engaged in an expansion of its membership as a tool of 'deliberate cooptation' (Larson 2002). The FASB joined the IASC in 1988, the European Commission in 1990, and the IOSCO in 1996, all with observer status. However, national public standard-setters remained somewhat sceptical of the activities of the IASC (Botzem and Quack 2006). Basically, the IASC was 'a collegial, private interest association dominated by accountants in common law countries and with cooperative links to other professional associations' (Donnelly 2007: 117).

In 2001, the IASC was transformed into the IASB to create close ties with national standard-setters and to reduce the influence of professional associations. A heated debate accompanied the transformation of the IASC into the IASB. It mainly concerned the governance structure of the IASB. The US (to be precise, the SEC) argued that the IASB members should be appointed on the basis of their technical expertise, as opposed to their geographical representativeness, which was the European Commission's preferred criteria (Camfferman and Zeff 2007; Martinez-Diaz 2005). The SEC proposed a two-tiered body modelled on the FASB, where trustees would select board members with relevant professional expertise. Board members would include individuals from the largest economies with rotating seats for other countries (Botzem 2012; Martinez-Diaz 2005).

As Martinez-Diaz (2005) notes, the SEC prevailed on all key points. Indeed, the SEC managed to upload its national model (the FASB model) to the international level: like the IASB, the FASB is a private organization (also funded by a private foundation) to which the SEC has delegated the setting of accounting standards in the US. Both the IASB and the FASB are based on the principles of independence and technical expertise. The main difference between the IASC and the IASB is that the latter is not controlled by the worldwide association of professional bodies, the International Federation of Accountants.

The IASB is the independent standard-setting body of the IFRS Foundation, which until 2010 was named the IASC Foundation. The IFRS Foundation is an independent, not-for-profit private accounting organization. There are twenty-two trustees, eighteen of whom represent the regions of North America, Europe, and Asia/Oceania (with six trustees per region), one from Africa, one from South America, and two from the rest of the world. They represent various professions, including accountants, auditors, users (financial institutions and public authorities), and academics. The trustees are publicly accountable to a monitoring board of public authorities.

The IFRS Foundation appoints the IASB members and oversees the board's activity. The trustees also appoint the members of two other bodies that are important to the IASB's work: the Standards Advisory Council and the International Financial Reporting Interpretation Committee. The sixteen members of the IASB are responsible for the development of the IFRS. They are chosen on the basis of expertise on reporting standards and financial markets. The authority to take decisions on standards is centralized in the board, which adopts standards in consultation with national standard-setters.

Shortly after the IASB was established, the EU adopted the International Accounting Standards regulation (2002), which made IFRS mandatory by 2005 for all publicly listed firms in the EU. Afterwards, the European Commission, with the support of European business, banks, and accounting organizations, put forward a series of requests to the IASB, with a view to increasing the influence of the EU on this body (Leblond 2011). The results were mixed. When the IASC Foundation completed its first constitutional review in 2005, it increased the number of trustees from nineteen to twenty-two in order to provide better geographical balance, though without changing the number of seats held by the EU and the US. The voting majority of the IASB was increased to nine from eight, as the EU had demanded, in order to reduce the influence of members from Anglo-Saxon countries (Leblond 2011).

The other important reform of the governance structure of the IASB took place in the wake of the financial crisis. In 2007, the European Commission, the SEC, the Financial Services Agency of Japan, and the IOSCO jointly proposed the establishment of a body that would monitor the IASC Foundation (later renamed the IFRS Foundation). In 2009, the monitoring board of public authorities was officially created: it was a way for public authorities, especially from the EU and the US, to exercise greater control over the IASB. This reform was possible because of the overlapping preferences and the equal distribution of power between the US and the EU. For the US, it was a quid pro quo whereby the SEC ended its reconciliation requirements in 2007, but required some sort of political control on the IASB. In the EU, the crisis empowered Germany and the European Parliament, who had criticized the IASB's lack of political accountability (Bengtsson 2011).

International Accounting Standards

The IASC passed twenty-six IAS in the first fifteen years of activity. However, these were mainly 'consensus standards', based on a minimum common denominator, permitting a wide range of options. In the late 1980s, the IASC began to review its standards, excluding alternatives that were not in line with capital market orientations. Rival approaches, such as historical accounting or replacement costs, were marginalized. Market values played an increasing role in financial reporting, most notably fair value accounting, which privileged the information needs of capital market actors (Botzem 2012). From 1987 onwards, the standard-setting activity of the IASC moved away from the lowest common denominator of the past. In 1989, the IASC adopted a conceptual framework that was uploaded by the US framework, and this was the only one in existence at that time (Camfferman and Zeff 2007; Whittington 2008).[7]

Within the IASC, the active engagement of national standard-setters from four countries (the US, the UK, Canada, and Australia), gathered in the so-called Group of Four, influenced international standard-setting on the basis of regulatory templates already established in these countries, promoting a capital market approach for accounting (Botzem and Quack 2009). The Group of Four, which operated from 1992 to 2001, was an embryonic standard-setter itself (Street 2006, cited in Botzem and Quack 2009: 991). Its members shared a similar conceptual framework and wanted to move faster than the rest of the IASC. Within the FASB, there was a pro-international accounting standards faction that was involved in the activities of the IASC (Posner 2010). Donnelly (2007) notes that the 'special relationship' between the FASB and the IASC (first) and the IASB (later) was criticized by national standard-setters and by the big accounting firms. This issue was raised by the EU when the IASB governance structure was debated.

US influence on international accounting standard-setting was exerted in two ways: by uploading US accounting templates to the IASC/IASB and via the IOSCO. As already mentioned, there was the (partial) uploading by the FASB of its Conceptual Framework to the IASC in 1989. Subsequently, in 1997, the IASC announced plans to use parts of the US GAAP as building blocks for its own rules (Martinez-Diaz 2005). Moreover, the 'IASC did not issue a single standard that was in fundamental opposition to US GAAP' (Flower 1997: 289).

In 1993, the IOSCO compiled a list of core accounting standards that the regulators considered crucial and the IASC set to work on them. Throughout the project, the SEC's preferences were the most influential. Indeed, Jean Saint Geours, chair of the IOSCO committee responsible for the list, described the core standards as perhaps 'too much influenced by the preoccupations of our North American colleagues' (cited in Eaton 2005: 4). In 1994, the IOSCO decided, under the influence of the SEC, to follow a step-by-step endorsement of the IASC's Core Standards, instead of voting on the completed set. By retaining the ability to endorse (or otherwise) each individual standard, the regulators secured their influence in the making of those standards (Eaton 2005). Eventually, the IOSCO recommended that its members should allow multinational issuers to use the IASC standards in cross-border listing, subject to reconciliation requirements, as in the US (Whittington 2005).

[7] As Whittington (2008) notes, the FASB's conceptual framework dated from the 1970s and consisted of seven substantial concepts statements. The IASC's framework was a brief single document, issued in 1989. Its content shows a strong affinity with the FASB's earlier work, although there are important differences of detail.

By 2001, when the IASC was transformed into the IASB, there were forty-one standards. After 2001, the new standards were called IFRS. The EU's decision to adopt international accounting standards, subject to an endorsement process at the EU level, was a milestone. Prior to this decision, no jurisdiction had made the use of international accounting standards compulsory, and only a few countries allowed the use of international accounting standards as an alternative to national standards. The neighbouring countries of the EU shifted to international accounting standards at the same time as the EU (Véron 2007). Other countries worldwide followed this move, making them truly global standards: 120 countries have adopted the IFRS.

After the EU's decision to adopt international accounting standards, the IASB worked to improve the standards issued by its predecessor. The intention was to avoid the revisions of theses standards shortly after their adoption by the EU (Leblond 2011). The revision of the IAS and the IFRS standards was completed in 2004, in time for the EU to endorse them. Hence, in this period the EU exercised considerable influence over the standard-setting agenda of the IASB, even though it did not necessarily have influence on the content of its standards (Botzem 2012; Leblond 2011).

Given the widespread adoption of the IAS and the IFRS, the US had a new incentive to negotiate mutual recognition with the IASB and the EU. The appointment of a new 'internationalist' chairman to the FASB in the summer of 2002 facilitated this process (Eaton 2005: 11). According to Eaton, Robert Herz's nomination received the crucial backing of senior figures at the SEC. In 2002, the Norwalk agreement between the IASB and the FASB was signed to foster convergence between GAAP and IAS/IFRS, whereby the IASB and the FASB pledged to '(a) make their existing financial reporting standards fully compatible as soon as is practicable and (b) to coordinate their future work programs to ensure that once achieved, compatibility is maintained' (FASB and IASB 2002).

After the Norwalk agreement, the FASB and the IASB met on a regular basis and worked on convergence projects. In some cases, the IASB adopted some FASB standards, an example being an exposure draft issued in 2006 with a view to aligning the IASB segment reporting requirements with the equivalent GAAP standard (Larson and Street 2006). In other cases, it was the FASB that issued or amended standards to be in line with the IFRS. The FASB and the IASB worked jointly to develop common standards in several key areas, including business combinations, revenue recognition, liability extinguishment, leasing, and financial performance reporting by business entities (Larson and Street 2006).

In 2005, the two boards undertook a joint project for the convergence of their conceptual framework. Whittington (2005) notes that the convergence project was truly a joint one, even though the bulk of the FASB's existing framework and its strong staff input meant that the initial point tended to be the FASB's standards rather than the IASB's. In most aspects, there was little difference between the two frameworks.

In 2005, the US agreed a roadmap with the EU to stop the requirement of reconciliation with GAAP for EU firms listing in the US by 2009.[8] The roadmap was a twenty-five-page document outlining a series of steps to be met before the IFRS could be accepted by the SEC as equivalent to US GAAP for non-US private issuers. In 2007, the US eliminated the requirement of US GAAP reconciliation for foreign issuers using the IFRS as published by the IASB, even though EU regulators had (unsuccessfully) requested the inclusion of the IFRS as adopted by the EU. The SEC considered that foreign standards had converged sufficiently with US standards to lift the reconciliation requirements and to allow mutual recognition. Afterwards, the SEC began consulting about the possibility of using the IFRS in the US, instead of the US GAAP. However, the global financial crisis moved this issue onto the backburner (*Financial Times,* 7 Oct. 2010, 27 Jan. 2011).

During the financial crisis, the debate mainly focused on accounting provisions for financial instruments, whereby the IASB and the FASB reinterpreted the existing standards. The key issue was the reclassification of assets held by financial institutions from the trading book (at fair value) to the banking book, to which fair value did not apply (Leblond 2011). This issue reopened the never-settled divide by those (mostly in the US and the UK) in favour of fair value in accounting and those in continental Europe who opposed it. In the midst of the crisis, the EU exerted considerable pressure on the IASB to prompt the revision of some of its standards (interview, Brussels, July 2013). This revision was done by the IASB without due process, on the ground that the financial crisis required prompt action. Moreover, the IASB feared that otherwise the EU would resort to new carve-outs (Bengtsson 2011), or even to issue its own standards (interviews, Brussels, June 2013).

Afterwards, the IASB began working on the IFRS 9, to replace IAS 39 on financial instruments. This work was divided into three phases: classification and measurement; impairment methodology; and hedge accounting. Most of the debate has focused on the use of fair value in accounting for financial instruments. The first phase, which was completed in 2011, was reopened afterwards, with a view to furthering convergence with US GAAP. The second and third phases have not been put forward yet. The view of several EU policy-makers, especially from the Commission, is that in the past convergence between the IFRS/IAS and the GAAP has moved too much towards the US position (interviews, Brussels, June 2013). Yet the US has not adopted

[8] See <http://www.sec.gov/news/press/2005-62.htm>; <http://europa.eu/rapid/press-release_IP-05-469_en.htm#PR_metaPressRelease_bottom> (both accessed Sept. 2011).

IFRS and is unlikely to do so in the near future. The Commission and some member states, such as France, are therefore keen to develop a stronger EU influence on the IASB standard-setting activity.

Over the years, the IASB was transformed from an arena into a player (Botzem 2012). Some authors argue that the relatively high degree of autonomy of the IASB from the EU and US in setting IFRS was achieved by maintaining a delicate balance between US and EU interests (Leblond 2011). However, it was also due to the success (meaning wide adoption) of its standards. Other authors (for example, Posner 2010) note that the IASB's relative autonomy and that of its predecessor, the IASC, had declined since the late 1990s, when many countries began to adopt the IAS and the IFRS. The establishment of the monitoring board under the auspices of the EU and US is the most recent example of the increasing influence of the public authorities on the activity of the IASB (Posner 2010).

Overall, together with banking standards, accounting standards have reached the furthest point in their adoption worldwide. There have been several reasons for the success of these standards: their adoption by EU (interviews, Brussels, July 2013); the corporate scandals, especially in the US, which raised questions about the quality of the US GAAP (Eaton 2005); the cooperation between the IASB and the FASB (interviews, Washington, Aug. 2011); the fact that international standards largely converged towards US standards, becoming more acceptable for the US (Martinez-Diaz 2005); the request from securities exchange regulators gathered in the IOSCO for comprehensive and detailed standards that the IASB was able to produce (Donnelly 2007); and lobbying from multinational corporations for one set of global standards, in particular, pressure on US multinationals to align to the rest of the world (Posner 2009a). There is also the constructivist argument, based on the dissemination of Anglo-Saxon principles for accounting in the IASB, with the endorsement of the IOSCO (Eaton 2005). Finally, international standards continue to coexist with national standards, which are often retained for the tax purposes. Using two standards avoids the politically contentious issues related to a country's tax system (Donnelly 2007), even though it represents a cost for companies that have to prepare two sets of accounts according to different standards.

The Downloading of International Accounting Standards by the EU

Standards are adopted in the EU after they have been published by the IASB, subject to a regulatory comitology procedure, which involves the European Commission, the member states, the European Parliament, and stakeholders.

The IAS can only be adopted in the EU if three conditions, stated in the 2002 regulation, are met: international accounting standards should not be contrary to the principle of true and fair view referred to in the 4th and 7th Directives; international accounting standards must be conducive to 'European public good' (this was something of a 'political' condition, which left some room for manœuvre to the EU authorities in the adoption of international accounting standards: Dewing and Russell 2008); and international accounting standards should conform the criteria of understandibility, relevance, and reliability.

Although the Commission can in principle refuse to adopt standards that do not meet the relevant criteria, this option has several disadvantages and has been used in very few (but important) cases. In 2003–4, the conflict concerning the endorsement of the IAS 39 on financial instruments stressed the difficulty of reaching an agreement within the EU and between the EU and the IASB. Basically, the use of the IAS 39 implied a move from 'historic cost' (valuing assets on the basis of the purchase costs) to 'fair value' accounting (valuing assets on the basis of their market price) (Dewing and Russell 2008). Some banks and continental standard-setters opposed this move, whereas the UK supported the full implementation of IAS 39 in the EU. This 'technical' issue became so politicized that French President Chirac wrote to Prodi, President of the European Commission, arguing that the international accounting standards 'were not sensitive enough to European interests' (Whittington 2005: 143).

The Commission carved out some provisions on the fair value option of the IAS 39 in 2004. This gave a way out of the impasse, given that the deadline for the adoption of the IFRS in the EU was approaching. The carve-outs were a pragmatic response by the Commission to ensure the support of key actors, such as the European banking industry, for the adoption of international accounting standards as the 2005 implementation deadline approached (interview, Brussels, July 2013). However, they also highlighted the fact that the EU endorsement process was subject to 'political' considerations (Dewing and Russell 2008).

Although the Commission presented its decision for the carve-outs as a technical one, it was influenced by intense lobbying by European vested interests (Nobes and Parker 2006; Whittington 2005). According to Leblond (2011: 453), 'For the EU, the use of carve-outs was clearly a way to influence the IASB's decision-making, without having to resort to abandoning IFRS altogether. Nevertheless, such a control mechanism was only of limited use since it negatively affected the IASB's legitimacy and made it more difficult for the SEC to accept the IFRS, which is something that the EU strongly supported.'

At the same time this episode, as well as the reaction of the EU to the global financial crisis, stressed that it is not easy for the IASB to understand the

EU's official view in a cacophony of European voices, often with different (even conflicting) objectives. Indeed, in the wake of the crisis a policy debate ensued on whether accounting standards should be designed to contribute to financial stability (the continental view as well as the view of several banking regulators) or provide reliable information to investors (the Anglo-Saxon view) (interview, Brussels, July 2013). Given this internal division, it was difficult for the EU to speak with one voice on this issue before and after the crisis.

The Regulatory Capacity of the EU in Auditing

The regulatory capacity of the EU in auditing developed very late (see Table 6.1), partly because of limited efforts by the Commission, partly because of different regulatory frameworks in the member states. The EU enhanced its regulatory capacity in auditing from the 2000s, following a process similar to, but distinct from, accounting.

The Institutional Framework for Auditing Regulation in the EU

The EU bodies set up to deal with auditing regulation were mainly advising the Commission on the implementation of auditing legislation in the member states and later on the adoption of international standards. The Committee on Auditing, which was composed of government experts nominated by the member states and representatives of the European accountancy profession, was established in 1998. It was an advisory committee that had the task of reviewing the international auditing standards and contributing to the regulatory debate in the IAASB. In 2005, this Committee was renamed the Audit Advisory Committee (Soltani 2007).

Mirroring the Lamfalussy architecture for banking, securities, and insurance, the new 8th Company Law Directive led to the establishment of the Audit Regulatory Committee in 2005. Like its counterpart in accounting, it has the task of assisting the European Commission in the adoption of implementing measures, following the comitology procedure. In the same year, the European Commission set up the European Group of Auditors' Oversight Bodies, with a view to ensuring the coordination of new public oversight systems of statutory auditors and audit firms across the EU.[9] Like the level 3 Lamflaussy committees, it provides technical input to Commission in the preparation of implementing measures of the Directive on Statutory Audit, such as the endorsement of the International Standards on Auditing (ISA), or

[9] http://eur-lex.europa.eu/LexUriServ/LexUriServ.do?uri=CELEX:32005D0909:EN:NOT (accessed Sept. 2011).

the assessment of third countries' public oversight systems. It is composed of high-level representatives from the entities responsible for public oversight of statutory auditors and audit firms in member states or, in their absence, of representatives from the competent national ministries.

The new EU audit legislation proposed after the global financial crisis envisaged that the European Securities and Markets Authority (ESMA) would take over the functions of the European Group of Auditor Oversight Bodies. The ESMA is assigned the task of issuing European certifications of firms performing audits of listed companies. It is to be responsible for issuing standards and guidelines with a view to harmonizing supervisory practices.

The Regulatory Templates of Auditing in the EU

Until the early 2000s, the EU regulatory templates in auditing were based on minimum harmonization through company law directives. There were two turning points in the development of EU regulatory capacity in auditing over the last decade: the new 8th Company Directive (2006), which mentioned the possibility of downloading international auditing standards in the EU, and the EU legislation proposed in the wake of the crisis.

EU-wide requirements for audited financial statements were first introduced by the 4th Directive on the annual accounts of certain types of companies in 1978. In 1983, the 7th Directive on consolidated accounts extended these requirements to companies producing consolidated financial statements. In 1984, the (old) 8th Directive specified common standards for the approval of persons undertaking statutory audits, even though several issues were left unresolved because of disagreements amongst the member states (Dewing and Russell 2004).

In 1998, the Commission issued *Statutory Audit in the European Union, The Way Forward*. This proposed the establishment of a committee on auditing composed of government experts from the member states and representatives of the European accountancy profession. The Committee was set up in 1998, as has already been mentioned. In 2003, the Commission's *Reinforcing the Statutory Audit in the European Union* proposed ten priorities for improving and harmonizing the quality of statutory audit throughout the EU. The plan, issued in the aftermath of the Enron scandal, announced an overhaul of EU accounting legislation. It also mentioned the possibility of adopting the ISA for all EU statutory audits from 2005 onwards and the creation of a Regulatory Committee on Audit, as already mentioned.

The Commission's proposal to reform EU auditing legislation was designed to facilitate the completion of the single financial market and to deal with the weaknesses exposed by the Parmalat scandals in Europe (Eberle and Lauter 2011). It was also an attempt to counterbalance US influence in this field, especially as a response to the extraterritorial provisions introduced by the Sarbanes-Oxley Act.

Internal Market Commissioner Frits Bolkestein stated:

> I want European solutions tailored to our needs... I do not accept the imposition of US standards on our firms and that is why the European Union strongly opposes registration of EU audit firms with the United States' Public Company Accounting Oversight Board. The EU will regulate its own businesses... Rapid progress on the priorities in the Communication will also be crucial to the EU–US regulatory dialogue on audit issues. A legally underpinned comprehensive audit regulatory and supervisory environment in the EU will be least equivalent to the regulatory systems currently being developed by the US Public Company Accounting Oversight Board. It will be a sound bedrock for exempting EU auditors from unnecessary and burdensome US regulatory outreach, which constitutes a barrier to an efficient transatlantic and global capital market.[10]

The new 8th Company Law Directive on statutory audit of annual accounts and consolidated accounts, which amended the Directives of 1978 and 1983, was proposed by the Commission in 2004 and was co-decided by the European Parliament and the Council at first reading in 2005. The Directive was designed to separate auditors' supervision from professional groups, ensuring public oversight of audit firms. It introduced a requirement for external quality assurance and set out principles for public supervision of auditing in the member states. The Directive left member states some room for manœuvre in shaping their own national regime. However, it required them to establish systems of public oversight for statutory auditors at the national level. The Commission set up an organization, the European Group of Auditors' Oversight Bodies, to facilitate the coordination of these public oversight systems (Humphrey et al. 2009).

During the negotiations for the Directive it was clear that both the auditing profession in Europe and the member states were not prepared to go as far as the Commission. Thus, several proposals were watered down in the drafting phase of the Directive, following intense lobbying from the profession (Eberle and Lauter 2011). The auditing profession in Europe, and in particular the Federation of European Accountants, pointed out that auditing in the EU did not apply only to listed companies, it applied to all companies for which statutory auditing was required, and that this was a much larger pool than in the US (interview, Brussels, July 2013). Some of the provisions envisaged by the Directive would have been too burdensome for the diversified EU audit market; for example a prescribed methodology on quality assurance or peer review and monitoring by public authorities (Eberle and Lauter 2011).

[10] <http://europa.eu/rapid/press-release_IP-03-715_en.doc> (accessed Sept. 2011).

Article 26 of the Directive foresaw the possibility of adopting the ISA in the EU through a regulatory comitology procedure. However, the Directive stressed that these international standards had to be developed 'with proper due process, public oversight and transparency'.[11] No timetable or deadline was mentioned for their downloading into EU legislation: the main obstacle to the adoption of the ISA in the EU was dissatisfaction with the governance structure of the International Federation of Accountants and its committees. The Commission complained that the IAASB's audit standard-setting processes were conducted 'by and for the audit profession' (Humphrey and Loft 2009: 221). This was one of the factors that triggered the reform of the International Federation of Accountants, which was approved in 2003.

The 2006 Directive applied not only to EU auditors and audit firms but also to audit firms from third countries. According to the Directive, an EU member state could exempt third-country auditors from national registration and oversight in Europe if: the third-country audit regime had been recognized by the European Commission as equivalent to the EU regime; and reciprocal exemptions were applied by the third country to the EU member states' auditors.

At the basis of these provisions, there was the Commission's support for international 'mutual reliance' on the supervision of auditors in third countries. As the Commission put it, 'Mutual reliance means that member states and the third countries can rely on each others' inspections of audit firms allowing for a more effective and efficient oversight of global audit firms' (Commission of the European Communities 2011c). It was similar to the concept of mutual recognition that the European Commission pursued *vis-à-vis* the SEC in securities trading in the same period.

The Directive was an attempt by the Commission to forge a common EU position *vis-à-vis* its main trading partner and to exert some pressure on the US authorities as a response to the extraterritorial effects of the Sarbanes-Oxley Act. As Charlie McCreevy Commissioner for the Internal Market and Services put it:[12]

> the EU's aim has always been to move towards full reliance on the audit inspections of the public oversight bodies in these third countries... In return, of course, EU oversight bodies would expect the same treatment for EU audit firms...we need more time to ensure that the United States is ready to cooperate with us fully, based upon mutual trust and mutual assistance.

[11] The article also stated that 'member states may apply a national auditing standard as long as the Commission has not adopted an international auditing standard covering the same subject-matter'.

[12] MEMO/09/79, Brussels, 19 Feb. 2009.

In 2007, the European Commission and the US Public Company Accounting Oversight Board agreed on an EU–US roadmap on cooperation concerning public oversight systems of auditors, similar to that in accounting.[13] The goal was to enable the EU and US authorities to move towards full mutual reliance by 2009. In January 2011, the European Commission recognized the equivalence of the audit oversight systems in ten third countries.[14] The decision on US equivalence was limited in time, because the US did not fully support mutual reliance on the oversight of auditors by their home country oversight system. As a way to keep pressure on the US authorities, the Commission reserved the right to reassess the situation in three years' time.

The European Commission's efforts to adopt international auditing standards in the EU continued during the global financial crisis. In 2009, the Commission undertook a public consultation on the formal adoption of ISAs in the EU, which was supported by the majority of respondents to the consultation.[15] An independent study commissioned by the European Commission and undertaken by the University of Duisberg-Essen (2009) concluded that 'on balance, an adoption of the ISAs in the EU would result in quantitative and qualitative benefits for companies, investors, and regulators'.[16] In 2009, the Commission also published an independent study on the evaluation of the differences between the ISA and the standards of the US Public Company Accounting Oversight Board. The study concluded that 'the number of areas for which substantive differences exist between the clarified ISAs and the US Public Company Accounting Oversight Board standards is limited'.[17]

As a response to the global financial crisis, in November 2011, the Commission proposed a regulation to increase the quality of audits of financial statements of public-interest entities and a directive to enhance the single market for statutory audits. Audit firms were required to rotate after a maximum engagement period of six years (with some exceptions). The rotation period was nine years in the case of joint audits, which were encouraged. Public-interest entities were obliged to have an open tender procedure to select a new auditor. Audit firms were prohibited from providing non-audit services to their audit clients. In addition, large audit firms were obliged to separate audit activities from non-audit activities in order to avoid risks of conflict of interest. The proposals required all statutory auditors and audit firms to comply with international auditing standards when carrying out

[13] <http://europa.eu/rapid/press-release_SPEECH-07-757_en.htm> (accessed Oct. 2011).

[14] Australia, Canada, China, Croatia, Japan, Singapore, South Africa, South Korea, Switzerland, and the United States of America.

[15] <http://ec.europa.eu/internal_market/consultations/2009/isa_en.htm> (accessed Mar. 2012).

[16] <http://ec.europa.eu/internal_market/consultations/docs/2009/isa/consultation_ISAs_en.pdf> (accessed Apr. 2012).

[17] <http://ec.europa.eu/internal_market/auditing/isa/index_en.htm#isastudy> (accessed Mar. 2012).

statutory audits. These proposals elicited a strong backlash from the auditing profession, in particular from the big players, which wished to retain the status quo and feared that the proposals would be detrimental to their business (interviews, Brussels, June 2012, July 2013).

The Commission proposed the creation of a single market for statutory audits by introducing a European passport for the audit profession, based on the mutual recognition of statutory auditors approved in member states to ensure the cross-border mobility of auditors. The mandate, powers, and independence requirements for audit supervisors were established at EU level, but supervision was to be carried out nationally. Cooperation and coordination at European level was to be ensured by ESMA, which took over the current functions of the European Group of Auditor Oversight Bodies.

As for the adoption of international standards in the EU, it is noteworthy that the Commission changed its strategy. The revised article 26 stated: '1. Member States shall ensure that statutory auditors and audit firms comply with... international auditing standards when carrying out statutory audits...' Hence, it is the responsibility of the member states, not the Commission, to adopt the ISA domestically. What can explain the change of strategy since 2006? Most likely the EU authorities wanted to avoid the repetition of what happened with the controversial adoption of accounting standards in the EU through the endorsement process. The European Parliament felt marginalized in that process, which was also subject to political lobbying that resulted in the carve-outs. Hence, the burden of the adoption of international auditing standards in the EU was passed on to the member states (interview, Brussels, June 2012).

The Regulatory Capacity of the US in Auditing

Historically, the US had weak regulatory capacity in auditing, unlike in accounting. The main turning point in the development of regulatory capacity in auditing in the US was the Sarbanes-Oxley Act in 2002, following the Enron scandal, which underscored several auditing irregularities, and led to the demise of Arthur Andersen, one of the main auditing firms worldwide.

The Institutional Framework for Auditing Regulation in the US

Prior to the Sarbanes-Oxley Act, auditors in the US were subject to self-regulation: the SEC was responsible for oversight, but the professional organization of American auditors (the American Institute of Certified Public Accountants) set audit standards and rules of professional ethics.

The Sarbanes-Oxley Act created the Public Company Accounting Oversight Board, which is an independent private non-profit body funded by levies on audit firms and public companies. It maintains a register of accounting firms that provide audit services to companies publicly traded in the US, sets auditing and ethics standards for auditors, and carries out disciplinary actions against audit firms. It is subject to SEC oversight and the SEC appoints the members of the board. The SEC is responsible for approving rules and disciplinary actions and has appeal functions for audit firms unhappy with the Public Company Accounting Oversight Board decisions (Gadinis 2008).

Regulatory Templates for Auditing Regulation in the US

The Sarbanes-Oxley Act and the establishment of the Public Company Accounting Oversight Board had significant extraterritorial effects. Any firm that offered audit services to companies whose stocks were publicly traded in US markets had to register with the Public Company Accounting Oversight Board and was subject to its jurisdiction. This created a problem for foreign issuers listed in the US stock exchange and audited by audit firms in their home countries. International branches or subsidiaries of US companies operating abroad also used local audit companies, on whose opinion US auditors relied when they audited parent companies in the US (Gadinis 2008). The provisions of the Sarbanes-Oxley Act raised the compliance costs for foreign firms that had to comply with the US Public Company Accounting Oversight Board rules. It was also expensive for the Public Company Accounting Oversight Board which had to carry out inspections outside the US, creating enforcement problems (Gadinis 2008).

Moreover, it was problematic for foreign auditors to release certain information that was regarded as confidential in their home jurisdiction to the US Public Company Accounting Oversight Board. For inspections outside the US, the Public Company Accounting Oversight Board partly relied on foreign regimes to different degrees. The greater the independence of a national regime from the profession, the greater the reliance of the Public Company Accounting Oversight Board on it (Eberle and Lauter 2011; Gadinis 2008). This was because the end of self-regulation by the profession was at the core of the reforms introduced in the US. The diversity of audit regimes within the EU, where some member states relied on self-regulation by professional associations, prevented mutual recognition with the US. It also made difficult international harmonization, which was supported by large, multinational audit companies (Gadinis 2008).

The EU, especially the European Commission, was vocal in its reaction to the extraterritorial effects of the Sarbanes-Oxley Act. Externally, there was a statement from the Council of Economic and Finance Ministers with a threat to retaliate (see Posner 2009a). Internally, the European Commission, with the support of the member states, set out to upgrade its regulatory templates in auditing. As Posner (2009a) notes, the issue was resolved with mutual regulatory adjustments, whereby the Public Company Accounting Oversight Board allowed foreign auditors to omit information if these disclosures violated home countries rules. EU policy-makers also made regulatory adjustments, trying to increase intra-EU harmonization on auditing and reducing reliance on self regulation, through the new 8th Company Law Directive. In 2008, the Public Company Accounting Oversight Board proposed mutual recognition, whereby it would accept inspections by some non-US counterparts (PCAOB 2008).[18]

International Auditing Standards

As in the case of accounting, the main international standard-setters in auditing are private bodies. The predecessor of the International Auditing and Assurance Standards Board began issuing auditing standards in the late 1980s. Over time the number of standards steadily increased. Nowadays, over 100 countries adopt or incorporate ISAs in their national auditing standards.

The Institutional Framework for Audit Regulation Internationally

The ISAs are developed by independent committees of the International Federation of Accountants, which is the global, private organization representing the accounting profession. Its members are primarily national professional accountancy bodies from more than 120 jurisdictions. The most relevant committee is the IAASB, which was set up in New York in 2002. Its predecessor was the International Auditing Practices Committee, which was established in 1977.

In 2003, the International Federation of Accountants approved a series of reforms designed to strengthen its standard-setting processes, including those of the IAASB, so as to make them responsive to the public interest.[19] The timing of this reform is explained by the Sarbanes-Oxley Act in the US, as well as the possibility that the EU would adopt international auditing standards. The Monitoring Group was established to oversee the implementation of the reform: its members are the BCBS, the IAIS, the IOSCO, the World Bank, and the European Commission. In cooperation with the International Federation of Accountants it decided to create the Public Interest Oversight Board for the oversight of the standard-setting activities, including that of the IAASB, and this was established in 2005. It has a small full-time secretariat

[18] <http://www.sec.gov/news/press/2008/2008-9.htm> (accessed Apr. 2013).
[19] <http://www.sec.gov/news/speech/2009/spch120709amp.htm#foot2> (accessed Mar. 2013).

with a secretary-general. For the ten members of the Board, it is a part-time job. The Monitoring Group is responsible for the selection and appointment of the Board members, including its chairman. The main objective of the Public Interest Oversight Board is to ensure that the standard-setting activities are responsive to the public interest. It oversees the IAASB and two other standard-setting committees of the International Federation of Accountants, namely, the International Ethics Standards Board for Accountants and the International Accounting Education Standards Board.

In 2006, national audit regulatory agencies and oversight boards formed a new international body, namely the International Forum of Independent Audit Regulators. The Forum facilitates coordination and information sharing amongst its members. It includes member bodies from thirty-eight countries. The formation of national agencies had been the result of the move away from self-regulation of the auditing profession towards a system of independent oversight, as explained in the previous sections.

International Regulatory Templates in Auditing

The predecessor of the IAASB began to issue auditing standards as early as the 1980s. Its initial work focused on three areas: object and scope of audits of financial statements; engagement letters; and general auditing guidelines. In 1991, the guidelines of the International Auditing Practices Committee were recodified as the ISA. An updated codified version of the ISA was issued in 1994. Despite its support for international high-quality audit standards, the IOSCO was reluctant to endorse the ISA. It did not agree with the division of text in the standards between basic principles and essential procedures because significant components appeared to be advisory rather than mandatory (Humphrey et al. 2009). The IOSCO was also concerned about the excessive role of the auditing profession in the standard-setting process in the International Auditing Practices Committee (Humphrey et al. 2009). From 1994 onwards, the IOSCO, the BCBS, the IASC, and the European Commission became involved in the activities of the International Auditing Practices Committee as a consultative advisory group.

In 2001, the Financial Stability Forum, now FSB, included the ISA amongst the key standards for financial stability. In so doing, public authority underpinned private standards, giving them a different status. In 2004, the IAASB began the Clarity Project, reviewing the conventions used in its international standards in order to improve the clarity, and thereby the consistent application, of these standards worldwide. The project was completed in 2009. The reform of the governance structure of the International Federation of Accountants and the completion of the Clarity Project with a view to improving ISAs convinced the IOSCO to endorse the ISAs for the audit of cross-border offerings and listing in 2009. However, it recognized that 'the decision on whether to do so will depend on a number of factors and circumstances in their jurisdiction' (IOSCO 2009b: 2).

Overall, the reforms made to the constitution of the International Federation of Accountants, the establishment of the Public Interest Oversight Board, and the completion of the IAASB's Clarity Project seem to have had an impact on the perceived standing of the ISAs (Humphrey et al. 2009). To date, thirty-six international standards on auditing and twenty international auditing practice statements have been published. Over 100 countries adopt or incorporate the ISA in their national auditing standards.

The Industry and International Accounting and Auditing Regulation

The financial industry, the accounting profession, and the big auditing firms have played an important role in the development of accounting and auditing standards in the EU, as well as globally. Three main considerations are, however, important. First, prior to the regulatory changes of the 2000s, accounting and auditing were prime examples of private-sector governance. Professional associations were delegated by the public authorities the power to set the rules and monitor their compliance. As a reaction to the policy failures of the early 2000s and later as a response to the global financial crisis, the public authorities in the EU, the US, and elsewhere have strengthened the monitoring of these private-sector bodies.

Second, the main transnational players inside and outside the financial industry were by and large in favour of international regulatory convergence. So were the accounting profession and the big audit firms. The renewed impulse for accounting harmonization in the EU in the late 1990s came mainly from the big financial players, as well as large non-financial companies that had much to gain from a harmonized set of accounting standards across the EU and *vis-à-vis* the US (Camfferman and Zeff 2007). However, some divergences remained (often along national lines) about the specific content of those standards, as suggested by the extensive lobbying that led to two carve-outs in the EU. As for auditing, responses to consultations conducted by the Commission also revealed overwhelming support by companies and the profession for the adoption of international auditing standards in the EU in the 2000s.

In the US, pressure on the SEC to back international accounting standards came mainly from American stock exchanges hoping to attract new foreign listings. The New York Stock Exchange lobbied the SEC and the Congress (Martinez-Diaz 2005). Subsequently, US multinationals that would benefit from a single set of standards raised the issue of filing their statements in accordance with the IFRS (Lütz and Eberle 2008; Posner 2010). In 2005, 37 per cent of the world's largest publicly listed companies listed in the US and reported only under the US GAAP; 39 per cent were listed in the EU, Australia, China, or Singapore, which mandated the IFRS or near-identical standards, and 20 per cent were in countries such as Canada or Japan that were converging towards the IFRS (Véron 2007: 16).

Third, the dominance of the accounting profession within the IASC and the IASB provided some glue to the professional epistemic community active in these bodies (Botzem 2008), even though the influence of the profession diminished over time. The big audit firms were also important players. Four multinational corporations dominate the auditing market: Ernst & Young, Deloitte, KPMG, and PricewaterhouseCoopers. The vast majority of the world's largest companies are audited by one of these four firms. The market share of the Big Four for audits of listed companies exceeds 85 per cent in the vast majority of member states. In the UK, the Big Four audit 99 per cent of the FTSE. In Germany, two Big Four firms have the audit mandates for 90 per cent of the companies listed on the DAX 30 (KPMG and PricewaterhouseCoopers). In Spain, all IBEX 35 companies are audited by the Big Four.[20] These companies have their headquarters in the US or the UK and are organized as networks, each of which is a separate and independent legal entity under the global firm. The Big Four have offices worldwide because the knowledge of local accounting standards and proximity to the clientele are important in the auditing market (e.g. PricewaterhouseCoopers has offices in 150 countries) (Humphrey et al. 2009).

Conclusion

In accounting, a combination of weak EU regulatory capacity and strong US regulatory capacity led to the uploading of the US regulatory templates and governance model to the IASB, until the early 2000s. In the same period, the US also cross-loaded some of its accounting rules to the EU, and in particular to EU firms listing in the US. International accounting standards were subsequently downloaded by the EU, taking into account some European specificities, through 'carve-outs'. After the global financial crisis, given the fact that the EU is the largest jurisdiction to adopt the IFRS, the EU has tried to exert greater influence on the IASB standard-setting process and governance

[20] <http://europa.eu/rapid/press-release_MEMO-11-856_en.htm?locale=en> (accessed Mar. 2014).

structure. The results so far have been limited, but the issue has gained political momentum. The beefing up of EU regulatory capacity in accounting and the coming to a halt of the convergence process between IFRS and GAAP raise the possibility that they might become potential rival standards.

In auditing, a combination of weak EU and US regulatory capacities meant that international auditing standards were set by private-sector bodies at the national level until the early 2000s. International auditing standards did not carry much weight. Once the US beefed up its regulatory capacity, some disputes emerged between the US and the EU because of the cross-loading effects of the Sarbanes-Oxley rules. Consequently, the European Commission, with the support of the member states, attempted to step up the EU regulatory capacity in auditing in order to be better positioned to negotiate with the US counterparts. The European Commission also proposed the downloading of the ISA in the EU, but left this task to the member states.

The US, and to some extent the UK, were very influential in shaping international accounting standards. Nobes and Parker (2006: 97) argue that the IASB 'is heavily dominated by former Anglo-Saxon standard-setters'. Moreover, the support of the FASB for the convergence of US accounting standards and international standards made it more likely that international accounting standards would be developed according to the Anglo-Saxon model (Dewing and Russell 2008).

In the EU, there were deep-seated divisions along national lines concerning accounting. The different preferences of member states slowed down intra-EU negotiations and re-emerged with reference to the IASB, whereby the British authorities sided with the US. Over time, this division was reduced by the spread of Anglo-Saxon accounting and the completion of the single financial market in the EU. Dewing and Russell (2008: 257) also point out the influence of the profession and the main players therein: 'Standing behind the accountancy profession are the big four global accountancy firms which dominate the market for listed company audit, national professional bodies and associated institutions and have strong Anglo-American origins.' Big companies, in particular, called for a harmonized set of accounting standards across the EU and across the Atlantic. However, after the global financial crisis, the global convergence of accounting standards lost momentum.

Market size is a necessary but not a sufficient condition for influencing global accounting and auditing rules. The large US securities market was an important potential power resource for the US authorities (see Table 4.2). In accounting, where the US had a strong regulatory capacity, the US authorities were able to actively cross-load domestic rules to the EU. They also uploaded domestic institutional and regulatory templates to the international level. In auditing, where the US has a large domestic market but no strong regulatory capacity prior to the Sarbanes-Oxley Act, the US did not cross-load or upload rules. Following the Act, the US authorities attempted to actively cross-load some of their new rules to the EU. The EU, however, was in the process of completing its single financial market and beefing up its regulatory capacity in auditing, hence it was better positioned to counteract US pressure.

7

An Overall Cross-Sectoral Assessment Over Time

This chapter begins by discussing the various combinations of regulatory capacity in the EU and the US, as well as the sequencing effects in the development of domestic regulatory capacity and international standard-setting. Subsequently, it discusses alternative or complementary explanations for international regulatory convergence. This is followed by an explanation of the development of regulatory capacity in the EU. It also briefly compares financial services regulation to other economic policies. The final section discusses the proposal for Banking Union, elaborating its implications for the EU and international financial regulation.

The Combinations of Regulatory Capacities in the EU and the US Across Sectors and Over Time

Using the concept of 'regulatory capacity', defined as 'a jurisdiction's ability to formulate, monitor, and enforce a set of market rules' (Bach and Newman 2007: 831), this research argues that different combinations of 'strong' and 'weak' EU and US regulatory capacities account for the uploading, cross-loading, and downloading of rules by these jurisdictions and hence their ability to influence global regulatory convergence in finance over time. A two-by-two explanatory matrix was outlined in Chapter 2, with weak/strong EU regulatory capacity on one side and weak/strong US regulatory capacity on the other (Table 2.1).

If EU regulatory capacity is weak and US regulatory capacity is strong, the EU mainly downloads international rules uploaded by the US, as in the case of Basel I. Or it passively cross-loads rules from the US, as in the case of securities trading in the 1990s and early 2000s (Table 7.1). Or both, as in the case of accounting standards, whereby several national authorities in Europe

Table 7.1. The analytical framework applied to banking, securities, insurance

		US regulatory capacity	
		Strong	Weak
EU regulatory capacity	Strong	Banking (2000s) US and EU upload rules in Basel IIII (2010) EU and US download Basel III into national legislation (ongoing) *UK sides with US* Securities trading (2000s) and rating agencies, hedge funds, OTC derivatives (post-crisis) EU and US mutually cross-load rules *UK sides with the EU and US*	Insurance (2000s) EU uploads Solvency II and reinsurance rules to IAIS standards (ongoing) and actively cross-loads rules *UK sides with EU*
	Weak	Banking (pre-2000) US upload Basel I (1989) EU downloads Basel I into legislation (1993) *UK sides with US* Securities trading (pre-2000) US actively cross-loads rules to the EU *UK sides with the US*	Rating agencies, hedge funds, OTC derivatives (pre-crisis) industry self-regulation *UK sides with US*

allowed companies based in their territory but listed in the US to prepare their financial statements according to the Generally Accepted Accounting Principles (GAAP), de facto cross-loading these rules into their jurisdictions (Table 7.2). The US authorities were also influential in shaping the international accounting standards issued by the International Accounting Standards Board (IASB), uploading US accounting templates. International accounting standards were subsequently downloaded by the EU. In these cases, the EU performs mainly a 'passive' role in international regulatory convergence. It is a rule-taker rather than a rule-maker.

If the EU regulatory capacity is strong and US regulatory capacity is weak, the EU is able to upload its regulatory templates internationally, as in the case of solvency requirements for insurers. Or the EU cross-loads its rules to the US, as in the case of collateral rules for reinsurers. In both instances, the EU performs an 'active' role in international regulatory convergence. It is a rule-maker rather than a rule-taker.

If both EU and US regulatory capacities are strong, there is an exchange of rule elements vertically and/or horizontally. These jurisdictions upload parts

Table 7.2. The analytical framework applied to accounting and auditing

		US regulatory capacity	
		Strong	Weak
EU regulatory capacity	Strong	Accounting (post-crisis) US and EU increase monitoring power on the IASB EU seeks to influence revision of international accounting standards End of IFRS–GAAP convergence, potential for rival standards Auditing (post-2005) US actively cross-loads rules EU resist cross-loading EU exerts greater influence on revision of international auditing standards EU downloads international rules *UK sides with EU*	
	Weak	Accounting US uploads international standards and actively cross-loads them to the EU EU downloads international standards (2005–) with carve outs *UK sides with the US*	Auditing (pre-2005) Industry self-regulation (pre-2005) at the national and international level

of their regulatory templates into international standards and then download these standards domestically, sometimes with significant adaptations—this was the case with Basel III. There can also be reciprocal cross-loading of rules between the EU and the US, as in the case of the proposed mutual recognition of rules concerning securities trading, as well as the Norwalk agreement on accounting standards and the convergence process that ensued from it. Other examples of potential cross-loading are the post-crisis rules on rating agencies, hedge funds, and over-the-counter derivatives. Alternatively, the EU and the US could set up rival standards (see Drezner 2007), instead of converging. After the global financial crisis, the convergence of IFRS (adopted by the EU) and US GAAP has come to a halt. Potentially, they could become rival standards, with the proviso that the EU allows US companies listed on EU stock exchange to use GAAP and vice versa.

If EU and US regulatory capacities are weak, these jurisdictions do not have domestic regulatory templates to upload or cross-load. Standard-setting activity is likely to be delegated to industry through self-regulation, as was the case for auditors, rating agencies, hedge funds, and over-the-counter derivatives prior to the financial crisis. As will be explained, these financial players were often successful in preventing the development of statutory rules, either domestically or internationally. After the global financial crisis, they were no longer able to do so.

The temporal dimension—the sequencing of the development of domestic regulatory capacity—is important: to be precise the setting in place of robust regulatory templates in the EU and the US and the development of international standards creates a process of path-dependence (for a similar argument see Mügge 2011a; Posner 2010). If the EU has strengthened its regulatory capacity in a given sector by establishing its own regulatory template prior to international standard-setting, then it is better positioned to influence the making of international standards by uploading its regulatory templates, as in the case of solvency rules for insurers. Vice versa, if international standards have already been developed in a given sector, the EU will continue to download international standards, in a path-dependent way, as in the case of the Basel accords and, to some extent, accounting standards.

If the US has developed regulatory capacity on a given financial service prior to the EU, as was the case with securities trading, accounting standards, and some aspects of banking legislation, then the US enjoys a first-mover advantage in international standard setting and *vis-à-vis* the EU. Similarly, if the EU has strengthened its regulatory capacity on a given financial service prior to the US, as in the case of insurance, it is better able to influence the making of international standards. If the EU and the US develop domestic rules at the same time, as in the cases of most post-financial-crisis legislation, they will have an incentive to consider the potential cross-loading effects of their respective regulatory templates.

Overall, does the EU act as a rule-maker in regulating global finance, or is it mainly a rule-taker and why? Has this changed over time, especially after the completion of Economic and Monetary Union (EMU) and the single financial market, or after the global financial crisis? Taking a dynamic historical approach, in the past the US had a predominant role in global financial regulation because of the size of its market and its strong regulatory capacity in banking, securities trading, and accounting, less so in insurance and auditing. The EU has increasingly become an active player in international regulatory convergence, whereby the main turning points were the completion of EMU and of the single financial market in the early 2000s, and the post-crisis period. These periods coincided with important developments in the regulatory capacity of the EU.

Amongst the member states, the UK deserves special attention because in international standard-setting this country sometimes sided with the rest of the EU, as in the case of insurance solvency requirements in the 2000s. At other times, it sided with the US, as in the case of the (non-)regulation of hedge funds and rating agencies prior to the crisis, and capital requirements for banks. Depending on where the UK sat in international standard-setting, it either strengthened the EU's ability to shape those standards—if the UK sided with the rest of the EU, as in the case of insurance—or it weakened it, when the UK sided with the US, as in the case of Basel I, Basel III, and pre-crisis self-regulation for hedge funds and rating agencies. In the passive cross-loading of US rules to the EU, the UK often sided with the US, as in the cases of accounting standards and templates for securities trading in the 1990s and 2000s. In the active cross-loading of EU rules to the US, the UK was particularly concerned about the equivalence clauses introduced in EU financial legislation in the 2000s (especially post-crisis), given the strong financial transatlantic ties of the City of London.

The empirical chapters showed that the EU should be decomposed into different 'components' (or 'actors') in the uploading, downloading, and cross-loading phases. In the downloading process, the European Commission proposed the incorporation of international rules into EU legislation, which was co-decided by the European Parliament and the Council of Ministers. In uploading, the European Commission was present (as an observer) in the international fora into which EU regulatory templates were uploaded and was sometimes instrumental in this process.

In passive cross-loading, the Commission borrowed regulatory templates on securities trading from the US, and these pieces of legislation were then co-decided by the Parliament and the Council. The European Commission repeatedly asked the SEC to agree to mutual recognition, which the SEC called 'substituted compliance'. In active cross-loading, the Commission negotiated with third countries' authorities and was responsible for decisions concerning equivalence, following the advice of European supervisory authorities. In the post-crisis period, the Commission also liaised with the US authorities in the preparation of their respective domestic rules on rating agencies, hedge funds, and derivatives (interviews, Brussels, Apr. 2011, Washington, Aug. 2011).

Alternative and Complementary Explanations for International Regulatory Convergence in Finance

In the literature, some alternative or complementary explanations have been put forward for international regulatory convergence in finance. The first explanation focuses on *market size*, the argument being that access to (hence control of) a large domestic market increases a jurisdiction's ability to make rules for global finance (Drezner 2007; Simmons 2001; with reference to the EU, see also Damro 2012; Dür 2011). Unless financial firms in other jurisdictions comply with the rules of the jurisdiction with a large market, they will not be able to access that market. Moreover, a jurisdiction with a large market will have greater say in international regulatory fora, because its support is crucial for the making of international standards.

This explanation was used to account for the nearly hegemonic role of the US in international standard-setting in finance up to the late 1990s. However, after the (near) completion of the single financial market in the EU, the EU has a market size similar to that of the US in several financial services. The main exceptions are rating agencies, hedge funds, and fund managers. Indeed, the main rating agencies are North American and operate in the EU with subsidiaries. Hedge fund managers are mostly located in the US, and to some extent in the UK. Hedge funds are generally domiciled offshore (see Table 4.4). Nonetheless, it is not straightforward to define the market size for these financial services because their products (credit ratings or hedge fund investments) are widely used outside the US, including in the EU.

As noted by Bach and Newman (2010), the size of the financial market is a potential capability or a power resource that can be deployed by a given jurisdiction. It is a necessary but not sufficient condition for a jurisdiction to be able to influence international regulatory convergence: regulatory capacity is also needed. This is especially true in the EU, which is a regional jurisdiction that has a true single market only when it is regulated by uniform sets of rules. Otherwise it is a collection of national markets in Europe, not a single market. On its own, regulatory capacity is not a sufficient condition because unless a jurisdiction controls a large internal market it is likely to have limited weight in the uploading of its rules to international standard-setting bodies and its possibilities for active cross-loading are very limited. Hence, a large internal market and regulatory capacity are two necessary and complementary conditions for a jurisdiction's ability to influence international regulatory convergence in finance (and elsewhere).

The second alternative or complementary explanation for international regulatory convergence concerns *lobbying from the financial industry* (see Lall 2012; Underhill et al. 2010; Young 2012). This explanation can be combined with the explanation based on regulatory capacity because the financial industry located in a given jurisdiction (be it the US or the EU) generally has a vested interested in supporting the uploading of (national or regional) rules to the international level, so as to minimize the costs of complying with international standards and to prevent regulatory arbitrage to their disadvantage.

Thus, if the EU has robust regulatory templates in place, the financial industry based in the EU has an incentive to lobby for the adoption of EU rules internationally or in third jurisdictions, or at least for EU rules to be subject to mutual recognition in third countries. A similar reasoning applies in the US. In the case of the Basel I accord, US banks stood behind the attempt of the US authorities to set in place international capital rules in line with those introduced in the US. US banks feared competition from Japanese banks, which were subject to lower domestic capital requirements (Kapstein 1989; Simmons 2001). In the case of Basel III, European banks lobbied their national regulators and the Basel Committee on Banking Supervision (BCBS) in order to maintain the definitions of capital in place at the domestic level (which, for example, included silent participations in Germany).

In the case of securities market legislation, the financial industry in the EU stood behind the European Commission's efforts to negotiate mutual recognition with the Securities and Exchange Commission (SEC) concerning several aspects of securities trading in the 1990s. Industry also supported the European Commission's request to end the (costly) reconciliation requirements in accounting standards for European companies listed in the US in the 2000s. In accounting and auditing standards, the main transnational financial and non-financial companies favoured harmonized international accounting standards, which would reduce their compliance costs across jurisdictions (Leblond 2011).

In insurance regulation, the EU reinsurance industry stood behind the European Parliament (EP) and the Commission concerning the request to change the treatment of European reinsurers in the US in the mid-2000s. The main EU insurance companies supported the uploading of the Solvency II requirements to the international level because they were already bearing the costs of adapting to this new piece of legislation in the EU. They also hoped that the activities of the International Association of Insurance Supervisors (IAIS) could be instrumental in easing the access of EU reinsurers to the US market.

If a jurisdiction has no domestic regulatory capacity concerning certain financial services, that part of the financial industry has a strong incentive to prevent public regulation, either domestically or internationally. Instead, industry will favour self-regulation, which can be instrumental in staving off public regulation, as hedge funds, rating agencies, and derivatives were able to do prior to the crisis. Self-regulation can promote international standardization, which facilitates cross-border activities, as in the case of derivatives trading, accounting, and auditing.

With the exceptions of the financial services subject to private-sector governance, namely accounting and auditing, amongst the cases examined, only in Basel II did the financial industry (to be precise, the main transnational banks) play a leading role in international standard-setting. Unlike in Basel I, in Basel II the two main jurisdictions (i.e. the US and the EU) did not upload domestic rules: the main regulatory changes were spearheaded by the main transnational banks.

The third alternative explanation for international regulatory convergence concerns the specific features of various *policy areas* or *financial services*.[1] This

[1] I wish to thank a reviewer for this point.

somewhat 'functionalist' explanation argues that certain financial services are more amenable to international financial harmonization because of their distinctive features. These features have to do mostly with systemic risk, externalities, investor protection, and regulatory competition.

One argument is that the higher the systemic risk posed by a financial service as well as the cross-border (negative) externalities it can cause, the higher the incentive for international regulatory convergence. This explanation, which is often subscribed to by economists, maintains that banks were more regulated (internationally as well as domestically) than investment firms, insurance, rating agencies, hedge funds, and derivatives because of the far-reaching implications of banking failures for systemic stability. Yet, during the financial crisis, the US government's rescue of several investment firms as well as of the insurance company AIG demonstrated that these activities can also have systemic implications and be in need of government financial support. Likewise, the poor performance of rating agencies and over-the-counter derivatives markets were at the origins of the global financial crisis.

Another version of this argument, which is used to explain the presence (or absence) of regulation in a certain financial service, has to do with the kind of customers (or investors) active in that sector. The argument is that sophisticated customers or wholesale investors need less protection than small unsophisticated investors. Hence, in the first case there is less need for public regulation. This argument was used, for example, to justify the absence of public regulation of hedge funds or derivatives. However, several hedge fund scandals demonstrated that ordinary non-sophisticated investors were also directly affected by hedge fund failures and so were supposedly sophisticated investors, including US municipalities that subsequently needed to be rescued through public financial support.

Finally, a *constructivist* or *sociological institutionalist* explanation would argue that there has been a remarkable ideational convergence in the world of finance over the past thirty years or so. Indeed, prior to the global financial crisis, the neoliberal paradigm in finance (Best 2003; Gamble 2009; Nesvetailova and Palan 2010) and the 'governance light' approach based on a benign view of financial markets and grounded in efficient market theories (Underhill et al. 2010) were in good currency in the US, the EU, and other main jurisdictions. To some extent, there has been ideational convergence concerning finance worldwide, and the EU and the US have mostly cooperated in global financial regulation. However, within the shared neoliberal paradigm, the EU and the US have kept their distinctive regulatory models, often competing for influence in regulating global finance by uploading their rules to international regulatory fora and by actively cross-loading their rules to other jurisdictions, as explained in this book.

Explaining the Development of Regulatory Capacity in the EU Across Financial Services

In the first part of the explanation put forward by this research, the regulatory capacities of the EU and the US are the independent variables, the combinations of which explain the uploading, downloading, and cross-loading of rules for global finance, or industry self-regulation. But what explains the development (or the lack) of regulatory capacity across financial services in a given jurisdiction?

This issue is particularly complex with reference to the EU, which is a regional jurisdiction. The main explanatory factors for the building up (or otherwise) of the regulatory capacity of the EU in given financial services were: the activity of policy entrepreneurs—generally the Commission and one or two large member states (the UK or France and Germany), and the support of member states with similar (or at least compatible) preferences. In turn, member states' preferences were mostly shaped by their domestic political economies, in particular the configuration of the national financial sector and its link to the real economy. In some cases, the opposition of the entities or activities to be regulated (e.g. rating agencies, hedge funds) also played an important role in preventing EU rules.

Let us consider these components in turn. The European Commission often performed the function of policy entrepreneur in finance as well as in other policy areas. Nonetheless, the Commission was mindful of the preferences of the member states. For this reason, until the late 1990s, the strategy chosen by the Commission was based on minimum harmonization, coupled with mutual recognition and national supervision (Padoa-Schioppa 2004b). In banking, the Commission, with the support of the member states, promoted market integration early on. However, it was more difficult for the national authorities to agree on prudential rules, such as capital requirements for banks. At that time, the member states had different national banking systems and different domestic regulatory templates. As a way out of the impasse, the European Commission suggested the downloading of the Basel accord into the EU, which was endorsed by the member states. A similar strategy was followed with reference to accounting and auditing standards in the 2000s.

Until the late 1990s, securities market integration and regulation was a sensitive issue for the member states, which had different preferences rooted in their domestic political economy. The configuration of national capital markets and their regulation differed across the EU. Moreover, securities market regulation was linked to other sensitive policy areas, such as corporate finance, corporate governance, and taxation (Story and Walter 1997). The Commission was reluctant to put forward significant regulatory initiatives.

When it did, as in the case of the Investment Services Directive, the complexity of the negotiations resulted in the adoption of EU regulatory templates based on minimum harmonization, as a result of several compromises. In accounting, despite the Commission's efforts, even minimal harmonization was difficult: member states had incompatible preferences, based on different national accounting systems (Botzem 2012).

By the late 1990s, the Commission, the member states, and their financial industries were well aware that the single financial market was far from being completed. For example, different prospectuses had to be prepared by issuers for different European markets, despite the Listing Particulars Directive (Ferran 2004). The Investment Services Directive had not dismantled the privileged position granted to certain national stock exchanges by the concentration rule. In insurance, solvency rules were not harmonized and there were no EU rules for reinsurers. No progress had been made on the harmonization of accounting standards in the EU, despite the Commission's efforts (van Hulle 2004). The Commission hardly tried to promote auditing harmonization in the EU in that period.

It became clear to the Commission, which enlisted the support of the member states, that for the completion of the single market two reforms were needed (Mügge 2006; Quaglia 2007). First, a reform of the institutional framework for financial services regulation and supervision—the Lamfalussy reform, designed to speed up the rule-making process. Second, a wave of new EU legislation was required, as outlined by the Financial Services Action Plan (FSAP), and was to be based mostly on maximum harmonization. Hence, the strengthening of EU regulatory capacity in several financial services was instrumental to the completion of the single market.

Financial market integration in Europe had been a long-standing priority for the Commission (Jabko 2006). By the late 1990s, it became a priority for the member states and parts of their financial industries for two main reasons: the desire to complete the single European market, which would equal the size of the US market for many financial services; and the opportunities for cross-border expansion that the most competitive parts of national financial industries actively sought. In securities markets, large investment banks in the main member states and demutualized stock exchanges were keen to expand their cross-border activities (Mügge 2010). In insurance, EU reinsurers were eager to expand across the EU as well as in the US. The main insurers were to benefit from the harmonized set of solvency rules under Solvency II, especially the provisions on group support and supervision (Quaglia 2011b). In accounting, financial and non-financial transnational companies supported the adoption of harmonized standards across the EU and internationally (Leblond 2011).

In line with the light-touch regulatory philosophy that prevailed at the European Commission at that time, the EU rules issued following the FSAP in the early 2000s were mostly designed to complete the single financial market and foster market integration. No rules were proposed for some financial entities or instruments, such as rating agencies, hedge funds, and derivatives. Self-regulation by industry was encouraged. Accounting standards were also delegated by the EU to a private standard-setting body, as explained in Chapter 6.

Thus, the first Barroso Commission did not act as a policy entrepreneur in promoting the regulation of (unregulated) financial services. After the global financial crisis, the second Barroso Commission reversed its light-touch regulatory approach, proposing new legislation on all these activities. The turn-around of the Commission was the result of several factors: lessons drawn from the crisis; the desire of the President of the Commission to be reappointed, which encouraged him to adopt a 'tough' stance *vis-à-vis* the financial industry; the appointment of a Frenchman as Internal Market Commissioner in the second Barroso Commission; and the temporary setbacks for the financial industry and its weakened lobbying power in the wake of the crisis (see Quaglia 2012).

The changed balance of power in the EU and the realignment of preferences amongst the member states was very important in the building up of EU regulatory capacity in certain financial services after the crisis. The UK had a pivotal role before and after the crisis. Prior to the crisis, the British authorities were very influential in shaping EU financial regulation because the UK hosted the main global financial centres in the EU and had a large financial industry, in particular when compared to the rest of the British economy (Baker 2010). British policy-makers had widely recognized expertise in the financial field and were regarded as providing state-of-the-art regulation. As argued in the previous chapters, they were influential in shaping EU securities trading regulation (Posner and Véron 2010) and new solvency rules, as well as preventing legislation on rating agencies and hedge funds, in line with their light-touch approach to financial regulation.

After the crisis, alternative views about financial services regulation began to emerge in the UK, at least in some quarters. As the Turner Review acknowledged (Financial Services Authority 2009: 38–9), the global financial crisis robustly challenged on 'both theoretical and empirical grounds' the existing 'regulatory philosophy' and the 'intellectual assumptions' of 'efficient', 'rational', and 'self correcting markets' on which it was based. In his oral evidence before the Treasury Committee, Lord Turner spoke of 'an intellectual failure' of the international regulatory community in respect of the global set of rules in place (House of Commons 2009). Andy Haldane, Executive

Director at the Bank of England, authored some imaginative papers, demonstrating the very limited contribution of the financial sector to the real economy in the UK (a view echoed by Lord Turner)[2] and arguing that over time the banks have come to 'bank on' the state, with the state providing financial assistance to the banks in case of trouble (Haldane and Alessandri 2009).

The UK came to support the building up of EU regulatory capacity in previously unregulated financial services. The efforts of British policy-makers focused on modifying the most prescriptive or burdensome (for industry) aspects of the proposed EU legislation. The UK authorities remained concerned about the possibility of international regulatory arbitrage and relocation of the financial industry outside the EU. They were also mindful about the implications of the new rules for third countries, first and foremost the US. In the discussion on post-crisis EU legislation, UK and US policy-making often acted in concert on these issues.

By now the EU has developed a strong(ish) regulatory capacity in many financial services discussed in this book, with two partial exceptions: accounting and auditing. International accounting and auditing standards are set by private-sector bodies, although they are subject to monitoring from the public authorities, including the European Commission. In accounting, the EU has set up an endorsement process for the downloading of international standards that indirectly has given the EU a greater say in the making of these standards. In auditing, the EU has decided to download international standards without an EU endorsement process and left this task to the member states. However, the EU also proposed its own rules to deal with certain aspects of the auditing markets.

Ongoing Developments: Banking Union in the EU

Over the past year or so, the most important development in EU economic governance is the proposal for the establishment of Banking Union with a view to stabilizing the national banking systems exposed directly to the sovereign debt crisis in the euro area. Banking Union is seen as a way to break the dangerous link between the high and rising sovereign debt in the euro-area peripheral member states and domestic banks, which had come to hold an increasing amount of this debt. In June 2012, the European Council and Euro Area Summit agreed to deepen EMU by creating a 'Banking Union' (*Euro Area Summit Statement* 2012). Banking Union has five main elements: a single EU rulebook; an EU deposit guarantee scheme; an EU framework for

[2] Lord Turner, in an interview for *Prospect Magazine* in Aug. 2009, warned that a 'swollen' financial sector paying excessive salaries had grown too big for society (*Financial Times*, 27 Aug. 2009).

bank recovery and resolution; a Single Supervisory Mechanism (SSM) for banks; a Single Resolution Mechanism and a common fiscal backstop for struggling banks.

A single rulebook, advocated by the EU in the aftermath of the global financial crisis, means a set of fully harmonized EU rules applied consistently across the member states. EU financial legislation mainly comprises directives, which need to be adopted by the member states in order to be implemented. Some of these directives contain several national discretions, i.e. they leave open the possibility of national options or 'specificities' in the implementation of EU rules. For example, the Capital Requirements Directive III (CRD III) (2006) contained more than 100 national discretions (Quaglia 2010b). Partly for this reason, the proposed Capital Requirement IV legislation comprises a directive based on maximum harmonization, which therefore leaves little room for manœuvre in national transposition (Commission of the European Communities 2011a); and a regulation, which is directly applicable in the member states (Commission of the European Communities 2011b) (see Chapter 3).

The Deposit Guarantee Scheme Directive and the Directive on Bank Recovery and Resolution were legislative proposals put forward by the Commission prior to the proposal for Banking Union. The principal logic behind the establishment of national guarantee schemes—which reimburse part of the amount of deposits to clients of banks that have failed—is to prevent a 'bank run', i.e. panic withdrawals of customer deposits from a bank because of fear of collapse. The EU issued a Deposit Guarantee Scheme Directive in 1994, setting the minimum level of deposit protection schemes in the EU at €20,000 per depositor. The Directive was based on minimum harmonization, hence national deposit guarantee schemes differed in several important respects, such as the definition of eligible deposits, the level of cover, the types of funding mechanism, and the calculation of members' contributions.

The global financial crisis that began in late 2007 brought into the spotlight the inadequacy of the existing Deposit Guarantee Scheme Directive (Ayadi and Lastra 2010). To begin with, the minimum level (€20,000) was too low to placate fears of a bank run. Moreover, the depositor protection coverage varied remarkably across the EU, ranging from €20,000 in most of the new member states and the UK to more than €100,000 in Italy and France. In addition, uncoordinated decisions on deposit guarantees taken by some member states (e.g. Ireland and Germany) worsened the crisis (see Quaglia et al. 2009). It became evident that different national schemes across the EU potentially distorted competition and created the potential for 'bank runs' in the EU because customers were prone to shift deposits to a bank headquartered in another member state with more generous guarantee schemes in the event of financial crises.

At the peak of the crisis, the Commission proposed legislative changes concerning the Deposit Guarantee Scheme Directive. These changes, which were agreed in a rush in 2009, represented an emergency measure designed to restore depositors' confidence by raising the minimum level of coverage for deposits from €20,000 to €50,000 and subsequently to €100,000. The need for swift action meant that several controversial issues were not tackled and hence the Directive contained a clause providing for a broad review of all aspects of deposit guarantee schemes. By 2010, deposit guarantee schemes continued to vary markedly across the member states, and only sixteen out of twenty-seven applied the coverage level of €100,000, or had legislation in place to do so (Commission of the European Communities 2010).

In July 2010, the Commission put forward a legislative proposal to amend the Deposit Guarantee Scheme Directive with a view to promoting the 'harmonisation and simplification of protected deposits, a faster pay-out, and an improved financing of schemes' (2010: 5). The proposal aimed to establish a network of guarantee schemes as a first step towards a 'pan-European deposit guarantee scheme' to cover all European Union-based banks (Commission of the European Communities 2010: 5). Such a pan-European scheme, however, presupposed full harmonization of national schemes and could only enter into force after a minimum fund of 1.5 per cent of eligible bank deposits had been reached in all member states.

One of the most contentious provisions in the Directive was the establishment of a mandatory mutual borrowing facility, whereby if a national deposit guarantee scheme is depleted, it can borrow from another national fund. Several member states tried to take this provision out while discussing this piece of legislation in the Council (interviews, Brussels, July 2012). The mutual borrowing facility could be the first step towards a pan-EU deposit guarantee scheme, which was even more controversial. Indeed, in the preparation of the Directive, the Commission considered setting up a single pan-European scheme. However, it soon realized that there were complicated legal issues that needed to be examined (Commission of the European Communities 2010) and therefore the idea of a pan-European deposit guarantee scheme was shelved for the time being. Ultimately, the problem was political. The creation of a pan-European deposit guarantee scheme would have implied pooling national sovereignty to an extent not acceptable to the member states at that time (i.e. in 2010).

When the sovereign debt crisis broke out in the euro area and proposals for Banking Union were put forward, the issue of a common deposit guarantee scheme came back onto the agenda and is likely to be a controversial issue. The main line of division is between the countries that fear that they will be net contributors to the scheme, such as Germany, and the countries experiencing banking problems (e.g. Spain, Ireland) which are likely to resort to the scheme. Moreover, Germany has a high level of depositor protection and a rather complex domestic system of public and private deposit guarantee schemes.

After prolonged consultations, the Commission put forward a formal legislative proposal for a Directive on Banks Recovery and Resolution[3] in June 2012 (Commission of the European Communities 2012c). The proposed Directive had the same scope of application as the CRD IV (hence, credit institutions and certain investment firms). It distinguished between powers of 'prevention', 'early intervention', and 'resolution'. In the case of prevention, banks are required to draw up recovery plans and resolution authorities are required to prepare resolution plans both at group level and for the individual institutions within the group. Authorities can require a bank to change its legal or operational structures to ensure that it can be resolved with the available tools. Financial groups may enter into intra-group support agreements in the form of loans, or the provision of guarantees. The framework envisages early supervisory intervention, whereby the authorities could require banks to implement measures set out in the recovery plan and would have the power to appoint a special manager at a bank for a limited period (Commission of the European Communities 2012c).

The harmonized resolution tools and powers outlined in the Directive are designed to ensure that national authorities in all member states have a common toolkit and roadmap to manage the failure of banks. Amongst the tools considered, there is a bail-in tool, whereby banks would be recapitalized, with shareholders' stakes wiped out or diluted, and creditors would have their claims reduced or converted into shares. Resolution colleges are to be established under the leadership of the group resolution authority and with the participation of the European Banking Authority (EBA), which is to act as binding mediator if necessary (Commission of the European Communities 2012).

The legislation envisaged the creation of resolution funding, which would raise contributions from banks proportionate to their liabilities and risk profiles and would not be used to bail out a bank. There is a link between this piece of legislation and the Deposit Guarantee Schemes Directive, which will provide funding for the protection of retail depositors. Member states will be allowed to merge these two funds, provided that the scheme remains in position to repay depositors in case of failure (Commission of the European Communities 2012). The Commission noted that, ideally, a single pan-European fund should be established with a pan-European resolution authority to manage its disbursal, but the absence of a single European banking supervisor and insolvency regime would make this unworkable.[4] As in

[3] 'Bank resolution' is the organization of an orderly failure, which maintains the continuity of banking service. It is an alternative or complementary mechanism to deposit guarantee schemes in the event of bank failure.

[4] <http://europa.eu/rapid/pressReleasesAction.do?reference=MEMO/12/416&format=HTML&aged=0&language=EN&guiLanguage=en> (accessed Dec. 2012).

the case of the Deposit Guarantee Schemes Directive, the obstacles to these far-reaching changes were ultimately political, the main line of division running between potential net contributors and net beneficiaries.

The EU legislative activity on bank recovery and resolution regimes was in line with international regulatory initiatives in this field undertaken by the Financial Stability Board (FSB) and the BCBS. In November 2011, the FSB issued *Key Attributes of Effective Resolution Regimes for Financial Institutions* (FSB 2011), which mainly focused on global systemically important cross-border financial institutions. It set out twelve essential features that should be part of the resolution regimes of all jurisdictions concerning: the scope of application; the resolution authority and resolution powers; recovery and resolution planning; legal framework conditions for cross-border cooperation; crisis management groups; and institution-specific cross-border cooperation agreements.

In turn, the FSB drew upon the work carried out by the BCBS. In March 2010, the BCBS published a report and a set of ten recommendations prepared by its Cross-Border Bank Resolution Group (BCBS 2010d).[5] At the June 2010 Toronto Summit, the G20 leaders endorsed the BCBS recommendations and expressed their commitment to implementing them. Several of the FSB and BCBS standards or recommendations informed specific features of the EU legislation, such as recovery and resolution planning; resolution powers, including bail-ins; and crisis management groups.

Unlike the previous three components of Banking Union, the SSM applies only to the euro-area countries and to the non-euro-area countries that decide to join Banking Union. In the SSM, responsibility for banking supervision is assigned to the ECB (Commission of the European Communities 2012b). During the negotiations, the main issue was the scope of ECB supervision, in particular whether the ECB should directly supervise all banks in the euro area (plus the opt-in countries) or only the main (cross-border) banks and the relationship with non-euro-area member states, in particular those that would not opt in.

The Germans opposed a broad scope for ECB supervision; in particular, they resisted the ECB's supervision of the country's public Landesbanks and savings banks. These banks were seen as having a 'public' function in Germany with strong ties to local and regional governments and traditionally reliant on the Lander for financial backing (Howarth and Quaglia 2013b). The French government expressed concern over unequal treatment of member states, given that its banking system was dominated by five very large

[5] These recommendations concerned 'effective national resolution powers'; 'frameworks for a coordinated resolution of financial groups'; 'convergence of national resolution measures'; 'cross-border effects of national resolution measures'; 'reduction of complexity and interconnectedness of group structures and operations'; and 'planning in advance for orderly resolution'; 'cross-border cooperation and information sharing' (BCBS 2010d).

institutions which would all end up being directly supervised by the ECB (*Financial Times*, 14 Nov. 2012).

In the end, the agreement reached at the December European Council foresaw that the ECB would be 'responsible for the overall effective functioning of the SSM' and would have 'direct oversight of the euro area banks' (European Council 2012: 2). This supervision, however, would be 'differentiated' and the Bank would carry it out in 'close cooperation with national supervisory authorities'. Direct ECB supervision was to cover those banks with assets exceeding €30 billion or those whose assets represent at least 20 per cent of their home country's annual GDP. This direct supervision would concern approximately 200 euro-area banks. However, the agreement also permits the ECB to step in, if necessary, and supervise any of the 6,000 banks in the euro area to bring about the eventual restructuring or closure of banks that find themselves in difficulties.

As for the relationship with non-euro-area members, some euro outsiders were interested in participating in the SSM and therefore opposed the regulation proposed by the European Commission in September, which placed the ECB at the centre of the mechanism. The European Council eventually decided that non-euro-area member states could opt in to the SSM and that 'opt-in' countries should be able to sit on a new ECB supervisory board with equal voting powers but not on the decision-making Governing Council (*EU Observer*, 29 Nov. 2012). The majority of non-euro member states either sought to enter Banking Union or adopted a 'wait and see' policy (Howarth and Quaglia 2013b).

The British government had no intention of joining the SSM, hence its main priority in the building up of Banking Union was to avoid a potential euro-area bloc within the single financial market. Crucially, the British feared the adoption of subsequent financial legislation that would be detrimental to the British financial sector. They also feared that the activity of the EBA would be heavily influenced by euro-area member states. Hence, the British demanded an EBA voting reform, whereby any decision by the authority should be approved by a minimum number of member states outside Banking Union and thus effectively by a 'double majority' of member states inside and outside Banking Union. The outcome of the EU negotiations was a compromise involving the creation of a double-majority system until the number of non-Banking-Union member states dwindled to less than four (Howarth and Quaglia 2013b).

In July 2012, the Commission proposed the establishment of an SRM (Commission of the European Communities 2013), designed to complement the SSM. The Commission's draft regulation envisages the establishment of a Single Resolution Board, consisting of representatives from the ECB, the European Commission, and the national resolution authorities of the countries where the bank has its headquarters as well as branches and/or subsidiaries. A Single Bank Resolution Fund would be set up under the control of the Single Resolution Board to provide financial support during the restructuring process, and be funded by the banking sector.[6] The proposal gives the ultimate decision-making power to the Commission, which would decide whether and when to place a bank into resolution and would set out a framework for the use of resolution tools and the fund.

The German government challenged this proposal on legal grounds, arguing that the Commission had overstepped its authority and that a treaty change was required for such a sweeping reform. They favoured a two-step approach, starting with a network of national authorities, and creating a centralized authority once EU treaties had been changed (*Wall Street Journal*, 10 July 2013). Beyond the legal argument, there was a financial and ultimately political argument. As for the other elements of Banking Union involving financial assistance in one way or another, German policy-makers feared that their country would be the main contributor to the resolution mechanism and that the Commission would take decisions that might have fiscal implications at the national level. Should the Single Resolution Fund not have enough financial resources to intervene, national governments (and ultimately taxpayers) would have to step in.

As for the common fiscal backstop, a link was established between Banking Union and the European Stability Mechanism (ESM) in the event that temporary financial support was needed. The ESM is a new EU agency which was to replace the temporary European Financial Stability Facility (EFSF). It was established in September 2012 and was to have a full lending capacity of €500 billion by 2014. The member states of the ESM could apply for an ESM bailout if they were in financial difficulty or their financial sector was a stability threat in need of recapitalization. However, the ESM bailouts were to be based on strong conditionality and member states were required to sign the Memorandum of Understanding which would highlight which reforms needed to be undertaken or fiscal consolidation implemented in order to restore financial stability. The Commission proposed that the ESM be used to support failing banks directly (Howarth and Quaglia 2013b).

In June 2012, the EU leaders agreed on a bailout plan for Spanish banks using Spain's Fund for Orderly Bank Restructuring, permitting the transfer of €39.5 billion from the ESM to the Fund. This transfer was accompanied by a pledge by Spain to restructure its financial sector. Nonetheless, Wolfgang Schäuble, the German Finance Minister, insisted that the ESM would not be used for other bank recapitalizations until the Banking Union was in full

[6] <http://europa.eu/rapid/press-release_IP-13-674_en.htm> (accessed July 2013).

operation (*EU Observer,* 3 Dec. 2012). The European Council agreed that the SSM would allow the ESM to recapitalize banks in difficulties directly, subject to 'double-majority' voting by both the ECB and the EBA.

The proposal for Banking Union has far-reaching implications for economic governance in the EU. Yet the road to Banking Union is fraught with difficulties, first and foremost profound disagreements amongst the member states. Given its implications for fiscal policy (in the end, taxpayers' money is at stake), Banking Union goes to the heart of national sovereignty. That said, the regulation of financial services in the EU will not be directly affected by Banking Union. The first three elements of Banking Union—namely the adoption of a single rulebook, the Deposit Guarantee Scheme Directive, and the Directive on Banks Recovery and Resolution—were put onto the EU agenda by the global financial crisis and preceded the proposal for Banking Union. The SSM, which is one of the two main institutional innovations envisaged by Banking Union, represents a watershed change in banking supervision, not regulation. The second main institutional innovation, namely the SRM, concerns the resolution of ailing banks, not banking regulation.

Banking Union will not directly change the framework for and content of financial services regulation in the EU. Indirectly, EU financial services regulation might be affected by shifting political dynamics, i.e. by the creation of a euro-area bloc, or a bloc of Banking Union countries, comprising euro-area countries and non-euro-area 'opt-in' countries. The concern of countries such as the United Kingdom, which will not join Banking Union, is that Banking Union members will form a coalition that will pass financial regulation that is unpalatable for non-Banking Union members. As recorded, in order to mitigate this risk, the UK asked for and obtained the revision of the decision-making process in the EBA.

Overall, the concerns of the British authorities and the City of London seem to be somewhat overstated. After all, the establishment of EMU in 1999 did not lead to the formation of a euro-area bloc in EU financial services regulation, so it is far from clear that Banking Union will do so. To the extent that it might, this would mainly affect banking regulation, rather than financial services regulation *tout court.* As for the external representation of the EU in international regulatory fora in finance the most likely change is that the ECB will no longer sit on the BCBS as an observer but will be a full member, provided that the other non-EU members of the Committee agree. In the BCBS, the ECB might in the end replace the national banking supervisors of the countries in Banking Union, even though those member states are unlikely to relinquish willingly their (over-)representation in Basel.

8

Conclusions

This chapter begins by recalling the puzzles and the research questions set out at the beginning of the book and summarizing the main findings. Subsequently, it outlines the contributions of the research to the literature. Finally, some limitations and proposals for further research are put forward.

The Puzzle, the Research Question, and the Main Findings of the Book

This book began with a puzzle, outlined in Chapter 1: in some (very few) cases, the EU 'uploads' its financial rules to international regulatory fora. In other (very many) cases, the EU 'downloads' international financial rules. In other cases, the EU actively 'cross-loads' its rules to other jurisdictions, or passively 'cross-loads' rules from other jurisdictions (mainly the US). Finally, in some instances, there are no international or national rules set by (public) authorities. Often in these cases, private-sector rules are set by industry.

Using the concept of 'regulatory capacity', this research argues that different combinations of 'strong' and 'weak' EU and US regulatory capacities account for the uploading, cross-loading, and downloading of rules by these jurisdictions and hence their ability to influence global regulatory convergence. The temporal dimension is also important, i.e. the sequencing between the development of domestic regulatory capacities in the EU and the US and international standard-setting. The building up of regulatory capacity in the EU is explained by the role of policy entrepreneurs and the convergent (or at least compatible) interests of the main jurisdictions and their financial industries.

The US and, more recently, the EU have contributed to international regulatory convergence in three ways. First, they have uploaded their domestic regulatory templates to international standards. Second, they have actively cross-loaded their rules to third jurisdictions, through extraterritoriality (mainly with reference to US legislation) and equivalence clauses (mainly contained in EU legislation). Third, the US and the EU have downloaded international rules (sometimes with considerable domestic adaptation), and passively cross-loaded rules from other jurisdictions, mainly from each other. In all these cases, the EU and the US have fostered international regulatory convergence, but only in the first two cases have they actively shaped it—it was a form of 'power'.

A large market and a strong regulatory capacity are two necessary and complementary conditions for a jurisdiction's ability to influence international regulatory convergence in finance (and elsewhere). This explanation can be combined with an explanation based on the power of the financial industry because the financial industry located in a given jurisdiction (be it the US or the EU) generally has a vested interest in supporting the uploading of (national or regional) rules to the international level.

The theoretical framework developed in this book has three main blind spots. When both the EU and the US have strong regulatory capacities, the framework does not allow us to make clear predictions on whether rival standards with no convergence will emerge, or whether regulatory converge will take place as a result of uploading by both jurisdictions to international regulatory fora, or through mutual cross-loading. Amongst the cases examined, the only potential rival standards are in accounting, with the caveat that currently a sort of mutual recognition is in place between the EU and the US. Second, when neither the EU or the US have domestic regulatory templates in place because certain financial services are subject to self-regulation (e.g. hedge funds and over-the-counter derivatives prior to the global financial crisis), the framework does not allow us to make clear predictions as to what happens when these services need to be included within the perimeter of (public) regulation. In all the post-crisis cases examined in this book, the EU and the US set up their own domestic rules, which they tried to actively cross-load, but neither jurisdiction uploaded its domestic rules to international regulatory fora. Third, the framework does not fully explain what happens when existing templates are unfit for purpose and new rules are needed (e.g. revised capital requirements). The EU and US cannot upload or actively cross-load their unfit-for-purpose domestic regulatory templates, though a process of path-dependence is likely to be at work, namely the incremental reform of existing rules.

Contributions to the Literature and Comparison to Other Policy Areas

This research feeds into two main bodies of scholarly work. It contributes to the international political economy literature on international standard-setting in finance by arguing that the EU plays an active role and a passive role in international regulatory convergence. Until the 2000s, the EU more frequently played a passive role than an active role because it was in the process of building up its regulatory capacity in several financial services. Moreover, the US enjoyed a first-mover advantage in the regulation of several financial services, not only *vis-à-vis* the EU, but also in setting international standards. This trend began to change in the early 2000s, when the 'great leap forwards' (Grossman and Leblond 2011) took place in EU financial market integration and regulation. After the global financial crisis, the EU and the US seem to be keen to reap first-mover advantages in international standard-setting by putting in place domestic rules on rating agencies, hedge funds, and over-the-counter derivatives.

This research also develops the EU literature on financial regulation by explaining the building up of EU regulatory capacity over time across financial services, and by examining the EU's regulatory response to the global financial crisis. It argues that the great leap forward was possible because of the policy entrepreneurship of the Commission and one or two main member states. It also accounts for the increasing convergence of the preferences of the member states, linking this convergence to the development of the most transnational parts of their financial industry.

The concept of regulatory capacity can be applied and indeed has been applied to other EU policy areas beyond finance. It fits well with all regulatory policies concerning the single market (see Bach and Newman 2010). Basically, the argument is that a strong regulatory capacity, coupled with a large internal market, allows the EU to settle regulatory disputes (generally *vis-à-vis* the US) on more favourable terms than otherwise. This argument may have particular implications for trade policy, since regulatory issues have been considered of increasing importance in the EU's external trade relations since the late 1990s, and indeed the EU's recent trade agenda has revolved around attempts to upload its regulatory model to the multilateral level and to cross-load it through bilateral agreements—with mixed success (see Young and Peterson 2006).

Limitations and Proposals for Further Research

This work has investigated the influence of a regional jurisdiction, the EU, in international regulatory convergence, mainly in comparison to the US. Until the 2000s, the market size and domestic regulatory capacity of the US were greater than that of the EU, explaining the predominant role of the US in international standard-setting in finance. Most international regulatory convergence in that period took place on US terms. From the 2000s onwards, the strengthening of EU regulatory capacity and the completion of the single financial market have better equipped the EU with the resources to influence international standards by uploading its rules to the international level.

Three main caveats are in order. First, this research has mainly focused on rule-making, whereas there might be more subtle forms of influence, for example, through the promotion of influential policy ideas or norms to legitimize certain policies (see Mügge 2011b). The crisis, which originated in the US and was seen as having been triggered by the Anglo-Saxon model of financial capitalism, has undermined the legitimacy of the US in regulating global finance (Helleiner and Pagliari 2011). There is a consolidated body of literature on the international relations of the EU that considers the EU as a 'normative power' (Manners 2002), besides being a 'market power' (Damro 2012). This is an interesting venue for further research in the area of finance.

A second caveat is that, after the crisis, which had its epicentre in developed countries, other jurisdictions, especially rising powers, have acquired greater weight in the international regulatory arena, as witnessed by the fact that the BCBS was reformed so as to include the G20 members. On the one hand, this might predict a move from US–EU bipolarity to multilateral international financial governance, if not in the short term, at least in the medium term. On the other hand, some authors (e.g. Posner 2009a; Véron and Rottier 2010) maintain that the US and the EU will continue to play a pivotal role in international standard-setting.

Third, the EU has responded to the global financial crisis by strengthening its framework for financial supervision (the so-called de Larosière architecture) and by reforming its policy templates for the regulation of certain financial activities (such as hedge funds and credit rating agencies). Many of the post-crisis EU rules contain so-called 'equivalence' clauses that have the practical effects of encouraging third countries to change their domestic rules so as to make them equivalent to EU rules, or increase the cost for third-country firms to provide services in the EU, subjecting them to EU requirements in addition to their home regulation. More recently, there has been the proposal for Banking Union. It is too early to tell whether the crisis and the regulatory response to it have significantly changed the 'balance of power' between the US and the EU in international regulatory convergence. However, this research concludes that EU is now a (*sui generis*) player in the politics of international financial regulation and, although it does not (yet) fully exploit its potential, it can no longer be ignored when seeking a thorough understanding of international financial governance.

References

Abdelal, R. (2007). *Capital Rules: The Construction of Global Finance*. Cambridge, Mass.: Harvard University Press.

Acharya, V. V., Cooley, T. F., Richardson, M. P., and Walt, I. (2011). *Regulating Wall Street: The Dodd-Frank Act and the New Architecture of Global Finance*. Hoboken, NJ: Wiley & Sons.

Alexander, K., Dhumale, R., and Eatwell, J. (2005). *Global Governance of Financial Systems: The International Regulation of Systemic Risk*. Oxford: Oxford University Press.

Allen, F. and Gale, D. (2000). *Comparing Financial Systems*. Cambridge, Mass.: MIT Press.

Alternative Investment Expert Group (2006). *Managing, Servicing and Marketing Hedge Funds in Europe*. Brussels: European Commission Internal Market and Services DG, July.

Alternative Investment Management Association (2007). *AIMA's Guide to Sound Practices for Hedge Fund Valuation*, Mar. London: AIMA.

—— (2008). *AIMA's Roadmap to Hedge Funds*, Nov. London: AIMA.

—— (2009). 'AIMA Warns of Global Impact of EU AIFM Directive', 27 July, <http://www.aima.org/en/media/press-releases.cfm/id/6D509933-0F03-4D6B-B193ECB26D844F36> (accessed July 2013).

Amable, B. (2003). *The Diversity of Modern Capitalism*. Oxford: Oxford University Press.

Asset Managers' Committee (2009). *Best Practices for the Hedge Fund Industry*, Report of the Asset Managers' Committee to the President's Working Group on Financial Markets, 15 Jan. Washington, DC: Asset Managers' Committee.

Association of Private Client Investment Managers and Stockbrokers (2003). *Review of Capital Requirements for Banks and Investment Firms: Response to the Consultative Paper 3*, London, 1 July.

Associazione Bancaria Italiana (Italian Banking Association) (2003). *Position Paper of the Italian Banking System on the European Commission Consultative Document: CAD 3*, Rome, Oct.

Ayadi, R. and Lastra, R. M. (2010). 'Proposals for Reforming Deposit Guarantee Schemes in Europe', *Journal of Banking Regulation*, 11(3): 210–22.

Bach, D. (2010). 'The Domestic Institutional Roots of Global Governance', *Review of International Studies*, 36(3): 561–89.

Bach, D. and Newman, A. L. (2007). 'The European Regulatory State and Global Public Policy: Micro-Institutions, Macro-Influence', *Journal of European Public Policy*, 14(6): 1–20.

—— (2010). 'Transgovernmental Networks and Domestic Policy Convergence: Evidence from Insider Trading Regulation', *International Organization*, 64(3): 505–28.

Baker, A. (2006). *The Group of Seven: Finance Ministries, Central Banks and Global Financial Governance*. London: Routledge.

—— (2010). 'Restraining Regulatory Capture? Anglo-America, Crisis Politics and Trajectories of Change in Global Financial Governance', *International Affairs*, 86(3): 647–63.

Baker, A., Hudson, D., and Woodward, R. (eds) (2005). *Governing Financial Globalisation*. London: Routledge.

Barclays (2010a). *Response to the Consultative Document of the BCBS 'Strengthening the Resilience of the Banking Sector'*, London, 16 Apr.

—— (2010b). *Response to the Consultative Document of the BCBS 'International Framework for Liquidity Risk Measurement, Standards and Monitoring'*, London, 16 Apr.

Barth, J. R., Caprio Jr, G., and Levine R. (2006). *Rethinking Bank Regulation: Till Angels Govern*. Cambridge: Cambridge University Press.

Basel Committee on Banking Supervision (BCBS) (1999a). *A New Capital Adequacy Framework*, Basel, 2 June.

—— (1999b). *Banks' Interactions with Highly Leveraged Institutions*, Basel, Jan.

—— (1999c). *Sound Practices for Banks' Interactions with Highly Leveraged Institutions*, Basel, Jan.

—— (2001). *The New Basel Capital Accord: Consultative Document*, Basel, 8 Jan.

—— (2005). *Amendment to the Capital Accord to Incorporate Market Risks*, Basel, Nov.

—— (2006). *Basel II: International Convergence of Capital Measurement and Capital Standards: A Revised Framework*, Basel, Nov.

—— (2010a) *Basel III: A Global Regulatory Framework for More Resilient Banks and Banking Systems*, Basel, 16 Dec.

—— (2010b). *Assessment of the Macroeconomic Impact of Stronger Capital and Liquidity Requirements*, Basel, 18 Aug.

—— (2010c). *Assessing the Macroeconomic Impact of the Transition to Stronger Capital and Liquidity Requirements*, Basel, 17 Dec.

—— (2010d). *Report and Recommendations of the Cross-Border Bank Resolution Group: Final Paper*, Basel, 18 Mar.

Basel Committee on Banking Supervision (BCBS) and International Organization of Securities Commissions (IOSCO) (1995a). *Framework for Supervisory Information about the Derivatives Activities of Banks and Securities*, Basel, 28 May.

—— (1995b). *Public Disclosure of the Trading and Derivatives Activities of Banks and Securities*, Basel, 28 Nov.

Bengtsson, E. (2011). 'Repoliticization of Accounting Standard Setting: The IASB, the EU and the Global Financial Crisis', *Critical Perspectives on Accounting*, 22(6): 567–80.

Best, J. (2003). 'From the Top-Down: The New Financial Architecture and the Re-Embedding of Global Finance', *New Political Economy*, 8(3): 363–84.

Bieling, H.-J., (2003). 'Social Forces in the Making of the New European Economy: The Case of Financial Market Integration', *New Political Economy*, 8(2): 203–23.

Bini Smaghi, L. (2006). 'Powerless Europe: Why is the Euro Area Still a Political Dwarf?', *International Finance*, 9(2): 261–79.

BNP Paribas (2010). *Response to the BCBS Consultative Paper*, Paris, 16 Apr.

Börzel, T. (2002). 'Member State Responses to Europeanization', *Journal of Common Market Studies*, 40(2): 193–214.

Botzem, S. (2008). 'Transnational Expert-Driven Standardisation: Accountancy Governance from a Professional Point of View', in J.-C. Graz and A. Nölke (eds), *Transnational Private Governance and its Limits*. London: Routledge, 44–57.

—— (2012). *The Politics of Accounting Regulation*. Cheltenham: Edward Elgar.

Botzem, S. and Quack, S. (2006). 'Contested Rules and Shifting Boundaries: International Standard Setting in Accounting', in M.-L. Djelic and K. Sahlin-Andersson (eds), *Transnational Governance: Institutional Dynamics of Regulation*. Cambridge: Cambridge University Press, 266–86.

—— (2009). '(No) Limits to Anglo-American Accounting? Reconstructing the History of the International Accounting Standards Committee: A Review Article', *Accounting, Organizations and Society*, 34(8): 988–98.

British Bankers' Association (2003). *Comments on the Commission Services Working Document on the Review of Capital Requirements for Banks and Investment Firms*, London, 22 Oct.

Brown, P. (1997). 'The Politics of the EU Single Market for Investment Services: Negotiating the Investment Services and Capital Adequacy Directives', in G. R. D. Underhill (ed.), *The New World Order in International Finance*. London: Macmillan, 124–43.

Brummer, C. (forthcoming). 'The New Politics of Transatlantic Credit Rating Agency Regulation', in T. Porter (ed.), *The Fate of Transnational Financial Regulation*. London: Routledge.

Brummer, C. and Loko, R. (forthcoming). 'The New Politics of Transatlantic Credit Rating Agency Regulation', in T. Porter (ed.), *The Fate of Transnational Financial Regulation*. London: Routledge.

Buckley, J. and Howarth, D. (2011). 'Regulating the So-Called "Vultures of Capitalism"', *Journal of Common Market Studies*, 49(s1): 123–43.

Buckley, J., Howarth, D., and Quaglia, L. (2012). 'Internal Market: The Ongoing Struggle to "Protect" Europe from its Money Men', *Journal of Common Market Studies Annual Review*, 48(s1): 119–41.

Bulmer, S. and Radaelli, C. (2005). 'The Europeanization of National Policy?', in S. Bulmer and C. Lequesne (eds), *The Member States of the European Union*. Oxford: Oxford University Press, 338–59.

Bundesverband deutscher Banken (German Private Banks Association) (2003). *Response to the Consultative Paper 3 on the Basel 2 Accord*, Berlin.

Büthe, T. and Mattli, W. (2011). *The New Global Rulers: The Privatization of Regulation in the World Economy*. Princeton: Princeton University Press.

Calomiris, C. W. (2000). *U.S. Bank Deregulation in Historical Perspective*. Cambridge: Cambridge University Press.

Camfferman, K. and Zeff, S. (2007). *Financial Reporting and Global Capital Markets: A History of the International Accounting Standards Committee 1973–2000*. Oxford: Oxford University Press.

Cernat, L. (2004). 'The Emerging European Corporate Governance Model: Anglo Saxon, Continental or Still the Century of Diversity', *Journal of European Public Policy*, 11(1): 147–66.

Cerny, P. (1995). 'Globalization and the Changing Logic of Collective Action', *International Organization*, 49(4): 595–625.

—— (ed.) (1993). *Finance and World Politics: Markets, Regimes and States in the Post-Hegemonic Era*. Aldershot: Edward Elgar.

Christopoulos, D. and Quaglia, L. (2009). 'Network Constraints in EU Banking Regulation: The Case of the Capital Requirements Directive', *Journal of Public Policy*, 29(2): 1–22.

Chwieroth, J. (2010). *Capital Ideas: The IMF and the Rise of Financial Liberalization*. Princeton: Princeton University Press.

Claessens, S., Underhill, G. R. D., and Zhang, X. (2008). 'The Political Economy of Basle II: The Costs for Poor Countries', *World Economy*, 31(3): 313–44.

Coen, D. and Thatcher, M. (2008). 'Network Governance and Multi-Level Delegation: European Networks of Regulatory Agencies', *Journal of Public Policy*, 28(1): 49–71.

Coffee Jr, J. C. (2011), 'Ratings Reform: The Good, the Bad, and the Ugly', *Harvard Business Law Review*, 1: 231–78.

Cohen, B. (2008). 'The Euro in a Global Context: Challenges and Capacities', in K. Dyson (ed.), *The Euro at 10: Europeanization, Power, and Convergence*. Oxford: Oxford University Press, 37–53.

Cohen, B. J. (1996). 'Phoenix Risen: The Resurrection of Global Finance', *World Politics*, 48(2): 268–96.

Coleman, W. and Underhill G. R. D. (1998). 'Globalism, Regionalism, and the Emergence of International Securities Markets: The Case of IOSCO and EU Financial Integration', in W. Coleman and G. R. D. Underhill (eds), *Regionalism and Global Economic Integration: Europe, Asia, and the Americas*. London: Routledge, 223–48.

Collinson, S. (1999). '"Issue-Systems", "Multi-Level Games" and the Analysis of the EU's External Commercial and Associated Policies: A Research Agenda', *Journal of European Public Policy*, 6(2): 206–24.

Comité Européen des Assurances (CEA) (2005). *Topography of EU25: Description of Markets, Products and Distribution*. Brussels: CEA.

—— (2007). 'The Insurance Groups and Solvency II', *Briefing Note 2*. Brussels: CEA, May.

—— (2011). *European Insurance in Figures*. Brussels: CEA, Nov.

Commission of the European Communities (1995). *Communication from the Commission—Accounting Harmonisation: A New Strategy vis-à-vis International Harmonisation*. Brussels: European Commission.

—— (1998). *Statutory Audit in the European Union, The Way Forward*. Brussels: European Commission, 8 May.

—— (2000). *Communication from the Commission to the Council and the European Parliament—EU Financial Reporting Strategy: The Way Forward*. Brussels: European Commission, 13 June.

—— (2001). *Proposal for a Regulation of the European Parliament and of the Council on the Application of International Accounting Standards.* COM(2001) 80 final, Brussels: European Commission, 13 Feb.

—— (2002). *Considerations on the Design of a Future Prudential Supervisory System.* Brussels: European Commission, 28 Nov.

—— (2003). *Reinforcing the Statutory Audit in the European Union.* Brussels: European Commission, 21 May.

—— (2004a). *Financial Services: Turning the Corner, Preparing the Challenge of the Next Phase of European Capital Market Integration.* 10th progress report, Brussels: European Commission, 2 June.

—— (2004b). *Framework for Consultation on Solvency II.* Brussels: European Commission, 14 July.

—— (2004c). *Press Release: Insurance: Commission Proposes a Directive to Create a Real EU-Wide Market for Reinsurance.* Brussels: European Commission, 21 April.

—— (2004d). *Proposal for a Directive of the European Parliament and the Council on Reinsurance and Amending Council Directives 73/239/EEC, 92/49/EEC and Directives 98/78/ECand2002/83/EC{SEC(2004)443}/*COM/2004/0273final—COD2004/0097*/.* Brussels: European Commission, 21 April.

—— (2005a). *The White Paper on Financial Services Policy (2005–2010).* Brussels: European Commission, 1 Dec.

—— (2005b). *The Green Paper on Financial Services Policy (2005–2010).* COM (2005) 177. Brussels: European Commission, 3 May.

—— (2005c). *Considerations Concerning the Outline for a Framework Directive on Solvency II.* Brussels: European Commission, 23 Mar.

—— (2007). *Proposal for a Directive of the European Parliament and of the Council on the Taking-Up and Pursuit of the Business of Insurance and Reinsurance—Solvency II.* Brussels: European Commission, 10 July.

—— (2008a). *Proposal for a Regulation of the European Parliament and of the Council on Credit Rating Agencies.* COM(2008) 704 final. Brussels: European Commission, 12 Nov.

—— (2008b). *Proposal for a Regulatory Framework for CRAs.* Brussels: European Commission, 31 July.

—— (2009a). *Proposal for a Directive on Alternative Investment Fund Managers.* Brussels: European Commission, 29 Apr.

—— (2009b). *Feedback Statement—Summary of Responses to Hedge Fund Consultation Paper.* Brussels: European Commission, 12 Mar.

—— (2010). *Proposal for a Directive of the European Parliament and of the Council on Directive on Deposit Guarantee Schemes.* COM(2010) 369, SEC(2010) 834, SEC(2010) 835. Brussels: European Commission, 12 July.

—— (2011a). *Proposal for a Directive on the Access to the Activity of Credit Institutions and the Prudential Supervision of Credit Institutions and Investment Firms.* 2011/453/EC. Brussels: European Commission, 20 July.

Commission of the European Communities (2011b). *Proposal for a Regulation on Prudential Requirements for Credit Institutions and Investment Firms.* 2011/452/EC. Brussels: European Commission, 20 July.

—— (2011c). *Press Release: Commission Decision Lays the Foundation for Reinforced International Cooperation on the Supervision of Auditors.* Brussels: European Commission, 19 Jan.

—— (2012a). *Proposal for a Directive Establishing a Framework for the Recovery and Resolution of Credit Institutions and Investment Firms and Amending Council Directives 77/91/EEC and 82/891/EC, Directives 2001/24/EC, 2002/47/EC, 2004/25/EC, 2005/56/EC, 2007/36/EC and 2011/35/EC and Regulation (EU) No 1093/2010.* COM(2012) 280/3. Brussels: European Commission, 6 June.

—— (2012b). *Proposal for a Council Regulation Conferring Specific Tasks on the European Central Bank Concerning Policies Relating to the Prudential Supervision of Credit Institutions.* COM/2012/0511 final. Brussels: European Commission, 12 Sept.

—— (2013). *Proposal for a Regulation of the European Parliament and of the Council Establishing Uniform Rules and a Uniform Procedure for the Resolution of Credit Institutions and Certain Investment Firms in the Framework of a Single Resolution Mechanism and a Single Bank Resolution Fund and Amending Regulation (EU) No. 1093/2010 of the European Parliament and of the Council.* COM/2013/0520 final. Brussels: European Commission, 12 July.

Committee of European Securities Regulators (2005). *CESR's Technical Advice to the European Commission on Possible Measures Concerning Credit Rating Agencies.* Paris: CESR/05-139b, Mar.

—— (2006). *CESR's Report to the European Commission on the Compliance of the Credit Rating Agencies with the IOSCO Code.* Paris: CESR/06-545, Dec.

—— (2008a). *CESR's Second Report to the European Commission on the Compliance of the Credit Rating Agencies with the IOSCO Code.* Paris: CESR/08-227, May.

—— (2008b). *CESR's Response to the Consultation Document of the Commission Services on a Draft Proposal for a Directive/Regulation on Credit Rating Agencies.* Paris: CESR/08-671, 16 Sept.

Committee of Wise Men (2001). *Final Report of the Committee of Wise Men on the Regulation of European Securities Markets,* Brussels, 15 Feb. <http://ec.europa.eu/internal_market/securities/docs/lamfalussy/wisemen/final-report-wise-men_en.pdf> (accessed 2 March 2014).

Council of the European Union and European Parliament (2009). *Directive 2009/138/EC of the European Parliament and of the Council on the Taking-up and Pursuit of the Business of Insurance and Reinsurance (Solvency II).* Brussels: European Union, 25 Nov.

Culpepper, P. D. (2011). *Quiet Politics and Business Power: Corporate Control in Europe and Japan.* Cambridge: Cambridge University Press.

da Conceição, E. (2010). 'Who Controls Whom? Dynamics of Power Delegation and Agency Losses in EU Trade Politics', *Journal of Common Market Studies,* 48(4), 1107–26.

da Conceição-Heldt, E. (2011). 'Variation in EU Member States' Preferences and the Commission's Discretion in the Doha Round', *Journal of European Public Policy,* 18(3): 403–19.

Damro, C. (2006). 'Transatlantic Competition Policy: Domestic and International Sources of EU–US Cooperation', *European Journal of International Relations,* 12(2): 171–96.

—— (2012). 'Market Power Europe', *Journal of European Public Policy,* 19(5): 182–99.

De Bièvre, D. and Dür, A. (2005). 'Constituency Interests and Delegation in European and American Trade Policy', *Comparative Political Studies*, 38(1): 1271–96.

Deeg, R. (2010). 'Institutional Change in Financial Systems', in G. Morgan, J. Campbell, C. Crouch, O. K. Pedersen, and R. Whitley (eds), *The Oxford Handbook of Comparative Institutional Analysis*. Oxford: Oxford University Press, 312–51.

de Larosière Group (2009) *The High Level Group on Financial Supervision in the EU, Brussels*, 25 Feb.

Delreux, T. and Kerremans, B. (2010). 'How Agents Weaken their Principals' Incentives to Control: The Case of EU Negotiators and EU Member States in Multilateral Negotiations', *Journal of European Integration*, 32(4): 357–74.

Derivatives Policy Group (DPG) (1995). *A Framework for Voluntary Oversight of the OTC Derivatives Activities of Securities Firms Affiliates to Promote Confidence and Stability in Financial Markets*. Washington, DC: DPG.

Dermine, J. (2006). 'European Banking Integration: Don't Put the Cart Before the Horse', *Financial Markets, Institutions & Instruments*, 15(2): 57–106.

De Visscher, C., Maiscocq, O., and Varone, F. (2008). 'The Lamfalussy Reform in EU Securities Markets: Fiduciary Relationships, Policy Effectiveness and Balance of Power', *Journal of Public Policy*, 28(1): 19–47.

Dewing, I. P. and Russell, P. O. (2004). 'Auditing and Corporate Governance of European Listed Countries: EU Policy Developments Before and After Enron', *Journal of Common Market Studies*, 42(2): 289–319.

—— (2008). 'Financial Integration in the EU: The First Phase of EU Endorsement of International Accounting Standards', *Journal of Common Market Studies*, 46(2): 243–64.

Donnelly, S. (2007). 'The International Accounting Standards Board', *New Political Economy*, 12(1): 117–25.

—— (2010). *The Regimes of European Integration: Constructing Governance of the Single Market*. Oxford: Oxford University Press.

Drezner, D. (2010). 'Is Historical Institutionalism Bunk?', *Review of International Political Economy*, 17(4): 791–804.

Drezner, D. W. (2007). *All Politics is Global: Explaining International Regulatory Regimes*. Princeton: Princeton University Press.

D'Souza, F., Ellis, N. S., and Fairchild, L. M. (2009). 'Illuminating the Need for Regulation in Dark Markets: Proposed Regulation of the OTC Derivatives Market', *University of Pennsylvania Journal of Business Law*, 12(2): 473–516.

Dür, A. (2007). 'EU Trade Policy as Protection for Exporters: The Agreements with Mexico and Chile', *Journal of Common Market Studies*, 45(4): 833–55.

—— (2008). 'Bringing Economic Interests Back into the Study of EU Trade Policy-Making', *British Journal of Politics and International Relations*, 10(1): 27–45.

—— (2010). *Protection for Exporters: Power and Discrimination in Transatlantic Trade Relations, 1930–2010*. Ithaca, NY: Cornell University Press.

Dür, A. (2011). 'Fortress Europe or Open Door Europe? The External Impact of the EU's Single Market in Financial Services', *Journal of European Public Policy*, 18(5): 619–35.

Dyson, K. and Marcussen, M. (2009). *Central Banks in the Age of the Euro: Europeanization, Convergence, and Power*. Oxford: Oxford University Press.

Eaton, S. (2005). 'Crisis and the Consolidation of Accounting Standards: Enron, the International Accounting Standards Board (IASB) and America', *Business and Politics,* 7(3): 1–18.

Eberle, D. and Lauter, D. (2011). 'Private Interests and the EU–US Dispute on Audit Regulation: The Role of the European Accounting Profession', *Review of International Political Economy,* 18(4): 436–59.

Elgström, O. and Frenhoff Larsén, M. (2010). 'Free to Trade? Commission Autonomy in the Economic Partnership Agreement Negotiations', *Journal of European Public Policy,* 17(2): 205–23.

Elsig, M. (2002). *The EU's Common Commercial Policy: Institutions, Interests and Ideas.* London: Ashgate.

—— (2007). 'The EU's Choice of Regulatory Venues for Trade Negotiations: A Tale of Agency Power?', *Journal of Common Market Studies,* 45(4): 927–48.

—— (2010). 'European Union Trade Policy After Enlargement: Larger Crowds, Shifting Priorities and Informal Decision-Making', *Journal of European Public Policy,* 17(6), 781–98.

Eurex Clearing (2008) *European OTC Central Counterparty for Credit Derivatives,* 14 Nov., <http://www.ecb.int/paym/groups/pdf/COGESI_Eurex_CCP_proposal.pdf?518abfd defe25a21a4d1ae0575366781> (accessed 2 Mar. 2014).

Euro Area Summit Statement (2012). Brussels, 29 June. <http://www.consilium.europa.eu/uedocs/cms_data/docs/pressdata/en/ec/131359.pdf> (accessed 2 Mar. 2014).

European Banking Federation (2003). *Response to the Consultative Paper 3 on the Basel 2 Accord.* Brussels: European Banking Federation.

European Banking Federation, Institute of International Finance, International Swaps and Derivatives Association, London Investment Banks Association, and Bond Market Association (2004) Joint letter to the Basel Committee on Banking Supervision, *Trade Book Review,* 9 Dec.

European Central Bank (ECB) (2009). OTC Derivative and Post Trading Infrastructures. European Central Bank, Sept.

European Council (2008). *Presidency Conclusions.* Brussels: European Council, 11–12 Dec.

—— (2012). *Council Agrees Position on Bank Supervision,* 17739/12 PRESSE 528, Brussels: European Council, 13 Dec.

European Parliament (EP) (2004a). *European Parliament Resolution on Corporate Governance and Supervision of Financial Services: The Parmalat Case,* Brussels, 22 Apr.

—— (2007). *Draft Report with Recommendations to the Commission on Hedge Funds and Private Equity* (2007/2238(INI)). Rapporteur: Poul Nyrup Rasmussen, Brussels, 18 Apr.

—— (2008a). *Report with Recommendations to the Commission on Transparency of Institutional Investors* (2007/2239(INI)). Rapporteur: Klaus-Heiner Lehne, Brussels, 9 July.

—— (2008b). *Report on the Amended Proposal for a Directive of the European Parliament and of the Council on the Raking-Up and Pursuit of the Business of Insurance and Reinsurance (recast).* COM(2008) 0119. Rapporteur: Peter Skinner, Brussels, 16 Oct.

—— (2010). *Resolution on Basel II and Revision of the Capital Requirements Directives (CRD 4).* Brussels: Committee of Economic and Monetary Affairs, Brussels, 21 Sept.

—— (2011). *Draft Report on the Proposal for a Regulation of the European Parliament and of the Council on Prudential Requirements for Credit Institutions and Investment Firms*, COM(2011)0452—C7-0417/2011—2011/0202(COD), Committee on Economic and Monetary Affairs. Rapporteur: Othmar Karas. Brussels.

European Savings Banks Group (2003). *Response to the Consultative Paper 3 on the Basel 2 Accord*. Brussels: European Savings Banks Group.

European Securities Markets Expert Group (2008). *Role of Credit Rating Agencies: ESME's Report to the European Commission*. Brussels: ESME, June.

Farrell, H. and Newman, A. L. (2010). 'Making Global Markets: Historical Institutionalism in International Political Economy', *Review of International Political Economy*, 17(4): 609–38.

Faull, J. (2012). *Letter from Jonathan Faull, Director General Internal Market and Services, to Gabriel Bernardino, Chair of EIOPA*, Feb.

Fédération Bancaire Française (French Banking Federation) (2010). *Comments on the Consultative Documents Published by the Basel Committee on Banking Supervision*. Paris: FBF, 16 Oct.

Ferran, E. (2004). *Building an EU Securities Market*. Cambridge: Cambridge University Press.

—— (2011). 'After the Crisis: The Regulation of Hedge Funds and Private Equity in the EU'. *European Business Organization Law Review*, 12: 379–414.

Ferrarini, G. and Wymeersch, E. (eds) (2006). *Investor Protection in Europe: Corporate Law Making, the MiFID and Beyond*. Oxford: Oxford University Press.

Financial Accounting Standards Board (FASB) and International Accounting Standards Board (IASB) (2002). *Memorandum of Understanding: 'The Norwalk Agreement'*, 29 Oct. <http://www.ifrs.org/Use-around-the-world/Global-convergence/Convergence-with-US-GAAP/Documents/Norwalk_agreement.pdf> (accessed 2 Mar. 2014).

Financial Services Authority (FSA) (2009). *The Turner Review: A Regulatory Response to the Global Banking Crisis*. London: FSA, Mar.

Financial Stability Board (FSB) (2011). *Key Attributes of Effective Resolution Regimes for Financial Institutions*. Basel: FSB, Nov.

Financial Stability Forum (FSF) (2000). *Report of the Working Group on Highly Leveraged Institutions*. Basel: FSF, Apr.

—— (2007). *Update of the FSF Report on Highly Leveraged Institutions*. Basel: FSF, May.

Flanagan, S. M. (2001). 'Rise of a Trade Association: Group Interactions Within the International Swaps and Derivatives Association', *Harvard Negotiation Law Review*, 6: 211–38.

Flower, J. (1997). 'The Future Shape of Harmonization: The EU versus the IASC versus the SEC', *European Accounting Review*, 6(2): 281–303.

Frieden, J. (2004). 'One Europe, One Vote? The Political Economy of European Union Representation in International Organisations', *European Union Politics*, 5(2): 261–76.

Gadinis, S. (2008). 'The Politics of Competition in International Financial Regulation', *Harvard International Law Journal*, 49(2): 447–507.

Gamble, A. (2009). *The Spectre at the Feast: Capitalist Crisis and the Politics of Recession*. Basingstoke: Palgrave.

Gebhardt, G. (2000). 'The Evolution of Global Standards in Accounting', in R. E. Litan and A.M. Santomero (eds), *Brookings-Wharton Papers on Financial Services 2000*. Washington DC: Brookings Institution, 341–68.

Garbaravicius T. and Dierick, F. (2005). 'Hedge Funds and Their Implications for Financial Stability', ECB Occasional Paper No. 34, Aug.

Genschel, P. and Plümper, T. (1997). 'Regulatory Competition and International Co-operation', *Journal of European Public Policy*, 4(4): 626–42.

George, A. L. and Bennett, A. (2005). *Case Studies and Theory Development in the Social Sciences*. Cambridge, Mass.: MIT Press.

Gieve, J. and Provost, C. (2012). 'Ideas and Coordination in Policymaking: The Financial Crisis of 2007–2009', *Governance*, 25(1): 61–77.

Goldstein, J., Kahler, M., Keohane, R. O., and Slaughter, A.-M. (2000). 'Introduction: Legalization and World Politics', *International Organization*, 54(3): 385–400.

Goodhart, C. (2011). *The Basel Committee on Banking Supervision: A History of the Early Years 1974–1997*. Cambridge: Cambridge University Press.

Greenspan, A. (1998). Remarks Before the 34th Annual Conference on Bank Structure and Competition, Federal Reserve Bank of Chicago, 7 May.

Griffith-Jones, S. (2003). Letter to the *Financial Times*, 12 May.

Grossman, E. (2004). 'Bringing Politics Back In: Rethinking the Role of Economic Interest Groups in European Integration', *Journal of European Public Policy*, 11(4): 637–54.

Grossman, E. and Leblond, P. (2011). 'European Financial Integration: Finally the Great Leap Forward?', *Journal of Common Market Studies*, 49(2): 413–35.

Group of Twenty (G20) (2009a). *Declaration on Strengthening the Financial System*. London: G20, 2 Apr.

—— (2009b). *Leaders' Statement: The Pittsburgh Summit*. Pittsburgh: G20, 24–5 Sept.

Group of Thirty (G30) (1993). *Derivatives: Practices and Principles*. Washington, DC: Working Group on Global Derivatives.

Haas, P. M. (1989). 'Do Regimes Matter? Epistemic Communities and Mediterranean Pollution Control', *International Organization*, 43(3): 377–403.

Haldane, A. G. and Alessandri, P. (2009). *Banking on the State*. London: Bank of England.

Hall, P. and Soskice, D. (eds) (2001). *Varieties of Capitalism: The Institutional Foundations of Comparative Advantage*. Oxford: Oxford University Press.

Haller, A. (2002). 'Financial Accounting Developments in the EU: Past Events and Future Prospects, *European Accounting Review*, 11(1): 153–90.

Hancké, B., Rhodes, M., and Thatcher, M. (eds) (2007). *Beyond Varieties of Capitalism: Conflict, Contradictions, and Complementarities in the European Economy*. Oxford: Oxford University Press.

Hardie, I. and Howarth, D. (eds) (2013). *Market-Based Banking and the International Financial Crisis*. Oxford: Oxford University Press.

Harris, J. (2010). 'SEC Says US Unable to Meet Equivalence Criteria', *Hedge Funds Review*, 10 June.

Hedge Fund Working Group/Hedge Fund Standards Board (2008). *Hedge Fund Standards: Final Report*. London, Jan.

Helleiner, E. (1994). *States and the Reemergence of Global Finance: From Bretton Woods to the 1990s*. Ithaca, NY: Cornell University Press.

—— (2010), 'A Bretton Woods Moment? The 2007–2008 Crisis and the Future of Global Finance', *International Affairs,* 86(3): 619–36.

Helleiner, E. and Pagliari, S. (2010). 'The End of Self-Regulation? Hedge Funds and Derivatives in Global Financial Governance', in E. Helleiner, S. Pagliari, and H. Zimmermann (eds), *Global Finance in Crisis: The Politics of International Regulatory Change*. London: Routledge, 74–90.

—— (2011). 'The End of an Era in International Financial Regulation? A Postcrisis Research Agenda', *International Organization,* 65(1): 169–200.

Helleiner, E., Pagliari, S., and Zimmerman, H. (eds) (2010). *Global Finance in Crisis: The Politics of International Regulatory Change*. London: Routledge.

Her Majesty's Treasury (2003a). *The New Capital Adequacy Directive, CAD 3: The Transposition of the New Basel Accord into EU Legislation,* Consultation Document. London: HM Treasury.

—— (2003b). *Consultation on CAD3 Summary of Responses*. London: HM Treasury.

—— (2007). *Strengthening the EU Regulatory and Supervisory Framework: A Practical Approach*. London: Financial Services Authority, Nov.

Her Majesty's Treasury and Financial Services Authority (FSA) (2006). *Supervising Insurance Groups Under Solvency II—A Discussion Paper.* London: FSA, Nov.

Heron, T. and Siles-Brügge, G. (2012). 'Competitive Liberalisation and the "Global Europe" Services and Investments Agenda: Locating the Commercial Drivers of the EU–ACP Economic Partnership Agreements', *Journal of Common Market Studies,* 50(2): 250–66.

Herring, R. J. (2007). 'The Rocky Road to Implementation of Basel II in the United States', *Atlantic Economic Journal,* 35(4): 411–29.

Hodson, D. (2011). *Governing the Euro Area in Good Times and Bad*. Oxford: Oxford University Press.

Hopwood, A. (1994). 'Accounting and the Pursuit of Efficiency', in D. McKevitt and A. Lawton (eds), *Public Sector Management: Theory Critique and Practice*. London: Sage, 145–59.

Horsfield-Bradbury, J. (2008). 'Hedge Fund Self-Regulation in the US and the UK', <http://www.law.harvard.edu/programs/corp_gov/papers/Brudney2008_Horsfield-Bradbury.pdf> (accessed July 2013).

House Committee on Financial Services (2003a). *The New Basel Accord: Sound Regulation or Crushing Complexity?* Washington, DC: Government Printer, 27 Feb.

—— (2003b). *The New Basel Accord: In Search of a Unified U.S. Position.* Washington, DC: Government Printer, 19 June.

House of Commons (2009). *Lord Turner, Oral Evidence to the Treasury Select Committee.* London: Stationery Office, 25 Feb.

House of Lords (2008). *Solvency II: Report with Evidence,* European Union Committee. London: Stationery Office, 6 Feb.

House of Lords (2009). *Fourteenth Report: The Future of EU Financial Regulation and Supervision,* European Union Committee. London: Stationery Office.

Howarth, D. and Quaglia, L. (2013a). 'Banking on Stability: The Political Economy of New Capital Requirements in the European Union', *Journal of European Integration,* 35(3): 333–46.

—— (2013b). 'Banking Union as Holy Grail: Rebuilding the Single Market in Financial Services, Stabilizing Europe's Banks and "Completing" Economic and Monetary Union', *Journal of Common Market Studies*, 49(s1): 119–41.

Howell, K. (2004). *Europeanization, European Integration and Financial Services: Developing Theoretical Frameworks and Methodological Perspectives*. Basingstoke: Palgrave Macmillan.

HSBC (2010). *Consultative Document BCBS 165: International Framework for Liquidity Risk Measurement, Standards and Monitoring*. London, 16 Oct.

Humphrey, C. and Loft, A. (2009). 'Governing Audit Globally: IFAC, the New International Financial Architecture and the Auditing Profession', in C. S. Chapman, D. Cooper, and P. Miller (eds), *Accounting, Organizations, and Institutions: Essays in Honour of Anthony Hopwood*. Oxford: Oxford University Press, 205–33.

Humphrey, C., Loft, A., and Woods, M. (2009). 'The Global Audit Profession and the International Financial Architecture: Understanding Regulatory Relationships at a Time of Crisis', *Accounting, Organizations and Society*, 34(6–7): 810–25.

Institute of International Finance (2010). *Interim Report on the Cumulative Impact on the Global Economy of Proposed Changes in the Banking Regulatory Framework*. Washington, DC: IIF, June.

International Association of Insurance Supervisors (IAIS) (2008a). *Guidance Paper on the Mutual Recognition of Reinsurance Supervision*. Basel: IAIS, Oct.

—— (2008b). *Standard No. 2.1.1 on the Structure of Regulatory Capital Requirements; Standard No. 2.2.6 on ERM for Capital Adequacy and Solvency Purposes; Standard No. 2.2.7 on the Use of Internal Models for Regulatory Capital Purposes*. Basel: IAIS, Oct.

—— (2008c). *Principles on Group-Wide Supervision*. Basel: IAIS, Oct.

—— (2012). *Insurance Core Principles, Standards, Guidance and Assessment Methodology*. Basel: IAIS, Oct.

International Monetary Fund (IMF) (2011). *United Kingdom: 2011 Article IV Consultation—Staff Report; Staff Statement; Public Information Notice on the Executive Board Discussion; and Statement by the Executive Director for the United Kingdom*. Washington, DC: IMF Country Report, 11/220, Supplementary Report, July.

International Organization of Securities Commissions (IOSCO) (1999). *Hedge Funds and Other Highly Leveraged Institutions*, Technical Committee. Madrid: IOSCO, Nov.

—— (2000). *A Resolution on IASC Standards Passed by the Presidents Committee*. Madrid: IOSCO, May.

—— (2003). *IOSCO Statement of Principles Regarding the Activities of Credit Rating Agencies*, Technical Committee. Madrid: IOSCO, 25 Sept.

—— (2004). *Code of Conduct for Credit Rating Agencies*, Technical Committee. Madrid: IOSCO, Dec.

—— (2008). *Code of Conduct Fundamentals for Credit Rating Agencies (Revised)*, Technical Committee. Madrid: IOSCO, May.

—— (2009a). *Final Report on Hedge Funds Oversight*. Madrid: IOSCO, June.

—— (2009b). 'Statement on International Auditing Standards', Madrid: IOSCO, 11 June, <www.iosco.org/library/statements/pdf/statements-7.pdf> (accessed 2 Mar. 2014).

Jabko, N. (2006). *Playing the Market: A Political Strategy for Uniting Europe, 1985–2005*. Ithaca, NY: Cornell University Press.

Jackson, G. and Deeg, R. (2008). 'From Comparing Capitalisms to the Politics of Institutional Change', *Review of International Political Economy*, 15(4): 680–709.

Jackson, H. E. and Pan, E. J. (2001). 'Regulatory Competition in International Securities Markets: Evidence from Europe in 1999—Part 1', *Business Lawyer*, 56: 653–96.

Journal of Common Market Studies (2007). 'Special Issue: The EU in International Trade Negotiations', 45(4).

—— (2009). 'Special Issue: European Perspectives of the Global Financial Crisis', 47(5): 939–1158.

Journal of European Public Policy (2006). 'Special Issue: The European Union and the New Trade Politics', 13(6): 795–957.

Kapstein, E. (1989). 'Resolving the Regulator's Dilemma: International Coordination of Banking Regulations', *International Organisation*, 43(2): 323–47.

Kapstein, E. B. (1992). 'Between Power and Purpose: Central Bankers and the Politics of International Regulation', *International Organization*, 46(1): 265–87.

Karmel, R. S. (2007). 'The EU Challenge to the SEC', *Fordham International Law Journal*, 31: 1692–712.

Kerremans, B. (2004). 'What Went Wrong in Cancun? A Principle-Agent View on the EU's Rationale Towards the Doha Development Round', *European Foreign Affairs Review*, 9(3): 363–93.

Kerwer, D. (2005). 'Rules That Many Use: Standards and Global Regulation', *Governance*, 18(4): 611–32.

Khademian, A. M. (1992). *The SEC and Capital Market Regulation: The Politics of Expertise*. Pittsburgh: Pittsburgh University Press.

—— (2002). 'The Securities and Exchange Commission: A Small Regulatory Agency with a Gargantuan Challenge', *Public Administration Review*, 62(5): 515–26.

Knill, C. (2005). 'Cross-National Policy Convergence: Concepts, Approaches and Explanatory Factors', *Journal of European Public Policy*, 12(5): 764–74.

Lall, R. (2010). 'Reforming Global Banking Rules: Back to the Future?', paper prepared for seminar at the Danish Institute for International Studies (DIIS), 18 May.

—— (2012). 'From Failure to Failure: The Politics of International Banking Regulation', *Review of International Political Economy*, 19(4): 609–38.

Larson, R. K. (2002). 'The IASC's Search for Legitimacy: An Analysis of the IASC's Standing Interpretations Committee', *Advances in International Accounting*, 15: 79–120.

Larson, R. K. and Street, D. L. (2006). 'The Roadmap to Global Accounting Convergence: Europe Introduces "Speed Bumps"', *CPA Journal* [online journal], <http://www.nysscpa.org/cpajournal/2006/1006/essentials/p36.htm> (accessed July 2013).

Leblond, P. (2011). 'EU, US and International Accounting Standards: A Delicate Balancing Act in Governing Global Finance', *Journal of European Public Policy*, 18(3): 443–61.

Lütz, S. (1998). 'The Revival of the Nation State? Stock Exchange Regulation in an Era of Globalised Financial Markets', *Journal of European Public Policy*, 5(1): 153–68.

Lütz, S. and Eberle, D. (2008) 'Varieties of Change in German Capitalism: Transforming the Rules of Corporate Control', *New Political Economy*, 13(4): 377–95.

Macartney, H. (2009), 'Variegated Neo-Liberalism: Transnationally Oriented Fractions of Capital in EU Financial Market Integration', *Review of International Studies,* 35(2): 451–80.

—— (2010). *Variegated Neoliberalism: EU Varieties of Capitalism and International Political Economy*. London: Routledge.

McNamara, K. R. and Meunier, S. (2002). 'Between National Sovereignty and International Power: What External Voice for the Euro?', *International Affairs,* 78(4): 849–68.

Managed Funds Association (2007). *Sound Practices for Hedge Fund Managers,* Washington, DC, and New York: Managed Funds Association.

Manners, I. J. (2002). 'Normative Power Europe: A Contradiction in Terms?', *Journal of Common Market Studies,* 40(2): 235–58.

Martinez-Diaz, L. (2005). 'Strategic Experts and Improvising Regulators: Explaining the IASC's Rise to Global Influence, 1973-2001', *Business and Politics,* 7(3): art. 3.

Mattli, W. and Büthe, T. (2003). 'Setting International Standards: Technological Rationality or Primacy of Power?', *World Politics,* 56(1): 1–42.

—— (2004). 'Global Private Governance: Lessons from a National Model of Setting Standards in Accounting', *Law and Contemporary Problems,* 68(3–4): 225–62.

Mayntz, R. (ed.) (2012). *Crisis and Control: Institutional Change in Financial Market Regulation.* Cologne: Max Planck Institute for the Study of Societies.

Meunier, S. (2000). 'What Single Voice? European Institutions and EU–U.S. Trade Negotiations,' *International Organization,* 54(1): 103–35.

—— (2005). *Trading Voices: The European Union in International Commercial Negotiations.* Princeton: Princeton University Press.

—— (2007). 'Managing Globalization? The EU in International Trade Negotiations', *Journal of Common Market Studies,* 45(5): 905–26.

Moloney, N. (2011a) 'The European Securities and Market Authority and Institutional Design for the EU Financial Markets—A Tale of Two Competences: Part (1) Rule-Making', *European Business Organization Law Review,* 12(1): 41.

—— (2011b). 'The European Securities and Markets Authority and Institutional Design for the EU Financial Market—A Tale of Two Competences: Part (2) Rules in Action', *European Business Organization Law Review,* 12(2): 177.

—— (2012). 'The Legacy Effects of the Financial Crisis on Regulatory Design in the EU', in E. Ferran, J. Hill, N. Moloney, and J. C. Coffee (eds), *The Regulatory Aftermath of the Global Financial Crisis.* Cambridge: Cambridge University Press, 111–202.

Moran, M. (1991). *The Politics of the Financial Services Revolution: The USA, UK and Japan.* Basingstoke: Macmillan.

Morgan, G. (2010). 'Legitimacy in Financial Markets: Credit Default Swaps in the Current Crisis', *Socio-Economic Review,* 8(1): 17–45.

Moschella, M. (2011). 'Different Varieties of Capitalism? British and Italian Recapitalization Policies in Response to the Sub-Prime Crisis', *Comparative European Politics,* 9(1): 76–99.

Moschella, M. and Tsingou, E. (eds) (2013). *Great Expectations, Slow Transformations: Incremental Change in Financial Governance.* Colchester: ECPR Press.

Moyer, H. W. (1993). 'The European Community and the GATT Uruguay Round: Preserving the Common Agricultural Policy at All Costs', in W. P. Avery (ed.), *World Agriculture and the GATT*. Boulder, Colo.: Lynne Rienner, 95–119.

Mügge, D. (2006). 'Reordering the Marketplace: Competition Politics in European Finance', *Journal of Common Market Studies,* 44(5): 991–1022.

—— (2009). 'Tales of Tails and Dogs: Derivatives and Financialization in Contemporary Capitalism, *Review of International Political Economy*, 16(3): 514–26.

—— (2010). *Widen the Market, Narrow the Competition: Banker Interests and the Making of a European Capital Market.* Colchester: ECPR.

—— (2011a). 'The European Presence in Global Financial Governance: A Principal-Agent Perspective', *Journal of European Public Policy,* 18(3): 383–402.

—— (2011b). 'From Pragmatism to Dogmatism: European Union Governance, Policy Paradigms, and Financial Meltdown', *New Political Economy*, 16(2): 185–206.

Nesvetailova, A. and Palan, R. (2010). 'The End of Liberal Finance? The Changing Paradigm of Global Financial Governance', *Millennium,* 38(3): 1–29.

New Political Economy (2010). 'Special Issue: The Political Economy of the Subprime Crisis: The Economics, Politics and Ethics of Response', 15(1): 1–164.

Nobes, C. and Parker, R. (2006) *Comparative International Accounting*. 9th edn, London: Prentice Hall.

Norton Rose Fulbright (2007). 'Preparing for the Reinsurance Directive', June, <http://www.nortonrosefulbright.com/tk/knowledge/publications/4606/preparing-for-the-reinsurance-directive> (accessed July 2013).

Oatley, T. and Nabors, R. (1998). 'Redistributive Cooperation: Market Failures, Wealth Transfer and the Basle Accord', *International Organization,* 52(1): 35–54.

Padoa-Schioppa, T. (2004a). *The Euro and its Central Bank: Getting United After the Union.* London: MIT Press.

—— (2004b) *Regulating Finance: Balancing Freedom and Risk.* Oxford: Oxford University Press.

—— (2007). Letter to the ECOFIN Council, 26 Nov. Included in K. Dyson and L. Quaglia (2010). *European Economic Governance and Policies*, ii. *Commentary on Key Policy Documents*. Oxford: Oxford University Press.

Pagliari, S. (2011). 'Who Governs Finance? The Shifting Public–Private Divide in the Regulation of Derivatives, Rating Agencies and Hedge Funds', *European Law Journal*, 18(1): 44–61.

—— (2013). 'A Wall Around Europe?: The European Regulatory Response to the Global Financial Crisis and the Turn in Transatlantic Relations', *Journal of European Integration*, 35(4): 391–408.

Paredes, T.A. (2006). 'On the Decision to Regulate Hedge Funds: The SEC's Regulatory Philosophy, Style, and Mission', *University of Illinois Law Review*, 5: 975–1006.

—— (2011). Remarks at the Symposium on 'Hedge Fund Regulation and Current Developments', Securities and Exchange Commission, 8 June.

Partnoy, F. (2001). 'Shifting Contours of Global Derivatives Regulation', *University of Pennsylvania Journal of International Economic Law*, 22: 421–96.

Paskelian, O. G. and Bell, S. (2013). 'The Take of Two Regulations—Dodd-Frank Act and Basel III: A Review and Comparison of the Two Regulatory Frameworks', *Review of Future Markets*, 21 (special issue): 7–30.

Patterson, L. A. (1997). 'Agricultural Policy Reform in the European Community: A Three-Level Game Analysis', *International Organization*, 51(1): 135–65.

Perry, J. and Nölke, A. (2006). 'The Political Economy of International Accounting Standards', *Review of International Political Economy*, 13(4): 559–86.

Pollack, M. A. (1997). 'Delegation, Agency and Agenda-Setting in the European Community', *International Organization*, 51(1): 99–134.

Porter, T. (1993). *States, Markets and Regimes in Global Finance*. Basingstoke: Macmillan.

—— (2003). 'Technical Collaboration and Political Conflict in the Emerging Regime for International Financial Regulation', *Review of International Political Economy*, 10(3): 520–51.

—— (2005). *Globalization and Finance*. Cambridge: Polity.

Posner, E. (2005). 'Sources of Institutional Change: The Supranational Origins of Europe's New Stock Markets', *World Politics*, 58(1): 1–40.

—— (2009a). 'Making Rules for Global Finance: Transatlantic Regulatory Cooperation at the Turn of the Millennium', *International Organization*, 63(4): 665–99.

—— (2009b). *The Origins of Europe's New Stock Markets*. Cambridge, Mass.: Harvard University Press.

—— (2010). 'Sequence as Explanation: The International Politics of Accounting Standards', *Review of International Political Economy*, 14(4): 639–64.

Posner, E. and Véron, N. (2010). 'The EU and Financial Regulation: Power Without Purpose?', *Journal of European Public Policy*, 17(3): 400–15.

President's Working Group (PWG) on Financial Markets (1999). *Hedge Funds, Leverage, and the Lessons of Long-Term Capital Management*. Washington, DC: PWG, Apr.

—— (2008). *Policy Objectives for the OTC Derivatives Market*. Washington, DC, 14 Nov.

PricewaterhouseCoopers (2004). *Study on the Financial and Macroeconomic Consequences of the Draft Proposed New Capital Requirements for Banks and Investment Firms in the EU*, Final Report. London, 8 Apr.

Public Company Accounting Oversight Board (PCAOB) (2008). *Rules on Periodic Reporting by Registered Public Accounting Firms*, PCAOB Release No. 2008-004. Washington, DC: PCAOB, 10 June.

Quaglia, L. (2007). 'The Politics of Financial Service Regulation and Supervision Reform in the European Union', *European Journal of Political Research*, 46(2): 269–90.

—— (2008). 'Committee Governance in the Financial Sector in the European Union', *Journal of European Integration*, 30(3): 565–80.

—— (2010a). 'Completing the Single Market in Financial Services: The Politics of Competing Advocacy Coalitions', *Journal of European Public Policy*, 17(7): 1007–22.

—— (2010b). *Governing Financial Services in the European Union: Banking, Securities and Post-Trading*. London: Routledge.

—— (2011a). 'The "Old" and "New" Political Economy of Hedge Fund Regulation in the European Union', *West European Politics*, 34(4): 665–82.

—— (2011b). 'The Politics of Insurance Regulation Reform in the European Union', *Comparative European Politics*, 9(1): 100–22.

—— (2012). 'The "Old" and "New" Politics of Financial Services Regulation in the European Union', *New Political Economy*, 17(4): 515–35.

—— (2013), 'The European Union, the USA and International Standard Setting by Regulatory Fora in Finance', *New Political Economy*, early view: DOI:10.1080/13563467.2013.796449.

Quaglia, L., Eastwood, R., and Holmes, P. (2009). 'The Financial Turmoil and EU Policy Cooperation: The Dog That Did Not Bark?', *Journal of Common Market Studies Annual Review*, 47(1): 1–25.

Reinhart, C. M. and Rogoff, K. (2009). *This Time is Different: Eight Centuries of Financial Folly*. Princeton: Princeton University Press.

Reinsurance Association of America (2000). 'Reinsurance Regulation in a Global Marketplace: A View from the United States', paper presented to the IAIS Reinsurance Subcommittee, June.

Review of International Political Economy (2010). 'Special Issue: Market Regulation', 17(4).

—— (2012). 'Special Issue: RIPE Focus on Governing Global Finance and Banking', 19(4).

Rhodes, M. and Van Apeldoorn, B. (1998). 'Capital Unbound? The Transformation of European Corporate Governance', *Journal of European Public Policy*, 5(3): 406–27.

Sami, G. (2009). 'A Comparative Analysis of Hedge Fund Regulation in the United States and Europe', *Northwestern Journal of International Law and Business*, 29: 275–308.

Sarkozy, President Nicholas and Merkel, Chancellor Angela (2009). Letter sent to Mirek Topolanek, Prime Minister of the Czech Republic, and José Manuel Barroso, President of the European Commission, 16 Mar.

Schammo, P. (2008). 'Regulating Transatlantic Stock Exchanges', *International and Comparative Law Quarterly*, 57(4): 827–62.

Schmidt, V. A. (2002). *The Futures of European Capitalism*. Oxford: Oxford University Press.

Scott, H. S. (2005). *Capital Adequacy Beyond Basel: Banking, Securities, and Insurance*. Oxford: Oxford University Press.

Shaffer, G. (2006). 'What's New in EU Trade Dispute Settlement: Judicialization, Public–Private Networks and the WTO Legal Order', *Journal of European Public Policy*, 13(6): 832–50.

Simmons, B. A. (1998). 'Compliance with International Agreements', *Annual Review of Political Science*, 1: 75–93.

Simmons, B. A. (2001). 'The International Politics of Harmonization: The Case of Capital Market Regulation', *International Organization*, 55(3): 589–620.

Sinclair, T. J. (2005). *The New Masters of Capital: American Bond Rating Agencies and the Politics of Creditworthiness*. Ithaca, NY: Cornell University Press.

Singer, D. A. (2004). 'Capital Rules: The Domestic Politics of International Regulatory Harmonization', *International Organization*, 58(3): 531–65.

—— (2007). *Regulating Capital: Setting Standards for the International Financial System*. Ithaca, NY: Cornell University Press.

Soltani, B. (2007). *Auditing: An International Approach*. Harlow: Pearson Education.

Spong, K. (2000). *Banking Regulation: Its Purposes, Implementation and Effects*. Kansas City: Division of Supervision and Risk Management, Federal Reserve Bank of Kansas City.

Story, J. and Walter I. (1997). *Political Economy of Financial Integration in Europe: The Battle of the System*. Manchester: Manchester University Press.

Stout, L. A. (2009). 'Derivatives and the Legal Origin of the 2008 Credit Crisis', *Harvard Business Law Review*, 1(1): 1–38.

Street, D. L. (2006). 'The G4's Role in the Evolution of the International Accounting Standard Setting Process and Partnership with the IASB', *Journal of International Accounting, Auditing and Taxation*, 15(1): 109–26.

Tafara, E. and Peterson, R. J. (2007). 'A Blueprint for Cross-Border Access to U.S. Investors: A New International Framework', *Harvard International Law Journal*, 48(1): 31–68.

Tarullo, D. K. (2008). *Banking on Basel: The Future of International Financial Regulation*. Washington, DC: Peterson Institute for International Economics.

—— (2011). 'Capital and Liquidity Standards', Before the Committee on Financial Services, US House of Representatives, Washington, DC, 16 June.

—— (2012). 'Regulation of Foreign Banking Organizations', speech at the Yale School of Management Leaders Forum, New Haven, Conn., 28 Nov.

TASS (2005). TASS database, *ECB Occasional Paper*, 34 (Aug.), 17.

Tickell, A. (2000). 'Dangerous Derivatives: Controlling and Creating Risks in International Money', *Geoforum*, 31(1): 87–99.

Tsingou, E. (2003). *Transnational Policy Communities and Financial Governance: The Role of Private Actors in Derivatives Regulation*, CSGR Working Paper, 111/03. Warwick: CSGR. <http://wrap.warwick.ac.uk/2009/1/WRAP_Tsingou_wp11103.pdf> (accessed 3 Mar. 2014).

—— (2008). 'Transnational Private Governance and the Basel Process: Banking Regulation, Private Interests and Basel II', in J. C. Graz and A. Nölke (eds), *Transnational Private Governance and Its Limits*. London: Routledge, 58–68.

—— (2010). 'Regulatory Reactions to the Global Credit Crisis: Analyzing a Policy Community under Stress', in E. Helleiner, S. Pagliari, and H. Zimmerman (eds), *Global Finance in Crisis: The Politics of International Regulatory Change*. Abingdon: Routledge, 21–36.

Underhill, G. R. D. (1995). 'Keeping Governments Out of Politics: Transnational Securities Markets, Regulatory Cooperation and Political Legitimacy', *Review of International Studies*, 21(3): 251–78.

—— (1997). 'The Making of the European Financial Area: Global Market Integration and the EU Single Market for Financial Services', in G. R. D. Underhill (ed.), *The New World Order in International Finance*. London: Macmillan, 101–23.

Underhill, G. R. D. and Zhang, X. (2008). 'Setting the Rules: Private Power, Political Underpinnings, and Legitimacy in Global Monetary and Financial Governance', *International Affairs*, 84(3): 535–54.

Underhill, G. R. D., Blom, J., and Mügge, D. (eds) (2010). *Global Financial Integration Thirty Years on: From Reform to Crisis*. Cambridge: Cambridge University Press.

University of Duisburg-Essen (2009). *Evaluation of the Possible Adoption of International Standards on Auditing (ISAs) in the EU*, Final Report, Markt/2007/15/5—Study on International Standards on Auditing. Essen, 12 June.

US Senate Committee on Banking, Housing, and Urban Affairs (2008a). *The State of the Insurance Industry: Examining the Current Regulatory and Oversight Structure.* Washington, DC: Government Printer, 29 July.

—— (2008b). *The State of the Banking Industry, Part II*, Washington, DC: Government Printer, 5 June.

van Apeldoorn, B. (2002). *Transnational Capitalism and the Struggle Over European Integration.* London: Routledge.

van den Burg, L. and Dăianu, D. (2008). *Report with Recommendations to the Commission on Lamfalussy Follow-Up: Future Structure of Supervision (2008/2148(INI)).* Brussels: European Parliament Committee on Economic and Monetary Affairs, 18 Sept.

van Hulle, K. (2004). 'From Accounting Directives to International Accounting Standards', in C. Leuz, D. Pfaff, and A. Hopwood (eds), *The Economics and Politics of Accounting: International Perspectives on Research Trends, Policy and Practice.* Oxford: Oxford University Press, 349–75.

Verdier, P.-H. (2011). Mutual Recognition in International Finance', *Harvard International Law Journal*, 52(1): 55–108.

Véron, N. (2007). *The Global Accounting Experiment.* Brussels: Bruegel Blue Print Series.

Véron, N. and Rottier, S. (2010). *Not All Financial Regulation is Global.* Policy Briefs PB10-22. Washington, DC: Peterson Institute for International Economics, Sept.

Whittington, G. (2005). 'The Adoption of International Accounting Standards in the European Union', *European Accounting Review*, 14(1): 127–53.

—— (2008). 'Fair Value and the IASB/FASB Conceptual Framework Project: An Alternative View', *Abacus*, 44(2): 139–68.

Woll, C. (2006). *Trade Policy Lobbying in the European Union: Who Captures Whom?* Cologne: Max-Planck-Institut für Gesellschaftsforschung Working Paper 06/07.

—— (2008). *Firm Interests: How Governments Shape Business Lobbying on Global Trade.* Ithaca, NY: Cornell University Press.

—— (2013). 'Lobbying Under Pressure: The Effect of Salience on European Hedge Fund Regulation', *Journal of Common Market Studies*, 51(3): 555–72.

Wood, D. (2005). *Governing Global Banking: The Basel Committee and the Politics of Financial Globalisation.* Aldershot: Ashgate.

Woolcock, S. (2005). 'Trade Policy: From Uruguay to Doha and Beyond', in H. Wallace, W. Wallace, and M. A. Pollack (eds), *Policy-Making in the European Union.* Oxford: Oxford University Press, 377–400.

Woolcock, S. and Hodges, M. (1996). 'EU Policy in the Uruguay Round', in H. Wallace, and W. Wallace (eds), *Policy-Making in the European Union.* Oxford: Oxford University Press, 301–24.

Woolley, J. T. and Ziegler, J. N. (2012). 'The Two-Tiered Politics of Financial Reform in the United States', in R. Mayntz (ed.), *Crisis and Control: Institutional Change in Financial Market Regulation.* Cologne: Max Planck Institute for the Study of Societies, 29–66.

Young, A. R. (2007). 'Trade Politics Ain't What it Used to Be: The European Union in the Doha Round', *Journal of Common Market Studies*, 45(4): 789–811.

Young, A. R. and Peterson, P. (2006). 'The EU and the New Trade Politics', *Journal of European Public Policy,* 13(6): 795–814.

Young, K. (2012). 'Transnational Regulatory Capture? An Empirical Examination of the Transnational Lobbying of the Basel Committee on Banking Supervision', *Review of International Political Economy,* 19(4): 663–88.

Zentraler Kreditausschuss (ZKA) (2010). *Position Paper on the Consultative Document of the Basel Committee 'Strengthening the Resilience of the Banking Sector'.* Berlin, 16 Apr.

Zimmermann, H. (2010). 'Varieties of Global Financial Governance? British and German Approaches to Financial Market Regulation', in E. Helleiner, S. Pagliari, and H. Zimmerman (eds), *Global Finance in Crisis.* London: Routledge, 121–38.

Zysman, J. (1983). *Governments, Markets, and Growth: Financial Systems and the Politics of Industrial Change.* Ithaca, NY: Cornell University Press.

Index